THE WOMAN WHO MURDERED BLACK SATIN

THE WOMAN WHO MURDERED BLACK SATIN

The Bermondsey Horror

By Albert Borowitz

OHIO STATE UNIVERSITY PRESS
COLUMBUS

Library of Congress Cataloging in Publication Data

Borowitz, Albert, 1930–
The woman who murdered black satin.

Bibliography: p.
1. Manning, Maria DeRoux, d. 1849.   2. Manning,
Frederick George, 1820–1849, defendant.   3. O'Connor,
Patrick, d. 1849.   4. Trials (Murder)—England—
London.   I. Title.
KD372.M36B67   345.42′02523   80-39756
ISBN 0-8142-0320-5

IN MEMORY OF

MAX AND HANNAH OSTERMAN

Contents

Illustrations		ix
1	: Bermondsey 1849	3
2	: What the Kitchen Hid	7
3	: The Odd Triangle	11
4	: The Disappearance of Patrick O'Connor	37
5	: Brokerage and Brandy	47
6	: Homicide Fair	79
7	: The Inquest at the Tavern	93
8	: A Month in Police Court	121
9	: The Mannings in Prison	149
10	: King Edward III's Jury	155
11	: The Case for the Crown	163
12	: The Arguments for the Defense	183
13	: Rue in the Dock	203
14	: Waiting for Mr. Calcraft	215
15	: Oh Mrs. Manning! Don't You Cry for Me!	235
16	: The Moral Lesson at Horsemonger Lane	255
17	: Homicide Fair Revisited	275
18	: The "Demise" of Black Satin	289
19	: Marie and Mademoiselle Hortense	297
20	: The Second Murder Plot	313
	Acknowledgments	329
	Selective Bibliography	331

Illustrations

Illustrations on pages i and ii are details from "The Great Moral Lesson at Horsemonger Lane Gaol" and "Minver Place," below.

Title Page of Robert Huish's *The Progress of Crime*	14
Portrait of Marie Manning	15
Portrait of Patrick O'Connor	21
Portrait of Fred Manning	26
Minver Place	39
The Discovery of the Body	44
The Back Kitchen at 3 Minver Place	45
Portrait of Patrick O'Connor	98
The Mannings and Their Solicitors in Court, by Robert Cruikshank	134
Sketches of the Mannings by William Mulready	135
Lord Chief Baron Pollock	157
The Last Meeting but One	247
The Last Scene	251
John Leech's "The Great Moral Lesson at Horsemonger Lane Gaol"	263
Marie Manning	282

Fred Manning   283

Staffordshire Figure of Mr. Manning   284

Staffordshire Figure of Mrs. Manning   285

Mlle Hortense Impersonating Lady Dedlock   307

Inspector Bucket Investigating   308

Inspector Bucket's "Fat Forefinger"   309

The Gravestone of Fred Manning   314

The Gravestone of Marie Manning   315

Fred Manning's Sketch of O'Connor's Body
in the Kitchen   321

THE WOMAN
WHO MURDERED
BLACK SATIN

CHAPTER ONE

Bermondsey 1849

The Modern Babylon, so great in other things,
has a giant's appetite for mortality.
—Household Words, June 1850

Walk south across London Bridge, turn left, and you were in Tooley Street, the main east-west thoroughfare of Bermondsey. A predominantly working-class district with a population of thirty-five thousand in 1849, Bermondsey had for a century and a half been the center of London's leather trade. The local street names still bear witness to Bermondsey's age-old belief that "there's nothing like leather": Leathermarket Street runs into Tanner Street.

In 1833 the Leather Market was established at the intersection of Long Lane with New Weston Street, which in its northerly direction bent toward Tooley Street and the Thames. All phases of the trade were carried on in the vicinity. The skins of slaughtered animals were prepared by dealers called "fellmongers" and sold to the numerous tanneries that were in operation in Bermondsey and neighboring districts.

Under the best of circumstances Bermondsey was not one of the most salubrious areas of London for residents. In an 1850 survey of comparative death rates in London's various regions conducted by the Registrar-General, Bermondsey's mortality figures ranked well above the metropolitan average. *Household Words*, a journal edited by Charles Dickens, was not surprised with this result: "[Bermondsey was] just level with the water line, and poisoned by open drains and unsavoury factories." A particularly infamous area of Bermondsey bearing the name "Jacob's Island" lay to the east of St. Saviour's Dock, a narrow inlet from the river. The Island was so called because it was surrounded by polluted tidal ditches, and the *Morning Chronicle* dubbed the place "the Venice of the drains." It was to Jacob's Island that Bill Sikes, the murderer in *Oliver Twist,* fled after killing Nancy. In the novel Dickens sketched a memorable portrait of the slum:

> Crazy wooden galleries common to the backs of half a dozen houses, with holes from which to look upon the slime beneath; windows, broken and patched, with poles thrust out, on which to dry the linen that is never there; rooms so small, so filthy, so confined, that the air would seem too tainted even for the dirt and squalor they shelter; wooden chambers thrusting themselves out above the mud, and threatening to fall into it—as some have done; dirt-besmeared walls and decaying foundations; every repulsive lineament of poverty, every loathsome indication of filth, rot, and garbage; all these ornament the banks of Folly Ditch.

Life in Bermondsey was unusually precarious in 1849, when a cholera epidemic struck London and took its greatest toll among the poverty-ridden population of the low-lying regions of the south bank of the Thames. Londoners were stunned by the return of the plague, which had taken over one thousand lives in England in the last three months of 1848. The origins of the disease were not yet scientifically established, and all sorts of theories were proposed. The "zymotic" explanation related cholera to a noxious gas produced by the decomposition of water. In rebuttal, a newspaper correspondent proposed an "antizymotic" theory that the disease was caused by the absence of ozone in the atmosphere. *Punch* identified and attacked as breeding grounds of pestilence the open sewerage drains of the metropolis; the glue and soap factories and slaughterhouses situated in populous neighborhoods; and the overcrowded graveyards within city districts—the so-called intramural burial grounds.

The plague came on gradually in May and June, but by early September 10,142 had died, one out of every 192 of London's population. Bermondsey stood second in the death rate, having lost 591, or one out of 59, and neighboring areas were also hard hit. Statistics, however, tell us less of the tragedy than we learn from the commentaries of eyewitnesses. The novelist Charles Kingsley made a personal inspection of Jacob's Island, where the plague had done its worst. He was horrified by what he saw, "people having no water to drink, hundreds of them, but the water of the common sewer which stagnated, full of dead fish, cats and dogs under their windows." A writer for the *Illustrated London News* described the onslaught of the cholera on Newington, a parish hemmed in by Bermondsey and its devastated riverside neighbors, Lambeth and Southwark:

> All day long was that sullen bell tolling—from morning to night it scarcely ceased a moment; for as soon as it had rung the knell of another departed spirit, there was a fresh funeral at the churchyard-gate, and again that "ding-dong" pealed mournfully through the sad and sultry atmosphere. Those who were left behind, too ill to join the funeral procession, heard not always the returning footsteps of the muffled mourners, for sometimes Death again entered the house while they were absent; and when they reached home they found another victim ready to be borne to the grave.

The cholera passed over the Bermondsey household at 3 Minver Place, in New Weston Street near the Leather Market, but death paid a visit in another guise. It came in the costume of friendship.

CHAPTER TWO

What the Kitchen Hid

"'Ware that there mound by the yard-gate,
Mr. Jasper."
"I see it. What is it?"
"Lime."
"What you call quick-lime?"
"Ay! . . . quick enough to eat your boots.
With a little handy stirring, quick enough to
eat your bones."
— *The Mystery of Edwin Drood*

On Friday, 17 August 1849, Constables Henry Barnes and James Burton of the K and M Divisions of the Metropolitan Police decided to return to 3 Minver Place, Bermondsey. The house was in a row of new two-story villas in the middle of Weston Street, near the southwest corner of the intersection with Guy Street.

Their earlier search had been fruitless, and now Barnes suggested to Burton the necessity of digging up the garden. This cannot have been a pleasant prospect, digging about in the ground of a plague-stricken neighborhood. Months later crusty Thomas Carlyle was to pay reluctant tribute to the "Cholera Doctors, hired to dive into black dens of infection and despair, . . . rushing about all day from lane to lane, with their life in their hand."

The officers dug in the garden but found nothing to arouse their suspicion. They then agreed that the house deserved another inspection. Burton had obtained a key from the landlord and opened the front door. As one entered from the street, the front parlor was at the right of the passage; two kitchens were beneath the parlor. After looking around on the ground floor, the two men went downstairs to the basement level. Having found nothing of interest in the front kitchen, they walked into the back kitchen, which had a view to the garden through an iron-barred window. Barnes had noticed when they had been at the house previously that the back kitchen appeared remarkably clean and neat, and that the flagstones with which it was paved had been recently and very carefully rubbed white with hearthstone. The constable looked at the flagstones more closely now and observed something that had escaped his eye before—there was a damp mark between the edges of two of the stones. He pulled a clasp knife out of his pocket and, opening it to test the spot, he found it very soft.

The two stones were thick and heavy, measuring together about five feet across. Barnes told Burton he would not be satisfied until the two stones were taken up, and Burton borrowed a shovel, a crowbar, and a boathook from some laborers. Barnes wielded the crowbar and Burton assisted him with the boathook, and the flagstones yielded. There was a bed of mortar underneath, and earth. The soil was wet, resembling as Barnes later testified, "made earth," such as would be used to fill in the foundation of a house, a combination of lime-core and clay. The mortar was carefully spread across the entire bottom surface of the flags. Barnes remarked that the stones could not have been laid by a mason, who would have applied the mortar only around the edges. The men exchanged a brief glance and decided to remove the soil.

They found the earth beneath the layer of mortar very loose, and on digging to the depth of twelve inches, they found a linen rag about the size of two hands. Barnes put the rag to his nose and recognized the smell of death. Continuing to dig, they saw something white and thought at first it was another piece of rag. Barnes shook it and found that it was a human toe.

"We've found him," he said. Burton immediately ran off for the station to summon assistance, leaving Barnes to the grim disinterment. Tearing further into the loose ground, Barnes uncovered the man's loins, and when assistance arrived the whole body was unearthed. The corpse was lying naked upon the belly, with head pointed down, and the legs were drawn back and tied against the thighs with a strong cord of the thickness of a clothesline. The body was completely imbedded in quicklime.

While the corpse still lay in its kitchen grave, Samuel Lockwood, a nonpracticing surgeon who happened to be in the neighborhood, arrived with a newspaper reporter at his heels. From the very outset this was to be a case where the press would never be left far behind.

Lockwood was afraid of injury being done to the head and himself disengaged it from the earth. He felt an extensive fracture on the upper part of the skull toward the back, so large that he could introduce two fingers into it; the scalp was cut through. The surgeon remembered the placard he had seen announcing that the missing man had worn false teeth. Raising the head carefully, he pulled out a full set of dentures, which he washed and gave to the summoning officer, Mr. Slow, one of the representatives of the law who were now crowding the kitchen. Shortly thereafter the body was raised and moved into the front kitchen, where Lockwood assisted George Odling, a police surgeon of the M division, in a preliminary medical inspection.

A two-inch coat of lime clung to the body, which was quite blue, decomposing and excoriated. Lockwood found another fracture at the back of the head, extending to the right side. Odling having called his attention to a small protuberance over the right eye, Lockwood felt it through the unbroken skin and found that it was hard and moveable. He cut down upon it and found it to be a large slug. The bullet had made an aperture in the skull directly in the middle over the right eye above the frontal bone. The slug was about an inch under the skin. No further examination of the body was made at the time; a more careful study was deferred until a postmortem could be arranged.

While the doctors were examining the body in the front kitchen, the police searched the house for the weapons but had no success. The reporter left the officials to their duties and was soon engrossed in his own speculations. He looked out through the bars of the kitchen window into the garden. The window had neither shutter nor blind, and at the end of the garden was the landlord Coleman's timber yard, with a saw pit close to the wall of No. 3. The saw pit was so close to the window, the reporter thought, that motions of any person in the kitchen could be observed by daytime, and the sound and light of a nocturnal interment could hardly have escaped the attention of neighbors.

When the inspection was over and the police were ready to leave, their task was clear before them. The victim was undoubtedly the missing Patrick O'Connor, and they must track and apprehend the pair of murderers who had fled from their lodgings at 3 Minver Place after burying him. The police were searching for Frederick George Manning and his wife, Marie.

CHAPTER THREE

The Odd Triangle

*[Murderers are] served up in their whole
biography and adventures—so many live
romances with a bloody ending.*
— Charles Dickens, letter to the
Daily News, 28 February 1846

xtraordinary Discovery of a Murder," the *Times*
headline cried discreetly the next morning,
and the national passion for the O'Connor
murder had begun. The "penny-a-liners" of
the metropolis, reporters paid by the line for coverage of crime
and other news stories, took themselves off to Minver Place or,
just as likely, stayed home and exercised their journalistic
fantasy. An anonymous member of the press corps gave the
case its gaudy sobriquet, "the Bermondsey Horror," a name
that was in its way a tribute to the macabre appeal of a single
mysterious death in a neighborhood whose residents were
dying by hundreds of a plague the doctors could not explain.

The public could not read enough in the ensuing months of
the past of the three characters in the drama or of the tortuous
paths of their lives that had their final dramatic convergence in
a Bermondsey kitchen.

We begin with Marie Manning, not out of lost notions of
gallantry, but because the insatiable public obviously looked
first for her name when the day's news stories, true and false,
were fed to them as daily breakfast and Sabbath fare. It is Marie
alone of the three principal figures of the case who has rated an
entry in the *Dictionary of National Biography* founded by Sir Leslie
Stephen, and Manning and O'Connor, husband and victim,
have become a part of her biographical data.

One of the appropriate definitions of a "beauty" in the dictionary of the English language would be "any accused murderess particularly when wearing a veil." Marie (or Maria, as she called herself in England) was predictably hailed by many newsmen as a beauty from the very outset, but as opinion hardened against her, her portrait changed as dramatically as the picture of Dorian Gray. We would therefore do best to introduce ourselves to her as she is described in the police bulletin circulated immediately after the discovery of O'Connor's body: "Maria Manning, a native of Geneva, 30 years old,* 5 feet 7 inches high, stout, fresh complexion, with long dark hair, good looking, scar on the right side of her chin, extending towards the neck, dresses very smartly, and speaks broken English. Has been a lady's maid and dressmaker."

Neither the police nor the responsible portion of the press could find out much about Marie's early life. It was known that her maiden name was de Roux and that she was born near Lausanne, Switzerland. Her parents, who had left her a small inheritance, were both deceased. But where facts were lacking, the journalistic retailers of gossip and purveyors of sensational literature rushed into the breach. Although most of their "revelations" are undoubtedly fictional, their writings were not without significance because they reflected a vision of Marie shared not only by the public at large but very likely also by the twelve men who were ultimately to serve as jurors in her trial.

The most voluminous surviving example of the Marie Manning sensation literature is a novelized account of her life and trial, *The Progress of Crime; or, The Authentic Memoirs of Maria Manning,* by Robert Huish. Its author had specialized in novels based on lurid crimes or the lives of royalty and nobility, two subjects he was able to combine in his book on the Manning case. The *Memoirs of Maria Manning,* which runs to more than eight hundred pages, was published in 1849 in penny-numbers of sixteen pages each. In his narrative of Marie's early life, Huish, while continually protesting pious disapproval of Marie's

---

*I have not attempted to reconcile the inconsistent contemporary accounts of the ages of the three principal figures in the Manning case. The Mannings were each about thirty and Patrick O'Connor was about fifty.

conduct, sought to cast her in the romantic, and not wholly unappealing, role of a headstrong girl who surrenders to the temptations of the world because of strong sexual passion and filial disobedience. The story is heavily larded with appeals to the anti-Catholic feelings Huish calculated could be automatically aroused among his readers.

According to Huish, Marie "first beheld the light of this glorious world" at the eastern end of the Lake of Lausanne and lived in a chalet right out of the travel guides. The household included her parents, three brothers, and a sister. M. de Roux, whom Huish calls a "rigid Catholic," destined one son for the priesthood and Marie for a convent. The fourteen-year-old girl, however, had her mind less on religion than "on those glorious and sublime works of nature which are presented by the Alpine mountains." Her thoughts were brought back to earth by the arrival on the scene of a handsome stranger who won Marie's heart by staring at her in church and then introduced himself to her parents as Ludovico Sangallo, a Florentine nobleman. The awful truth was that the young man was a disguised bandit chieftain named Montano. Despite the fact that one of Marie's brothers, who had sniffed out Sangallo's true identity, thwarted a rendezvous of the brigand with his sister by shooting him and inflicting a serious wound, the check was only temporary. On the very eve of her scheduled departure for the nunnery, Marie decamped, and though Huish is rather vague at this point in the narrative, he would apparently have us believe that Marie began her amatory career at the thieves' den established by Sangallo/Montano in a ruined palace in the Alps. To add insult to injury, Sangallo's bandits also made off with M. de Roux's ancestral silver plate after accepting a bag of money that the bewildered householder offered them in place of the heirlooms.

Somehow Huish, in musing about this undoubtedly mythical romance, found the bandit more lovable than the wayward girl. Sangallo "was a contradictory mixture of great virtues and great vices" and had only taken to crime because "his parents had been driven from their patrimonial estates by the accursed acts of the Holy Inquisition." Marie had at this period of her life "as yet been only faulty, not criminal," but would "always appear as

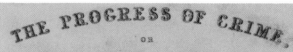

Title page of Robert Huish's *The Progress of Crime; or, The Authentic Memoirs of Maria Manning* (London, 1849).

MARIE MANNING,

As she appeared at Union Hall Police Court, Sept.r 15th 1849

Portrait of Marie Manning, from Huish's *The Progress of Crime*.

a lamentable example of the PROGRESS OF CRIME." She was "amongst all women perhaps the last, who in her emancipation from the unwelcome restraint of parental control, would remain long in the sober and regular paths of virtue and modesty." Marie lacked the one ingredient Huish regarded as essential to the "amelioration of the character of woman"—a sense of shame. Writing these early chapters before the trial for the murder of O'Connor took place, Huish was "not at present in a position publicly to state that Mrs. Manning was in reality the murderer of O'Connor, but that she was an accessory in the atrocious deed, cannot for a moment be questioned."

In the novel Marie is given a series of picaresque adventures on the Continent and in the British Isles before she makes her first appearance in a historically verifiable role, that of lady's maid to Lady Palk and then to Lady Blantyre, daughter of the Duchess of Sutherland. In Huish's pages Marie, after putting her fascination with Alpine banditry behind her, next turned up as a maid at an inn in Strasbourg, where she caught the eye of an amorous Irish tourist, Mr. Wentworth, who was traveling with his disagreeable wife. Wentworth convinced his competitive spouse that she could outdo all her neighbors' coiffures if they took Marie home with them as a lady's maid, although Mrs. Wentworth voiced her doubt as to how much a chambermaid would know about fashion. When the Wentworths, with Marie in tow, returned to their mansion of Ballincraig, in County Kilkenny, Mr. Wentworth's uncommon solicitude for his wife's hairstyling was put aside for a more personal interest in Marie. One night Mrs. Wentworth, "opening the door of the library in the softest manner," discovered "her beloved and continent husband sitting on the sofa with her chaste and immaculate servant affectionately seated on his knee." The outraged spouse, after leaving the marks of her fingernails on Marie's face and gown, ordered that the "vicious, abominable hussey sleeps not in my house to-night." Pretending to obey, Mr. Wentworth instructed Marie to take refuge in the cottage of an old tenant, Martin, a mile away, where he promised to communicate with her as soon as he could escape Mrs. Wentworth's jealous vigil. Unfortunately, he could not shake his suspicious wife from his heels, and when he set out for the cottage, she insisted on accompanying him even though he chose the muddiest route he could find. When the couple reached Marie's hiding place, the resourceful girl, Huish writes, expelled Mrs. Wentworth by extemporizing the role and costume of a witch and dousing her adversary with a pitcher of nauseous black liquid. In fact, Marie was no witch but a "tall masculine woman, who was completely shrouded in a white garment . . . abstracted from old Martin's bed," and the liquid that flowed down Mrs. Wentworth's dress was not a hellish brew but a blend of water and chimney soot.

According to Huish, Marie eventually took her revenge on the importunate Mr. Wentworth as well. After she read a newspaper advertisement announcing the death of her father and requesting that she apply to the estate's London solicitors for her inheritance, she no longer looked with favor on Wentworth's persistent offer to settle her in a comfortable establishment as his mistress. She accepted his proposal with her fingers crossed, pocketed "with delicacy" the compensation they had agreed on—a bond of three hundred pounds per annum and a tip of one hundred pounds in cash to be used for appropriate mistress's apparel—and immediately made off for London to escape Wentworth and to collect her legacy.

In about 1843 Marie de Roux finally freed herself from the shrouds of Huish's fiction and emerged on the stage of the real world. She entered the employ of the family of Sir Lawrence Vaughan Palk, at Haldon House, Devonshire, as maid to Lady Anna Palk. Sir Lawrence, M.P. for Devonshire, was the grandson of Sir Robert Palk, who had given over a chaplaincy at Fort St. George in India to enter the civil service of the East India Company. He became governor of Madras in 1763 and was created a baronet in 1772, after returning to England hugging a great fortune. In 1815 Sir Lawrence Palk, who had become the third baronet, married Anna Eleonora Hartopp, the widow of a gentleman of Leicestershire and the eldest daughter of Sir Bourchier Wrey.

According to Huish's account, Lady Palk was in a precarious state of health at the time of Marie's employment, and "her

ladyship had all the fretfulness and peevishness of the valetu-
dinarian, the chief object of her life appearing to be to travel
from place to place in search of some new doctor who could
successfully prescribe for her numerous ailments." Marie,
though, was not disenchanted with her situation, taking
pleasure in the opportunity to display her beauty "whether it be
in a box at the Opera-house, a pew in a conventicle, or on the
fashionable parade of a watering place."

Lady Palk died in January 1846. Despite the lurid tales that
Huish had spun about her earlier career, the real Marie de
Roux must have garnered a favorable letter of recommendation from Sir Lawrence, because she was soon accepted in the
service of Lady Evelyn Blantyre, daughter of the Duchess of
Sutherland. The Sutherlands were an old and distinguished
family that traced their lineage to Anglo-Saxon origins and held
titles in the peerages of England and Scotland; the dukedom
had been created in 1833. The family biographers tell us little
about Lady Evelyn except that in 1843 she had married the
twelfth Lord Blantyre, an ardent agriculturalist. Marie was
probably with the Blantyres when they left London at the close
of the season of 1846 to visit the Hebrides at the invitation of
Lady Blantyre's brother-in-law the Duke of Argyll. The
Blantyres rusticated in a farmhouse at Knock, and Argyll and
Blantyre found the local sheep farmer to be an ideal tenant, a
former banker who was expending money on stone dikes to
enclose the small precious area of level land.

Not only Lady Blantyre but the entire Sutherland family was
in the shadow of Harriet, Duchess of Sutherland, the wife of the
second duke. If the portraits by Lawrence and Winterhalter
and the memoirs of her descendants do not flatter her beyond
pardonable measure, she was a beautiful and brilliant woman.
Her grandson wrote of her: "She was tall, stately, and fair, with
large blue eyes, a nose the slight high curve of which was rather
dovelike than aquiline, and full lips whose frequent pleasant
smile spoke the lovable nature of a mind charmingly receptive
and benevolent. There was no cause which her judgment told
her was good that she did not feel impelled to help. There was
no fault or vice that could make her believe the offender was

wholly lost." Marie did not know when she entered the family's service that one day she would have occasion to test this last appraisal.

Appointed mistress of the robes by Queen Victoria on her accession, the duchess maintained a majestic London residence at Stafford House, and her receptions there were visited by the young queen and Prince Albert, by Whigs and Tories alike, and luminaries of the literary and art worlds. "It was during one of these receptions," one of the duchess's sons wrote, "that her Majesty, on entering the great hall, paid her hostess a compliment worthy of Louis XIV: 'I have come from my house to your palace.'" In fact, Stafford House (now named Lancaster House and used for government and diplomatic meetings) still stands as an elegant Palladian-style neighbor of Buckingham Palace, from which it is separated only by a short stretch of Green Park.

Marie de Roux had at last entered the marble halls scarcely dreamt of by young girls in Swiss chalets. If we wish to imagine the glories of Stafford House in the early Victorian years, we can turn to the pages of Benjamin Disraeli's novel *Lothair,* where the mansion is named Crecy House: "one of the half-dozen stately structures that our capital boasts of . . . an edifice not unworthy of Vicenza in its best days, though on a far more extensive style than any pile that city boasts." Marie also attended her employers during their stays at the principal family seat at Trentham, in Staffordshire, which Disraeli has described in the same novel under the slightly altered name Brentham: "It would be difficult to find a fairer scene than Brentham offered, especially in the lustrous effulgence of a glorious English summer. It was an Italian palace of freestone; vast, ornate, and in scrupulous condition; its spacious and graceful chambers filled with treasures of art, and rising itself from statued and stately terraces. At their foot spread a garden domain of considerable extent, bright with flowers, dim with coverts of rare shrubs, and musical with fountains."

Donald Nicoll recalls aristocratic gossip that Marie was selected by the Sutherlands for "all benevolent missions to the impoverished of her sex" in the neighborhood of the family mansions. Writing in the late nineteenth century with a memory of the O'Connor murder intervening, Nicoll added: "So well concealed was the cruel nature of the tigress, and so purring and soothing were the tones of her voice, aided also by brilliant eyes, expressing pity as powerfully as they could anger, that . . . the graceful and winning manner of the distributor of gifts almost appeared to make the poor believe they were not the persons most obliged by the transaction."

Somewhere along the way Marie Manning met Patrick O'Connor. About twenty years her senior, O'Connor was born in Clonkelly, in County Tipperary, in about 1798. Huish, whose novel follows O'Connor's career in great detail—in fact, in greater detail than his knowledge can possibly have justified— reports that Patrick's father was a respectable farmer who rented fifty acres from a proprietor of considerable lands in the south of Tipperary. Following the same anticlerical bent he had shown in recounting Marie's upbringing, Huish reports that Patrick's parents destined him at an early age for the church "before it was ascertained that Patrick had in himself the slightest inclination to be enrolled in the rather numerous fraternity of the Irish priesthood." As it turned out, Patrick had not the least aptitude for the profession chosen for him but early gave signs of "the general depravity of his character." He fell in love with sixteen-year-old Mary O'Connell, which was in itself forgivable since at her tender age she had already developed, Huish tells us, "one of those full, voluptuous figures, which are so often seen amongst the peasantry of Ireland" and, like her young countrywomen, could not be persuaded that the celibacy that priests professed "is not a decided fraud and imposition." But Patrick did not tackle the impressionable Mary fairly; instead he accomplished an easy seduction with the aid of some powerful drug he obtained from a local widow who dispensed herbs and remedies for all sorts of ailments including passion.

Huish suggests that Mary O'Connell died as a result of her dishonor, and that suspicion of O'Connor's role in the tragedy was the first cause of his eventual disqualification from ordination. He was also accused of participating in a rebellious prank in which a policeman was waylaid and disarmed. But Huish

PATRICK O'CONNOR.

From the likeness at Madame Tussaud's Exhibition

Portrait of Patrick O'Connor, from Huish's *The Progress of Crime*.

cited a more serious allegation against him: according to the novelist, there was a rumor implicating Patrick in the death of a tithe collector, O'Shaughnessy, whose body was found one day by the roadside riddled with bullets. Huish purports to place little faith in this rumor, and in light of the ease with which he customarily accepts, and invents, the wildest fantasies, we have no reason to set Patrick O'Connor down as a murderer. As events will show, there are quite enough other reasons to dislike him.

Huish reports that by this point Patrick had become persona non grata with his entire family and, no doubt to their great relief, left for London to seek his fortune. We are told that Patrick was given a small measure of just punishment for the seduction of Mary O'Connell when a gang of London thieves robbed him as he lay unconscious under the influence of an English equivalent of the Mickey Finn he had administered to Mary back home. Sources more reliable than Huish place the arrival of O'Connor in London in early 1832.

Despite what Huish tells us of the irritation of the O'Connor family with their prodigal son, Patrick came armed with a letter of introduction from his brother, a priest of a prosperous parish near Thurles in Tipperary, to an influential Irish barrister occupying chambers in the Temple, the district housing two of London's Inns of Court. The lawyer, who was a good friend of Father O'Connor, received Patrick kindly and asked him what sort of position he was looking for. O'Connor's answer is surprising if Huish's account of his character has any truth to it—he said he would like to enter the police. The lawyer gave Patrick a letter of introduction to Commissioner Richard Mayne of Scotland Yard. It appears that the letter was never delivered, for Patrick soon changed his mind; he found that it would be degrading for him to become a "thief-taker."

Besides, it had not taken Patrick long to decide which side of the law was better suited to his talents. About six weeks after his first introduction to the lawyer in the Temple, he paid another visit. Much to his host's surprise, he produced a fifty-pound note and asked him to take care of it for him. The lawyer accepted the note and, knowing that Patrick had been without funds when he came from Ireland, asked where the money had come from. Patrick, who had already displayed his fatal candor about his financial affairs, replied that he had received 15 pounds from his mother by mail and had quickly built it into 50 pounds by dealing in smuggled tobacco and cigars. The barrister had no reason to disbelieve the story, and knowing that Patrick was applying for a position in the customs service, he remarked drily that Patrick's practical knowledge of smuggling should, if known, prove a great point in his favor. Meanwhile, the trade in contraband goods prospered, and by the end of the year Patrick had deposited with the obliging lawyer in the Temple at least 184 pounds, of which 100 pounds was invested at Patrick's request.

In the meantime, O'Connor, ever one to hedge his bets, thought the time had come to supplement his illegal income with regular employment. In the winter of 1832–33 Patrick was given a customs post in the port of London, that of a "tidewaiter." The tidewaiter waited for incoming ships and boarded them to assure compliance with customs regulations.

Hardly had he begun his new work than, like a pendulum, his thoughts swung back to crooked schemes. He had a "lawyer's letter" sent to the barrister who had served as his depositary, demanding payment of the full sum of 184 pounds. The barrister had in fact returned 84 pounds to O'Connor, but, believing he was dealing with an honest smuggler, had not demanded a receipt. The matter might have gone to trial except that O'Connor tripped himself with his habit of dishonorable dealings with the female sex. He had made a proposal of marriage to his depositary's laundress on learning that she not only was a widow with a pension of 26 pounds but earned about 100 pounds a year as laundress to several lawyers in the Temple. Patrick, talkative as ever about his money matters, made the mistake of confiding in her about his withdrawal of 84 pounds from her employer. Whether this evidence of dishonesty shocked her or whether Patrick had also tried his old trick with the seduction drug we do not know, but the wooing went off the tracks and the laundress reported Patrick's confession to the barrister. His solicitor passed this news along to Patrick's solicitor, and the claim was quietly dropped.

One result of Patrick's clumsy atempt at fraud was that it spurred the Temple barrister to investigate the source of O'Connor's income. He found that O'Connor had wangled an introduction to the bishop of Llandoff, a member of Parliament named Darby, and other proselytizing Protestants who financed efforts for the conversion of Catholics to the Church of England out of the coffers of the Bexley Fund. O'Connor showed great nimbleness in using both religious camps for the advancement of his career. He offered his services to the Protestant group, claiming that he was being persecuted for his religious doubts by his brother and other Catholic clergymen. His reward was not only sums of money but also (so the London journalists believed) appointment to his job as tidewaiter. Having his foot inside the door of the Customs House, Patrick then turned back to his brother and family friends for further sponsorship. It was reportedly through the efforts of Richard Lalor Shiel, whose election as Member of Parliament for Tipperary had been backed by Father O'Connor and friends of the O'Connor family, that Patrick gained a better position in the customs service. He was now a "gauger," who measured the contents of casks and other containers. Patrick may have been tempted more than once to skim off a bit of rum for his private trading, but in any event he had found a new resource for putting a little butter on the daily bread—he engaged in usury among his fellow employees.

Patrick also found his inclination to fraud hard to resist. In about 1846 a case was heard in the Thames police court charging a man named Michael Lee with attempting to obtain money from O'Connor by threats. Lee testified that he had given O'Connor five pounds to get a job for him at the docks, but that no position was obtained and O'Connor would not give him his money back. Lee threatened to expose O'Connor if the money was not returned, and Patrick put him off, saying that he did not have the money with him but would pay it if Lee called at his lodging the same evening. At the agreed hour Lee came and repeated his threat, which was overheard by a constable whom O'Connor had stationed in an adjoining room. Lee was convicted on the constable's evidence and given twelve months' imprisonment, and O'Connor, who reportedly had been suspended at the Customs House for similar employment frauds, was reinstated.

It is not at all clear how the paths of Marie de Roux and Patrick O'Connor first crossed. Robert Huish, "having no particular data to go on," falls short of affirming that they "were sent from Heaven as a pair to hunt each other out through all the defiles, windings and sinuosities of this very best of all possible worlds." He contents himself with a conventionally romantic tale of their meeting: that Patrick was in the service of the Wentworths when they came upon Marie at the Swiss inn, and that, immediately smitten with her, he convinced Wentworth that she would be the very model of a lady's maid. Huish would have us believe that when the complicated foursome returned to Ireland, it was Patrick who first pursued Marie, but that, persistently unlucky in love, he was caught in flagrante delicto (or nearly so) by Wentworth and expelled from the household.

The journalists generally placed the first encounter of Marie and Patrick much later (in 1846) but in an equally romantic setting. They reported that the couple met on a Channel crossing to Boulogne, O'Connor having been given a two-week leave and Marie being on her way to join her mistress, Lady Blantyre, on the Continent; that one fateful evening they met in the ship's saloon, all the other passengers having retired. Marie is supposed to have been free with her name and position, for O'Connor, on his return home, was reputed to have told friends that he intended to call on Marie at Stafford House. The trouble with this delightful story is that it may be untrue. Marie, as will be seen, asserted that she had known Patrick since about 1842, long before her service to Lady Blantyre began.

We read that the road of the love affair did not run smooth. O'Connor showed friends letters from Marie that inquired bluntly: "Of what good is it to continue our correspondence? You never speak of marriage." Of what did O'Connor speak?

C. F. MANNING,

As He appeared at Union Hall Police Court, Sept.ʳ 15.ᵗʰ 1849.

Portrait of Fred Manning, from Huish's *The Progress of Crime*. The common reversal of his initials is probably an unconscious tribute to G. F. Handel.

He said that Marie's charming accent resembled that of Madame Celeste, a very popular actress. It was truly remarkable, he told friends, how much Madame Celeste's pronunciation of English was like that of his darling Mauridhe Rhua, as he called Marie in an Irish pun on her name. The Irish words meant Red Mary. This was all very gallant, but his friends did not gather that Patrick had any intention of marrying.

However fictitious her shipboard romance with O'Connor may be, it was very likely train travel that led to Marie's first acquaintance with Frederick George Manning, who was a guard on the Great Western Railway. Manning's father had been a sergeant in the Somerset militia and resided for many years in Taunton, where he collected market tolls. He was also for some time the keeper of the "Bear," a public house in Taunton, and was highly respected. He died about 1845, survived by his wife, Frederick, and other children.

It is reported that Lady Palk traveled frequently on the Great Western line and that it was on these travels that Marie came to know Frederick Manning. The reconstruction of their courtship is pure conjecture. Perhaps Marie had given up on the elusive Patrick O'Connor, who praised her accent but could never bring himself to pledge to live within eternal earshot of her voice. When Frederick met her, Marie's attractions were enhanced by an aristocratic aura lent by her service to Lady Palk; and she may already have adopted the genteel black satin that was to become her trademark. Huish writes that Frederick was a hard-working young man who had conserved a legacy of at least four hundred pounds under his father's will and had added money of his own through dealings in poultry and real estate, only to lose his state of respectability "by his fatal marriage with a female fiend."

Marie does not seem to have rushed into the arms of the railway guard. She entered the employ of the Sutherland family and for a time was visited at Stafford House by both Manning and O'Connor. Eventually, Frederick proposed marriage and she accepted. Rumor had it that Frederick did not rely solely on personal charm in pressing his suit (and indeed, after the fact at least, Marie did not rate his charm highly) but represented falsely that he was entitled to property worth about six hundred pounds under his mother's will. The wedding was celebrated in style at St. James's Church, Piccadilly. Manning now drew a will leaving his at least partly imaginary property to his "very dear and beloved wife" and appointed her coexecutor with his friend Henry Poole. Marie and all England would hear Mr. Poole's name again.

Marie's married life suffered a series of early surprises. The first was the arrival at Stafford House shortly after the marriage of a letter from O'Connor belatedly protesting his love and asserting (now that it was safe) that he had just been at the point of making his own proposal:

> Customs, St. Katherine's Docks
> June 11, 1847

MY DEAR MRS. _____. Not knowing your real name, I have addressed this note *as usual.* I hope it will find you. I cannot describe to you my feelings and what I suffered since I saw you last evening. If you were to know half, you would have compassion for me, if I were the greatest enemy you ever had. I have spent a solitary and a dreary winter, and a dull and melancholy spring, in anticipation of having a jovial and pleasant autumn. I had given up going into all society, and cut the acquaintance of every friend I had, on your account, being anxious to economise and secure for ourselves the means of making us happy and comfortable the rest of our lives. I had my month's leave of absence settled, to commence on the 6th of August, when I thought you might be returning from the continent, and hoped to get married on the 7th, leave London for Boulogne on the 8th, and there spend the honeymoon. But alas! all these arrangements are now blighted. You have all those comforts now that your heart can wish for, and I am glad of it. For poor me there is none of these consolations left, but the sad reflection of being disappointed. Ah, Maria! you have acted cruelly to me. Why not, like a true professor of what you avowed, write and say what you intended before you acted so, then, at the risk of losing my situation, I would have gone every step that man could, and got married to the only being on the face of the earth who could make me happy. And, Maria dear, if you could only read the feelings of my heart, you would not do as you did.

After this outpouring, Patrick cheered up and offered Marie and her husband a tour of the docks, including a visit to a ship from China. He concluded by hoping she would call on him as promised the next Sunday:

> You may be able to give some explanation on this matter which may smooth it down a little. I wish I could acquit you of infidelity on the occasion. I hope that every happiness may accompany your proceedings, and believe me under any circumstances till death,
>
> Yours very affectionately,
>
> PATRICK O'CONNOR

Marie, though, was accustomed to dealing with her triangular love life, and she no doubt found an early opportunity to make matters less complicated by introducing O'Connor and Manning to each other. They shook hands but would never be friends.

The next surprise for Marie was more severe: Manning was fired by the Great Western Railway. The newspapers reported after the O'Connor murder that Manning's dismissal was prompted by his implication (presumably with insufficient evidence for prosecution) in a series of robberies of gold bullion, in a total amount of four thousand pounds over a period of twelve months, from the train of which he was guard. We are not told the precise date on which Manning was dismissed.

The Great Western's troubles with gold robbers and inadequate guards continued into early 1848. On 10 January a box of gold coin with a total value of fifteen hundred pounds was stolen from a day-mail between Paddington Station and Bristol. The 10:15 A.M. train had been chosen for the shipment so that the parcel could be transmitted to its destination, a firm at Taunton, by daylight. The strong box, well secured with iron clamps, was brought by a special confidential messenger to Paddington and delivered into the hands of the guard immediately before the train started. The guard placed the box in a parcel compartment next to his own post on the train, from which he could keep the treasure under observation through an aperture in the wall of the compartment. On receiving the box, the guard said reassuringly, "All right—I'll take care of it," but the cautious messenger stayed on the platform until the train was in motion.

Upon the arrival of the train at Bristol, the superintendent searched for the box and found that all the gold had been removed. The box had been "dexterously cut by means of a circular saw, or some similar instrument, and the work was that of some practised hands." It was reported that the compartment adjoining that in which the gold was deposited had been hired by six persons of fashionable appearance, whom the police now surmised might be a part of London's "swell mob." However, the case was not solved. Still, the *Times* reporter could not resist dropping a suspicion about the guard: "The forcing open of the box whilst under the charge of the company's servant could not have been anticipated, it being an operation attended with difficulty and much noise." This guard, whom the *Times* supposed to be incredibly hard of hearing, may have been Manning, but this conclusion is far from clear. First, the robberies with which Manning was reportedly linked were of bullion, but the booty of the January 1848 robbery, though first described as bullion, was in a later report said to be coin. Also, Manning may well have been out of the railway service in 1847, since he soon turned up in a new position, that of keeper with his wife of the White Hart Inn at Taunton. Most important, there is another likely candidate for the role of the guard of the coin shipment—Henry Poole, a close friend of Manning's who, as we have seen, was named coexecutor in Manning's will.

Poole was soon to win an undisputed niche in the history of English train robberies—by daring mail thefts from both the up- and down-trains on the Great Western line on the same night of 1 January 1849.

The up-train left Plymouth for London at 6:35 P.M. On the arrival of the train at Bristol shortly before midnight, the guard went to the mail tender immediately at the rear of the post-office car in order to deliver the Bristol bags and was astonished to find that all the bags had been cut open or disturbed. When the mutilated bags were examined at the London Post Office in

St. Martin's-le-Grand, it was found that not only had registered letters and bankers' parcels been stolen but in many cases bills listing the valuable mail were also missing so that it was impossible to determine the full scope of the theft. While officials were still pondering these baffling discoveries on the afternoon of 2 January, the news reached London that a similar robbery had been perpetrated on the down-mail that had left London on the same evening of 1 January at 8:55 P.M., and that two suspected robbers had been arrested on the train. The suspects, who were eventually tried and convicted for the robbery of the down-train, were Henry Poole and Edward Nightingale, who had boarded the train at Bristol. On leaving Bristol, the train consisted of two second-class carriages next to the engine tender, then the "travelling post office" followed by the mail tender, and next the first-class carriage. The mail robbery was discovered after the down-train reached Bridge-water; some of the bags in the tender were found to have been opened and rifled, seals were torn off, strings untied, and different strings used to retie some of the parcels. The Bristol-Bridgewater segment of the run was the most convenient stretch for robbery attempts since it took two hours. It occurred to Barrett, the railway guard, that although it might be danger-ous for a first-class passenger to get to the mail tender while the train was moving, it would be almost impossible to get there from the second-class carriages, which were much farther away and were separated from the post office car by a gap of five feet. He therefore ordered a search of the first-class car, and Poole and Nightingale were found in a compartment with blinds drawn and in possession of a variety of incriminating objects: two crape masks, a piece of candle, a pocket hook that could be used to grapple a carriage roof, and a pair of false mustaches. After the prisoners were removed at Exeter to be searched, their compartment was gone over more carefully, and fourteen pieces of stolen mail were found bundled in a hand-kerchief under Poole's seat. The parcels contained six rings, ring mountings, a watchcase, and other articles. The police theorized that the robbers had stowed the proceeds of their up-train robbery somewhere at Bristol and then, after a stop-

over of only an hour and a half, coolly bought tickets at Bristol
Station for the down-train to pull off a repeat performance.
Their counsel, Mr. Cockburn, in his unsuccessful closing argument to the jury, described the agility and courage that would
have been required to accomplish the robbery: ". . . it was
alleged that when the train was proceeding at a velocity of from
20 to 50 miles an hour these men had got out of the window of
their own carriage, had then passed the windows of three
compartments, and then had got upon the buffers of the two
carriages, had proceeded from one carriage to another, and,
having only the shelving roof of the carriage to hold on by, they
had only the ledge of the panel on which to step for six feet
three inches. Why a cat could not have done it."

Poole was a former guard of the Great Western and had
worked on the mail trains. He had been discharged, one witness
stated, about eight or nine months before the mail robberies,
which would put the date of his firing in April or May of 1848.
Therefore, he was still in service at the time of the gold coin
robbery in January of that year, and just could have been the
negligent guard of whom the *Times* complained in that case, or
the guard's confederate.

The haul of Poole and Nightingale from the robbery of the
down-mail seems puny, but their theft from the up-train may
have been more impressive. One report valued the contents of
one of the missing registered letters at four thousand pounds,
and none of the lost mail had apparently been recovered by the
time of the robbers' trial. Poole's criminal career must have
been extraordinarily lucrative, because the auction of his
property, ordered by his friends in February 1849, included
furniture described by the *Exeter Gazette* as "fit for the mansion
of any nobleman . . . magnificent mahogany and rosewood
sideboards, chiffoniers, bedsteads, splendid feather beds,
Brussels and Turkey carpets, etc."

It is likely that Poole and Manning had shared the secrets of
earlier robberies, but their connection was first referred to by
the press in the accounts of the mail thefts. On 18 January 1849
the *London Times* quoted a piece of startling news from *Trew-
man's Flying Post* to the effect that the plan of the robbery of the

down-train had been known to the authorities for some four or five months before its commission. The detail of the plot, which was said to have been communicated first to two highly respectable persons in Taunton known to the *Flying Post*, was so accurate as to give the name of one of the prisoners, the description of the disguise, and the manner in which the robbery was to be accomplished. The parties who received the communication immediately reported to the railway authorities, and the *Flying Post* expressed the hope that it might still lead to "the capture of as formidable a gang of ruffians as ever infested any community." The paper stated that the two persons who contacted the authorities were Mr. Eales White, proprietor of a brewery, and Mr. James Dyer, a surgeon. The reporter identified the source of their information as "the wife of one of the supposed accomplices in this and many other 'railway schemes.'"

The *Taunton Courier* had fresh comments and news to offer on the hometown robbery plot. The *Courier* confirmed the accuracy of the *Flying Post*'s story but proceeded to raise a question as to whether the railway directors to whom the robbery plan was communicated in great detail were not subject to censure or perhaps even legal redress for not having immediately commenced an investigation to determine the accuracy of the information. In partial defense of the directors, the *Courier* expanded on the disclosure that the original source of the communication was the wife of one of the accomplices: "It should be known, and is not among the incidents of the disclosures narrated in the above statement, that the communication was made by the wife of the man said to be implicated in the robbery while in a paroxysm of anger arising from the ill-usage she had experienced. He had, consistently with his accustomed brutality, turned her out of his house, and it was while consulting those to whom she had appealed for advice that the various and long-continued enormities of her husband had been disclosed."

It is known that Inspector Charles Field and Detective Sergeant Langley, who were dispatched from London to investigate the mail robbery, interrogated the Mannings about the

case, and later newspaper reports make it certain that the
"accomplice's wife" who revealed the details of the criminal
plans to White and Dyer was Marie. Robert Huish, in his novel,
explicitly identifies Marie as the woman who gave away the
secrets of the robbery conspiracy. He states that Langley and
Field "satisfied themselves, beyond any possible doubt, that the
robberies were concocted at the White Hart Inn" as long as
three months before the actual perpetration of the crimes, but
that "the confederates were at that time foiled in carrying out
their objective by Mrs. Manning, who it appears had a violent
quarrel with her husband, and at that time, from a mere spirit
of revenge, had communicated the intended robbery." Huish
attributed the Mannings' disharmony to mutual infidelities. A
"certain meddling, officious gossip" supposedly dropped some
"oblique hints" about Fred's conduct with certain ladies of
Taunton. Marie, according to Huish, had been far from oblique
in her own love life. She took off without warning for London
and was met with a warm embrace by O'Connor at the station.
They lived together as Mr. and Mr. Johnson at Queen Street,
Bermondsey; neighbors, who, according to Huish, were fascinated with the new tenants, daily clocked O'Connor out of the
apartment at 9:00 A.M. and back at 4:00 P.M. and concluded
from these hours that the employee of Her Majesty's Customs
Service must work at a public house.

Marie returned to Fred Manning at Taunton but ran away
again, Huish reports, this time to parts unknown. The *Times*
published a melodramatic account of one of Marie's flights and
its prelude. The couple's mutual jealousies often ended in
blows, and on one occasion "the wife was seen in pursuit of her
husband with a large dirk knife." Then one night Marie left by
mail train, having, Fred complained, robbed him of money,
plate, and other valuables to the extent of three or four
hundred pounds. It is not surprising that marital scuffling
behind the bar and Marie's night raid on the inn's capital caused
the business to founder, and the creditors closed in.

When Marie returned she found that Manning had abandoned the inn but ultimately tracked him down, in Huish's
words, at "an obscure lodging in a quarter of the town at a

considerable distance from the White Hart." He cannot have been delighted to see her.

Therefore, two facts stood quite plain about the Mannings in early 1849: Fred Manning very likely had criminal connections, and the Mannings' marriage was in trouble.

CHAPTER FOUR

The Disappearance of Patrick O'Connor

*All that day, again, the search went
on. . . . But to no purpose; for still no trace of
Edwin Drood revisited the light of the sun.*
    —*The Mystery of Edwin Drood*

For a time Marie maintained her odd triangle with Patrick and Fred. Neither man was an Adonis. It might almost appear that she had chosen her men by the oddness of their jaws. Patrick had a caricature of a face that defied exaggeration by the police court artists. He was a tall, thick-set man with a long nose bent downward toward the tip as if to call attention unnecessarily to an enormous angular jaw that projected as dramatically as Dick Tracy's. Fred's face was plump and weak, and his large, formless chin seemed to have grown out of the soft planes of his cheeks.

The Mannings drifted from Taunton to London in early 1849. Huish claims that Sergeant Langley and Inspector Field, after several weeks' pursuit, traced them at last to O'Connor's residence at 21 Greenwood Street in Mile End Road, the easterly extension of Whitechapel Road, which runs through Jack the Ripper's famed district. The officers acquainted the Mannings with the object of their call and requested permission to search the apartment; they were presumably looking for the missing loot of the up-train. Huish writes that Mrs. Manning "immediately exclaimed with all the pride of conscious innocence, 'Oh! by all means, here are our boxes—you are at perfect liberty to examine all we have.' But nothing incriminating could be found."

The gossip according to Huish tells us that the Mannings stayed on briefly with O'Connor, and Huish adds censoriously that had Fred "been in the slightest degree sensitive to the fame and reputation of his wife, his penetration must have been of the most obtuse character not to have perceived the very questionable relation in which she lived with O'Connor." Eventually, says Huish, the ménage à trois became too much even for Fred to bear, and he left O'Connor's place to live with his brother in Newington. The *Times* account treats Patrick more kindly, reporting that the Mannings' first London residence was with Fred's brother, and that Marie took flight again and was tracked down by her angry husband at O'Connor's lodgings. In any event, the couple's differences were patched up again, and Fred and Marie were soon back together as proprietors of the old King John's Head, in Kingsland Road, a pub tied to the Goding's brewery. Still there were troubling shapes of things to come. Manning had to deposit some shares and scrip (bearer securities) as collateral for his account with Goding's. Huish asserts that Marie paid a visit to the brewery, made an unsuccessful attempt to reclaim the securities, and, having failed in her mission, "became highly excited and left the premises in a violent passion."

The Mannings' tenure at the King John's Head was brief, and they eventually took lodgings at No. 3 Minver Place, in Bermondsey. Manning apparently now had no regular occupation, and Marie's effort to establish business as a dressmaker did not meet with any success. Their relationship with O'Connor followed its unstable course. Patrick had apparently promised to sublease a portion of the Minver Place villa, and when he changed his mind, Manning filed suit against him. Somehow that controversy was smoothed away, and Patrick was often a guest at the apartment he had refused to rent. The Mannings were also seen at O'Connor's place. Marie frequently went there alone.

Patrick continued his twin occupations as gauger at the Customs House and usurer. He was very regular in his attention to both his professions. Therefore, it occasioned some surprise to O'Connor's cousin and fellow customs officer, William Flynn, when on Friday 10 August 1849, Patrick did not report for duty at the London Docks at the usual morning hour.

Minver Place, from Huish's *The Progress of Crime*.

He did not turn up at all that day or on Saturday, and Flynn and other friends and relatives of O'Connor became uneasy. On Saturday morning Flynn went to O'Connor's lodgings to inquire whether anything had been heard of him; and two friends of O'Connor from the customs service, William Patrick Keating and David Graham, called at the same time. Keating and Graham told Flynn that they had last seen O'Connor when they met him by chance as he was walking south on London Bridge at about a quarter to five Thursday afternoon. Patrick had shown Graham a letter signed "Marie" inviting him to dinner. After Flynn had absorbed this mysterious news, the three men questioned O'Connor's landlady. She was able to tell them only that Mrs. Manning had been at O'Connor's apartment on both Thursday and Friday evenings while he was away. Their worries now confirmed, Flynn and the two friends proceeded to the police station at Arbour Square in the Stepney district, about a half mile south of Mile End Road. After explaining the circumstances Flynn asked the inspector in charge of the station to permit an officer in plain clothes to accompany him to the Mannings'. Constable Barnes was selected and, meeting Flynn by appointment the same afternoon, went with him to 3 Minver Place. They knocked on the door several times, received no answer, and went away.

Keating had better luck than Flynn. He called at Minver Place with Graham on Sunday and found Mrs. Manning home. She sat outside the front of the house with her back to the window and seemed "rather slovenly in her dress." When Keating asked for Mr. Manning, Marie said he was away. He then inquired after O'Connor, saying "Why, did he not dine here on Thursday?" She answered shortly, "He did not." It struck Keating as strange that she appeared to show no anxiety about her friend.

He questioned her about her visit to O'Connor's lodgings on Thursday, and she informed him that she had gone there that evening and had also called on Friday, to "inquire for his health." When Keating suggested that Mr. Manning might know something of O'Connor, she told him that her husband was at church. To his parting statement that he would come again in the evening, she said: "No, we are invited out to tea, and I am afraid we shall be from home." As they left, Keating remarked to Graham that Mrs. Manning was very nervous.

Meanwhile Flynn, despite the temporary check he had received, thought it would be appropriate to call at the Stone's End police station, the nearest station to Minver Place, and arrived there with Constable Barnes at five o'clock Sunday afternoon. He repeated his suspicions to the inspector in charge and requested that a special watch be placed on the Mannings' house. Flynn thought that his request was granted, but when he called again at the station on Monday morning, another inspector to whom he was introduced could give him no guarantee that the house was in fact under watch; he assured Flynn that prompt measures would be taken to make certain that nothing was removed from the house.

At Flynn's request a constable named Wright was directed to accompany him in a new call on 3 Minver Place. This time the door opened to their knocking and the two men were met in the doorway by Mrs. Manning. By prearrangement, Wright placed himself opposite her "in order to observe the workings of her countenance" while Flynn questioned her. After being told that Manning was not at home, Flynn came to the point: "Have you seen or heard anything of Patrick O'Connor these last few days?" No, Mrs. Manning replied, she had not seen him since Wednesday night (8 August), when he called at their house very tipsy and was seen home by his companion Mr. Walsh. She had called at his lodgings on Thursday night and was very much surprised not to find him at home. She had also heard that he was still missing on Sunday.

Flynn said that it was very strange, and Mrs. Manning remarked: "Yes, it is very strange indeed, the more so as he is a very regular man." She added, "I understand some friends of yours met him on Thursday on London Bridge, coming in the direction of this house." But O'Connor had not come that evening, Marie said, and she was not surprised by his apparent change of mind; O'Connor was a "very fickle man and would frequently come to see us and, after sitting down for a minute or two, he would jump up suddenly and go away." She added that Patrick had friends at Vauxhall and suggested that they would probably know something about his whereabouts.

After some conversation about Marie's recent visits to O'Connor's lodgings, she suddenly exclaimed: "Poor O'Connor! He was the best friend I had in London." "Why *poor* O'Connor?" wondered Flynn, and thinking he detected a slight expression of discomfort in her features that he had not noticed before, he asked whether the room was perhaps too warm for her or whether she felt ill. She raised a hand to her face for a moment, but immediately recovering her composure, she said: "No, thank you, I have been ill for six weeks, and dare say I look rather pale, but there is nothing the matter with me." Flynn and the officer ended the interview at this point, perhaps less out of feelings of delicacy than a realistic conclusion that they would gain nothing from further questions at the moment.

Over the weekend Flynn had handbills circulated offering a ten-pound reward for information about the missing man:

Ten pound Reward — Missing

Mr. Patrick O'Connor, an officer of the Customs, who left his residence, 21, Greenwood street, Mile-end road, on Thursday morning, the 9th inst., and was seen near Weston street at 5 o'clock on the same afternoon. Description—50 years of age. 5 feet 11 inches high, fair complexion, light hair, stout made, and wears a false set of teeth.

If one were to disappear mysteriously, it would be well to have a relative as persistent and energetic as William Flynn. Not satisfied with the police activity he had stirred at two local stations, he now went directly from Minver Place to Scotland Yard, where he was promised every assistance he required to trace his missing cousin. On Monday night Flynn went again to O'Connor's apartment to see whether any of his property was missing. He first opened a trunk in which he knew Patrick kept his cashbox, having little difficulty forcing the patent lock. Inside he found the cashbox in its usual place. It was an ordinary japanned box with three compartments. Flynn knew that Patrick used to keep securities in the end compartments and his loose gold coins in the center compartment, which was covered by a slide. He discovered on examining the box that it was empty with the exception of a few scattered IOUs and memoranda and that the slide, instead of being in place, had been carelessly thrown down on the middle compartment.

Flynn had just returned home from another day of fruitless searching on Tuesday when Mr. Meade, a friend of O'Connor's, called on him with the disturbing news that the bird had flown. From neighbors Meade had learned that Mrs. Manning had been seen leaving her house at about four o'clock on Monday afternoon. She later returned in a cab and, picking up a large amount of luggage, drove off again. By Tuesday, Meade added, all the furniture had been removed from the house, which was now empty. Meade had already alerted the police at Stone's End Station, and they were surprised and chagrined that for some reason their promised watch of the house had been either nonexistent or easily eluded.

At 8:30 P.M. Tuesday evening, in response to Meade's information, Constable Burton was sent with Meade and two other friends of O'Connor to Minver Place. Finding the house closed up, they went through the adjoining house and over the wall, but the gymnastics were unnecessary because Meade had meanwhile obtained the housekey and let Burton in at the back door. The house appeared to have been left in a very confused state. There was a pile of linen in the front kitchen, and in the back kitchen over two large Yorkshire flagstones a large box or portmanteau lay open. Women's wearing apparel had been scattered about the room, and Burton also spotted a railway guard's coat. Upstairs clothes lay about in the same disorder. The searchers found nothing that belonged to Patrick O'Connor.

The next morning Burton kept watch at the house to see whether anyone would come for the rest of the Mannings' things. About 8:00 A.M. a man came and tried the front door but could not open it since Burton had locked it the night before with the latchkey. The visitor went off immediately to the police station to find out why the house was locked, unaware that Burton was following him at a discreet distance. The

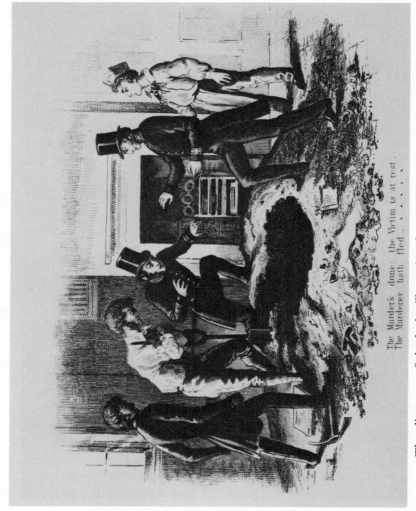

The discovery of the body; illustration from Huish's *The Progress of Crime*.

Left and right-hand Views of the Back-Kitchen where the Body was found.

A. Wall at the bottom of the kitchen-stairs, on which spots of blood were discovered, and near which it is supposed the air-gun was discharged.
C. Iron-barred window, through which the shadow of the Mannings was reflected on the garden-wall, late on the night of the murder.
D. Entrance to the kitchen where the body was found.

F. Fire-place where a goose was roasted, on the day after the murder, by Mrs. Manning.
G. Stone, under which the body was found.
E. The Sink in which O'Connor was in the habit of washing his hands.
H. Copper.

The back kitchen at 3 Minver Place, from *The New Wonderful Magazine*, vol. 2 (London, n.d.).

constable could not have been more pleased with the destination for which his quarry was heading. At the station it turned out that the man was a dealer named Bainbridge who had purchased the Mannings' household goods from Mr. Manning for thirteen pounds. Bainbridge had no interest in the linen, but he had come back to fetch away the railway guard's coat and some other things he had not yet had a chance to remove. He told the police that Manning had just left the Bainbridges' house.

Burton then accompanied Bainbridge back to Minver Place and watched him take away the remainder of his goods. Among the things Bainbridge took was a shovel that stood behind the door in the back kitchen. The courteous Constable Burton himself handed the shovel to Bainbridge.

On Friday Burton and Constable Barnes of the Stepney Division returned to 3 Minver Place for a more thorough inspection. They found Patrick O'Connor's body under the flagstones of the back kitchen where the open portmanteau had stood.

CHAPTER FIVE

Brokerage and Brandy

*If Slinkton had been running for his life
from swift-footed savages, a dozen miles, he
could not have shown more emphatic signs of
being oppressed at heart and labouring for
breath, than he showed now, when he looked at
the pursuer who had so relentlessly hunted him
down.*

—*Hunted Down*

Strange as it may seem now, the use of the
telegraph to pursue the fleeing Mannings
added an element of wildest romance to the
case. The "electric telegraph" then in its earliest days in England was not the Morse instrument but a device
jointly invented by William Fothergill Cooke and Charles
Wheatstone. In the Cooke-Wheatstone telegraph built in 1837,
a letter of the alphabet was transmitted through two of five
wires connecting the transmitter and receiver. The currents
deflected two electromagnetic needles in a set of five contained
in the receiver and caused them to point toward the designated
letter on the face of a diamond-shaped board. In a later model
the inventors reduced the number of wires and needles to two,
and the transmitted letter was indicated by a code based on the
number and direction of the deflections of the needles.

The telegraph was first developed along railroad rights-of-
way, which provided security and convenient placement for the
telegraph wires. Cooke, a great promoter, was able to arouse
the interest of rail executives and engineers in his invention
before governmental and public transmission of messages
began, because the telegraph was capable of performing significant operating and safety functions for the railroads. It could be

used in place of noisy pneumatic whistles to give advance notice of approaching trains to engine houses that powered rope haulage of trains up steep gradients. The telegraph also flashed warnings to avoid train collisions in tunnels and on single-track lines.

Even prior to the Manning case the telegraph had been applied to police work. Several detectives had been assigned to identify known criminals boarding trains at London's Paddington Station. The value of this procedure was triumphantly demonstrated on 3 January 1845, when John Tawell, dressed as a Quaker in a long brown greatcoat, was arrested at a London lodging house after committing a murder at Salt Hill in the neighboring town of Slough. He had traveled to Slough with a vial of cyanide in his pocket and used the poison to dispose of his unwanted mistress, Sarah Hart. Her dying screams alerted neighbors, who sent for a local surgeon. Unable to save her and hearing that a Quaker was the last man seen leaving the house, the surgeon proceeded to the Slough station where he thought the murderer might take a train. He saw Tawell pass through the office and communicated his suspicion to the station superintendent, Mr. Howell. When Tawell was observed boarding a London-bound evening train, Howell dispatched the following message by telegraph to Paddington Station 18 miles away: "A murder has just been committed at Salt Hill, and the suspected murderer was seen to take a first-class ticket for London by the train which left Slough at 7:42 P.M. He is in the garb of a Quaker, with a brown great coat which reaches nearly to his feet; he is in the last compartment of the second first-class carriage." The transmitting operator faced a bit of a puzzler in the word *Quaker,* since the receiving board in use on the Slough-Paddington line did not include a *q.* Nothing daunted, the operator proceeded to describe Tawell's pious costume phonetically as that of a "kwaker." The needle-watchers at Paddington could not believe that the first letters, *kwa,* were right and challenged them, but when the full word was transmitted, light dawned and Tawell was promptly arrested at a London boarding house. The capture of the criminal gave the public its first understanding of the sensational possibilities of the telegraph, and its wires were dubbed "the cords that hung John Tawell."

The debut of the electric telegraph in the Manning case was technologically impressive but the results were disappointing except in comic relief. Immediately after the discovery of O'Connor's body, a number of detectives were sent to several seaport towns to see whether any persons answering the description of the Mannings had taken passage on ships leaving for abroad, and telegraphic bulletins were also dispatched along the various railway lines.

One police constable placed his faith in serendipity. He went down from London to Portsmouth in the company of a man whose wife had run away with some of his property. On boarding a vessel, the constable saw a man who he thought matched Manning's description in every detail. The suspect was talking with "another party of Jewish appearance who spoke through his nose." The second man "made use of a low expression" and addressed his companion as Manning. It appeared that the two men were engaging a berth in a ship sailing for New York, and steamships were reportedly dispatched to overtake it. The two suspects were never heard of again.

The telegraphs, however, continued to work furiously. A wire was sent to Sir George Grey, the Home Secretary, regarding the murder, and his response was to order the immediate issuance of a reward of one hundred pounds for the apprehension of both the Mannings or fifty pounds for either of them. The Secretary promised a royal pardon to any accomplice coming forward with information who had not actually fired the shot or inflicted the mortal wound. The main attention for the moment, however, was still on heading off escape by sea. It was reported on Monday, 20 August, that a general belief now existed that the fugitives were on board the ship *Victoria* bound for New York. The source of the lead was a newspaperman who discovered at 3 Minver Place two cards, one of which was a list of times of sailing of a line of packet ships between London and New York, including the *Victoria*, advertised to sail from London Docks on Friday. The other card was plain, with these words written on it: "Mr. Wright, passenger to New York." The reporter gave the cards to a policeman, who tore them up, observing that it was unlikely that the Mannings would have left the cards behind if they had intended to go to New York. On Sunday the reporter, undiscouraged, called at the London Docks with a clerk of the *Victoria*'s agent to request that the passenger list be examined. Only the steerage list was available, and it did not show the Mannings among the passengers; but the baggage officials told them that six packages had been taken on board by a person named Manning. This discovery was related in triumph to the police, and Scotland Yard finally took interest in the *Victoria*. Two London detectives went to sea from Portsmouth in pursuit of the ship and attempted to stop her by signals to "hove to," but the *Victoria* for some reason refused to hove and proceeded on her way. At 4:00 Monday afternoon Detective Sergeant Edward Langley, who had been sent to the scene because he knew the Mannings by sight, received a wire from Inspector Haynes in London ordering that immediate pursuit of the *Victoria* should be undertaken. Langley communicated with the authorities at the Portsmouth Dockyards, and Admiral Capel immediately ordered the *Fire Queen,* a government steamer, to fire up its engines and proceed to the chase. The ship put to sea at 9:00 P.M. with Langley and Detective Sergeant Thornton aboard.

On Tuesday morning the *London Daily News* had a disappointing report on the *Fire Queen*'s mission. The *Victoria* had been overtaken off the Bill of Portland and boarded by Langley and Thornton. Two Mannings were indeed found on board, but they were not the parties searched for. They were mother and daughter, and the six parcels booked at the London Docks belonged to them.

The handwritten report of the detectives, which survives in Scotland Yard's dossier of the Manning case, tells of their pursuit in laconic terms: "We went on board [the *Fire Queen*] at 8 p.m. and by 9 p.m. Captain Allen had collected his crew and steamed out of the harbour—we overhauled several ships during the night and about 1/4 to 2 a.m. boarded the Victoria and found the parties on board were not the ones we were in search of. We then returned to Portsmouth." But the frustrations of the detectives cried out for the more detailed attentions of a humorist. A year later Charles Dickens could not resist poking a bit of fun at Detective Sergeant Thornton's fruitless search of the *Victoria* in his account in *Household Words* of a party for Thornton and other London detectives:

> One of our guests gave chase to and boarded the Emigrant Ship, in which the murderess . . . was supposed to have embarked. We learn from him that his errand was not announced to the passengers, who may have no idea of it to this hour. That he went below, with the captain, lamp in hand—it being dark, and the whole steerage abed and seasick—and engaged the Mrs. Manning who *was* on board, in a conversation about her luggage, until she was, with no small pains, induced to raise her head, and turn her face towards the light. Satisfied that she was not the object of his search, he quietly re-embarked in the Government steamer alongside, and steamed home again with the intelligence.

Fortunately, during all these dramatics on the high seas, the detective force was pursuing more substantial leads back in London. The first of many heroes in this phase of the police effort was Detective Sergeant Shaw. After the police had learned that Marie Manning left Minver Place on the afternoon of Monday, 13 August in a cab, their next task was to try to track down the driver. Shaw searched for the driver all week without success, but on the afternoon of the following Monday, 20 August, his inquiries led him to a man named Kirk, driver of Hackney Cab No. 1186. On being questioned, Kirk told Shaw that he had been called from the stand in Joiner Street, Southwark, to pick up a fare in the neighborhood of Weston Street. He could not describe the exact spot, nor could he remember his passenger in detail, but he recalled that she was "a female of very respectable exterior." When Shaw took him to Minver Place, Kirk immediately recognized No. 3 as the place where he had picked up his fare, and he was able to detail the route he had taken. His passenger, who had taken along three large boxes and a carpet bag, first directed him to drive to the London Bridge Station of the South Eastern Railway, but just as he was turning into the road leading from the "Borough" (the area of Southwark around Borough High Street) to the railway terminal, she pulled the cord and instructed him to stop at the door of Mr. Ash, stationer and printer at No. 5 Wellington Street. The woman got out and went into the shop, where she purchased, as the police later verified, six plain white cards. A pen being given to her at her request, she wrote directions on four of the cards. The fullest instruction read "Mrs. Smith, passenger to Paris. To be left till called for"; and the other notes were briefer variations. Having paid Mr. Ash for the cards, the woman reentered the cab and asked Kirk to drive her to the South Eastern Station. On her arrival there, she asked him to call a railway porter, and when a porter appeared, she requested that he obtain some tacks with which she might fasten the direction cards upon her boxes. The two boxes with the cards attached were conveyed to the luggage room with the instruction that they be taken care of until called for. The woman then reentered the cab and was driven by Kirk to the London and North Western Railway (Euston) Station, where she arrived at about a quarter to six o'clock. Kirk saw her remaining luggage, consisting of one box and the carpet bag, taken into the station.

Sergeant Shaw's discoveries were communicated to Inspector John Haynes at Scotland Yard. At an early hour on Tuesday, 21 August, Haynes proceeded to the South Eastern Railway terminal, where he found the two boxes exactly as described. No inquiry had been made for them since they were deposited on Monday of the week before. Haynes at once requested an interview with Mr. G. S. Herbert, the railway secretary. He explained the course of the police search and said that it was absolutely necessary for him to be permitted an immediate examination of the contents of the boxes. Herbert conferred with two or three of the railway directors who happened to be at the station, and they agreed to Haynes's request. The boxes were brought into the secretary's offices and were forced open; they were found to contain female wearing apparel marked with the name of Maria Roux, linens, dinnerware, and an array of household goods from toast rack to tea caddies. A skirt, a piece of muslin, and two toilette table covers appeared to be stained with blood. On further examination the searchers found a number of articles belonging to Patrick O'Connor and several letters he had written to Marie. Among the O'Connor property were several papers bearing witness to his money-lending activities—receipts for loans to various parties. There was also a document purporting to be the will of Frederick George Manning dated 6 June 1848. One of the attesting witnesses was known to the police—their old friend Henry Poole, who had by now been transported for the mail train robberies. Under the will, all of Manning's property was left to Marie.

Inspector Haynes then went to the London and North Western Station at Euston Square, where Marie had been dropped off by Kirk the week before. Here, too, his inquiries met with success. He found that a female passenger, whose luggage was marked with the name of Smith, had left Euston Station on the morning of Tuesday, 14 August by the 6:15 A.M. train, having booked a place to Edinburgh in the first-class carriage. Marie had fled in a style to which Lady Palk and the Duchess of Sutherland had accustomed her. Having resolved all doubt about Marie's escape route, Haynes at 12:50 P.M. sent a wire to the superintendent of the Edinburgh police alerting him to Marie's likely presence in the city and including a full description of the fugitive.

Marie had, in fact, arrived in Edinburgh on Wednesday, 15 August. She took lodgings with a woman named Hewart in Haddington Place. Marie had taken the same name she had given on her luggage, Mrs. Smith, which had become, according to one newspaper report, the "favorite cognomen nowadays with people who find themselves placed in any position of danger or difficulty." On Friday Marie called at the shop of a draper in the Lawnmarket and asked to see some stockings. The shopkeeper recalled her as "a woman of a somewhat elegant appearance and speaking with a foreign accent," who had had a quantity of stockings laid before her and chose one pair with obvious indifference. It was clear that the purchase was only a pretext for a question she put to the draper: Could he refer her to a respectable stockbroker in Edinburgh? He gave her the name and address of Messrs. Hughson and Dobson, members of the Royal Exchange.

Marie called on the brokers on Saturday and spoke first to one and then to both of the partners. She told them rather grandly that she had dealt in Spanish bonds and that at the present she held some shares in the Amiens and Boulogne Railway and also in the Sambre and Meuse Railway, which she would not mind disposing of if she could do so advantageously. The brokers told her that foreign stock was not traded much in Edinburgh but that they had no doubt that they could sell the stock through their London agents. Marie also confided that she had in her possession about three hundred to five hundred pounds in money that she was inclined to invest in railway preferred shares. In discussing this possible investment, she was anxious to know whether the dividends would be payable abroad. Messrs. Hughson and Dobson answered her questions and at the same time told her "in the most courteous and friendly manner" that it was unsafe for her to travel with so much money and that it would be better for her to deposit it in a bank account on which she could draw interest until she made an investment decision. To this suggestion she replied, pointing to her breast: "I keep it here, where it is quite safe."

In the course of her conversation, Marie informed Messrs. Hughson and Dobson that she had come to Edinburgh within the last few weeks. She told them expansively that she was highly pleased with the city as a place of residence and that she had enjoyed sea bathing in the neighboring town of Portobello. She added that her father resided in Glasgow and mentioned that his name was Robertson, which caused the brokers some surprise, since they had noticed that their new customer spoke in "a slightly foreign accent." According to Marie her father had done a great deal of business and had lost a lot of money in railway shares. The interview was brought to a close by Marie's handing the brokers a railway scrip certificate on which one pound per share had been paid, and, on her asking whether she could find out if any further payment was due, the brokers promised to correspond with their London agents and to get back to her in the next day or so. She left the scrip certificate with them and was given a receipt for it. Before leaving she left them a note of her Edinburgh address. Strangely, she had not told the brokers as much about her husband as she had about her father, but they later recalled her having mentioned that Mr. Smith was in England and would shortly visit her in Edinburgh.

On Monday, 20 August, while Sergeant Shaw was still searching for the elusive cabbie, Marie called again at the office of Messrs. Hughson and Dobson. Only Dobson was in at the time. After a few minutes of trivial conversation she stated that she wished to have the scrip certificate she had deposited returned to her. She did not give any reason at first but subsequently stated that she intended to leave that afternoon or the next morning for Newcastle to visit her mother, who was unwell. She added with an inappropriate smile: "Of course I must pay every attention to my beloved parents." She expected to return in a few days to Edinburgh and would then call on the brokers again. Mr. Dobson immediately give her back the scrip certificate and she tore up the receipt. Before leaving she also asked, as if in an afterthought, for the note of her name and address she had left on her first visit. However, Mr. Dobson could not find it.

On Tuesday morning, at the same time as Inspector Haynes was breaking open Marie's luggage at the South Eastern Station, Messrs. Hughson and Dobson received an enlightening circular in their mail. It was a printed letter advising that certain shares in foreign railways had been stolen in London and cautioning brokers against dealings in those shares. Their suspicions were immediately aroused that "Mrs. Smith" must in some way have been connected with the theft. Mr. Dobson searched again for the note Mrs. Smith had been so anxious to recover and this time he was successful. With the paper in hand he rushed to the Edinburgh police office and communicated his suspicions of Mrs. Smith to Richard Moxey, the police superintendent. Moxey consulted the wired description of Mrs. Manning he had just received from Haynes as well as another description given in the London papers, and he at once became convinced, as were the brokers, that "Mrs. Smith" was in reality Mrs. Manning. Since a train was just about to leave for Newcastle from the station of the North British Railway Company, Moxey and Dobson immediately proceeded there and personally inspected the passengers in all the carriages, without, however, discovering Mrs. Smith. They then went to the lodging house of Mrs. Hewart, where Mrs. Smith had stated in her note that she lodged. On arriving at the house Mr. Moxey and a police officer who accompanied him knocked at the door and asked the landlady after Mrs. Smith. Mrs. Hewart told him that Mrs. Smith was there and showed the oficers to her room with Dobson following close behind. As Moxey entered the room, he saw a young woman reading the *London Times* and said, "Mrs. Smith, I presume."

The woman rose politely. "Yes," she answered.

"I beg your pardon, but if you are Mrs. Smith, you are not the person of whom I am in request."

The woman claimed that her husband's name was indeed Smith and that he was dead. She could give no references to persons who knew her; she had come from Newcastle to benefit her health by bathing at Portobello. Moxey then called Dobson into the room and asked whether the woman was the Mrs. Smith who had called at his office; he replied without hesitation that she was. The superintendent then identified himself and acquainted Marie with the crimes of which she was accused. After cautioning her against making any statements that might prejudice her, Moxey asked her if she had any scrip. "Oh, yes," she replied, "I have scrip of my own; you will find it in my trunk."

Her luggage, consisting of a carpetbag, a trunk, and a box, was then examined by the two police officers whose findings convinced them that they had now come upon the greater part of the valuables said to have been stolen from the lodgings of Patrick O'Connor. Marie's purse contained seventy-three sovereigns in gold; one fifty-pound note; a five-pound note; and six ten-pound notes, five of which bore numbers previously advertised as having been paid to Manning on Saturday, 11 August, as part of the proceeds of sale of certain of O'Connor's securities. In addition, the officers found all the missing scrip of the Sambre and Meuse and Boulogne and Amiens Railways, which was known to have been owned by O'Connor, and they also discovered some clothing that belonged to him. It was soon established that the fifty-pound note and one ten-pound note in Marie's posession belonged to Fred Manning, representing proceeds of sale of the King John's Head public house, and certain French securities (rentes) she had were likely hers. A Spanish bond was also found in the trunk, and it was assumed, without any strong reason, to be O'Connor's property.

When the securities and money had been examined, the police proceeded to make a careful inventory of Marie's jewelry and her elegant wardrobe, including two black merino gowns, three black satin dresses, a colored figured sarsenet dress, and a black lace pelerine. They also noted the papers she had packed in her luggage, including correspondence with the Blantyres, a volume of sacred poetry, and the "Psalms of David in French with music."

Marie asked their permission to retire to an adjoining apartment for a few minutes, but being refused she consoled herself with a glass of wine and took several more while the examination of her luggage was going on. When the search was completed, she was taken from her lodgings to the police office in a cab. After she was safely in hand at the station, Superintendent Moxey wired news of her arrest to Scotland Yard.

The telegram was delivered to Inspector Haynes shortly after his return to the Yard from the railroad station. Between the time of Haynes's wire to Edinburgh and the return message from Moxey announcing the arrest, only about an hour had expired. The electric telegraph had more than redeemed the fiasco of the pursuit of the *Victoria* and had made an even more stunning showing than in the Tawell case of four years before.

The news of Mrs. Manning's capture caused intense excitement in London. The immense crowds that had surrounded the Minver Place house for the first few days after discovery of the murder now converged on Scotland Yard. Their first treat was the sight of Marie's boxes that had been discovered at the South Eastern Railway Station. The luggage brought a shock of recognition to one detective. "I've seen these boxes before," he said. "We searched them at the time of the Bristol mail robbery."

Meanwhile, the arrival of Mrs. Manning was momentarily expected, and a large throng packed Euston Square Station early on Wednesday, 22 August. However, the technicalities of Scottish law kept the crowd on tenterhooks. Prisoners taken in Scotland could not be sent across the very real border into England until an authorized English officer was sent to Edinburgh for the purpose of claiming the prisoner. Marie had been brought after her arrest before Sheriff Arklay of Edinburgh and charged with O'Connor's murder. Having received again the usual warning that any incriminating statements could be used against her, she replied that she had nothing to say and was sent back to jail for removal to London as soon as the English officers should arrive. The *Edinburgh Courant* reported that Marie's demeanor before the sheriff was calm and self-possessed, but that she was somewhat paler than at the time of her arrest. The Edinburgh reporter was the first to mention the prisoner's stylish dress: "She was attired in an elegant black satin dress, and white crepe bonnet. . . . We understand that her manner and accomplishments are most lady-like, and that she talks French with great fluency." (The British even then were clearly amazed by the ease with which French natives picked up the French language.)

While the Scots had their day in court with Mrs. Manning, the *London Times* reporter fretted about the delay in her return to England and wished that the police authorities had again made use of the electric telegraph or at least remembered that "England and Scotland are not governed by the same system of jurisprudence." Mrs. Manning finally arrived at the Euston Square Station at five o'clock Friday morning accompanied by Superintendent Moxey. She was taken by cab from the station to the Southwark Police Station at Stone End, where a charge of the murder of O'Connor was immediately made against her by John Wright, the police constable who had accompanied Flynn in his visit to her on the day of her flight from London. Before the charge was made she asked for a cup of coffee and sipped it while the accusation was registered. Observers did not find her in the least flurried by the customary questions that were addressed to her or alarmed by her dangerous situation. She gave her address as No. 3 Minver Place without hesitation and answered "yes" with great firmness when asked if she was married. To the question of Superintendent Evans of the Stone End Station whether she knew what crime she was accused of, she replied "with perfect composure: 'No, I know nothing.'" She addressed herself with great appetite to the substantial breakfast that was then served her and afterward became drowsy. During a fitful sleep that followed she was heard several times to mutter, "Oh dear, oh dear, where am I?"

Mr. Secker, a magistrate, arrived at Southwark police court at half past ten, and Marie was immediately placed before the bar of the court. The courtroom was jammed and the entrance besieged by men and women anxious to obtain a glimpse of the accused. The crowd did not show any reaction when Marie appeared in the dock. The *Times,* which had in an earlier report from Edinburgh expressed preliminary doubts of Marie's reputed beauty, now gave its first eyewitness description to its readership:

> She wore a white straw bonnet with a white lace veil, which was tied under the chin, and disposed in such a manner as partially to conceal her forehead. She also wore a black silk *visite* [loose mantle], with satin stripes, and a gown of the same colour and fabric. She is rather above the middle height, and her figure is stout, without being clumsy. It would, however, be a mistake to call her either handsome or beautiful. Her manners and appearance are very much what might be expected in a domestic in one of the town establishments of our nobility. Her features are neither regular nor feminine, yet the general expression of her face is rather pleasing than otherwise and she has evidently been a comely woman.

The reporter then proceeded to make ungallant speculations about Marie's age:

> Her age is entered on the charge sheet as 28, but she looks five or six years older at the least, and would be put down by a critic in these matters as decidedly *passée.* She has dark hair and eyes,

and by her cast of countenance would be set down as either a German or an English woman. She speaks slowly and distinctly, with a slight foreign accent, her voice having nothing harsh or disagreeable about it.

Although the reporter immediately envisioned her as a "foreign intriguer," the first impression of Marie's manner in court and of her response to the dreadful charges against her does not seem to have been wholly unfavorable:

> There is nothing about her which can be considered indicative of the monstrous crime with which she stands charged; and though there is little difficulty in seeing that she has been a woman of intrigue, no one from her appearance would fancy her a murderess. Her manner in the dock was suitable to her position in life, being submissive and respectful, without any trace of alarm about herself. She did not appear at all agitated, and her eye moved freely and without embarrassment around the court. When first brought in her face was pale, but the colour soon returned to it.

The police had decided to submit as little evidence as would be necessary to support Marie's retention in prison. It was their hope that Manning would soon be captured and that the couple could then be confronted with each other in court.

Magistrate Secker opened the proceedings by addressing the prisoner: "This is a most serious offence with which you are charged; have you any professional man in attendance?" Marie answered: "I have sent for one, but he is ill." Inspector John Yates was then called and charged Marie with the murder of Patrick O'Connor on Thursday, 9 August at 3 Minver Place, Bermondsey. In support of the charge, he testified that he had seen the body of the murdered man. Fourteen wounds had been inflicted on top of his head "as if with a plasterer's hammer," and a bullet had been taken from the front part of his head. The magistrate asked Marie whether she wished to ask any questions of Inspector Yates, advising her that it was not necessary for her to do so since this was merely a preliminary examination. Marie said in a firm tone: "I have no question to ask him at present." Constable Wright then testified as to Mr. Flynn's interview with Mrs. Manning and concluded his evidence by saying: "I also believe the prisoner to be concerned in the murder, and I ask for a remand until evidence can be produced against her." Marie again declined to ask any questions.

Magistrate Secker granted the request for a remand of Marie to prison and ordered that she be held for a week. He permitted Superintendent Moxey to return to Edinburgh and agreed that for the time being he should keep the property the Edinburgh police had taken from the prisoner. Moxey then told the magistrate that the prisoner had expressed a strong desire to see him again before he left town, and he asked whether he would be permitted to see her in the presence of the officer in charge of her. The permission granted, the superintendent withdrew to the inspectors' room, where Mrs. Manning was being held, and asked her what she wanted to communicate to him, cautioning her against self-incrimination. Perhaps the caution had been expressed effectively, because Mrs. Manning replied that she had nothing to say except that she was quite innocent of the charge. Her only request was for a change of clothes and for some of the money that had been taken from her. The magistrate granted the first request but not the second, feeling that there was strong reason to believe that all the money in Marie's possession had belonged to O'Connor. Marie was then quietly removed to Horsemonger Lane Gaol in Southwark. She rode in a covered van, which shielded her from the eyes of her public.

Frederick Manning remained at large. Marie had been tripped up by her passion for stock transactions but Fred Manning, it was to appear, was more interested in drink. If we are to judge by the immensely greater difficulty the police had in tracking him down, it must be concluded that, for a fleeing criminal, brokerage is more dangerous than brandy.

The police were quick to find the beginning of the trail that Manning had left. Bainbridge, the furniture dealer, had told them that Manning had slept at the Bainbridges, on Tuesday night, 14 August. The next morning when Bainbridge raised the blinds to let in the daylight, his guest showed sudden alarm. Explaining that he had a two hundred pound note that fell due that day, Manning unceremoniously left in a cab. On Sunday morning, 19 August, Inspector Perkins located the cabman, who recalled picking up a fare in Bermondsey Square on Wednesday morning. Manning had instructed him to drive to the Waterloo Station of the South Western Railway and insisted that he take a devious route through back streets. The mysterious passenger got off at Waterloo with two carpet bags, one of which, according to Bainbridge, contained two new suits of clothes. Manning had received only thirteen pounds for the furniture, and the police were counting on his quickly running out of funds unless he joined his wife. But they had not reckoned with the cheap tourist accommodations of Manning's chosen refuge.

Manning's unflattering description was advertised in the police bulletin, *Hue and Cry,* as well as in the general newspapers, and it was also posted in towns throughout England: "Frederick George Manning, 35 years old, 5 feet 8 or 9 inches high, stout, very fair and florid complexion, full bloated face, light hair, small sandy whiskers, light blue eyes, and a peculiar form of eyelids at the corners, and large mouth. Was dressed in an invisible-green [very dark green] overcoat, brown trousers, black hat, and wore a small-plaited linen shirtfront." During the chase Fred was to give a convincing demonstration of how his face had come to be florid and bloated. However, many of his countrymen must have shown the same bad habits in their faces because a disconcerting string of false identifications led his pursuers astray. From the time Manning's description was first publicized, the police received many reports from people who claimed to have seen Fred in London. The governor of Bath Gaol thought he saw Manning pass Basingstoke in a third-class up-train to London, and the overworked telegraph summoned Inspector Haynes to the pursuit. A special engine hauled Haynes, and two or three other officers who knew Manning by sight, from Waterloo to Wimbledon, where the up-train was stopped and examined. The suspected party was thoroughly rattled by the search but he was not Manning. Another Manning look-alike was taken into custody while bloating his face at a beer shop in the Caledonian Road, Islington. On

Friday afternoon, 24 August, a man who had some resemblance to Manning was chased through woods near Carshalton but outran his pursuers. At Bagnigge Wells Road Station people alerted the local authorities about a man who jumped out of the wrong side of the Greenwich train. As far away as Dublin, police were excited by rumors that the murderer Manning had arrived.

Grasping at every straw, Scotland Yard scattered its detectives in all directions. The Scotland Yard dossier indicates that the police from the very beginning were looking for a "French connection." An undated draft of a letter destined for France carried out the instruction of Commissioner Richard Mayne to inquire whether the Mannings might have murdered a second man who had resided in Paris:

> It has been represented to the Commissioners that a gentleman had been in the habit of visiting the said Manning and his wife at their various residences in London and he not having been seen for some few months past it is conjectured that some foul play has been practiced towards him by Manning and his wife. The Commissioners beg to enclose the name, the signature and address [in Paris] of a gentleman cut from one of several letters from the same party addressed to M. Roux found in her boxes . . . and beg that you will be good enough to cause prompt inquiry to be made at the address given to ascertain if the gentleman is still living.

It was also thought at first that the Mannings might have escaped to France, and Inspector Field was sent to Paris to search for them. Field returned to London, empty-handed, but according to the *Gazette des Tribunaux*, his junket was not a complete failure. While he was waiting at the Paris terminus for the train to Le Havre, a passenger discovered that his pocket had been picked. Field, after casting an experienced eye over the crowd at the station, walked up to an elegantly dressed young man who was negligently playing with his cane and, seizing him, cried out in the manner of his famous successor Sherlock Holmes: "This is the thief—Wood, the celebrated Wood!" The young man was searched and the missing watch was found in his boot. Fresh from this unexpected triumph,

Field was now dispatched to Plymouth to check a report that Manning was bound for Australia on the emigrant ship *Constant*. The police had been informed that on 14 August a man answering Manning's description had applied for passage to Australia and, when told the price was fifteen pounds, exclaimed that thirteen pounds was all the money he had in the world. Were the passenger's pounds Mr. Bainbridge's well-publicized payment, or had the informant had his imagination jogged by too much newspaper reading? The energetic Field would not guess but had to search the ship; after all, the story might make sense if he could believe what Marie was just quoted as having said to a constable asking about her husband's whereabouts: "It's no use your looking after him, for he's a long way from here; in fact he is out of the country."

Then on 28 August it was reported that the police had come upon a clue indicating that the trail of Manning, which ended so abruptly at the South Western Station, led to the Channel Island of Jersey. An official communication was received from the Channel Islands that a young woman had recognized Fred Manning on a Channel steamship. The woman told the Island authorities that she was the sister of the keeper of a Guernsey lodging house where Manning had stayed for four days in March. She had not heard of the murder at the time she saw him on board and thought nothing of the chance meeting as she alighted at Guernsey, where she was greeted by headlines of the Bermondsey Horror. She was sure that Manning had gone on to Jersey. Scotland Yard noted her story with interest, because there were rumors that Manning had fled to Jersey on a previous occasion when he found it wise to lie low. The ubiquitous Sergeant Langley, who had been doggedly tracking Manning along the route of the South Western, was sent to Jersey. But Scotland Yard was not placing all its bets on the Jersey lead and proceeded with its plans to search the ship *Constant* on its arrival at Plymouth.

The young woman from the Channel steamer was, however, quite right. Manning had arrived in Southampton on the South Western at about two o'clock on Wednesday, 15 August, and took a room at the Oxford Arms Inn near the railway station.

He stayed there all afternoon and at midnight left for Jersey on the South Western Steam Packet Company's mail ship the *Despatch*. During the crossing he rarely appeared on deck, staying in the forecabin and drinking a large amount of brandy. At Jersey he disembarked with a fellow passenger named Turk, with whom he had become acquainted on board. The two men walked into the principal town of St. Helier and asked for rooms at the Navy Arms Inn near the harbor. The landlady, Mrs. Berry, told them that she only had a double-bedded room available, and they accepted this accommodation, Manning agreeing to pay. On Thursday Manning went out with Mr. Turk "to see the island." He returned in the evening and had tea with Mr. and Mrs. Berry, subsequently joining the other guests in the parlor and entering freely into conversation with them. It did not take long for Manning to make himself thoroughly disliked by all who were present, including Mr. Turk. He was overbearing and rude, and strangely, despite the small amount of cash he was carrying, he contemptuously twitted Turk with claims of greater affluence: "I can show more fifty pound notes than you can sovereigns," he told him. When Turk immediately put down five or six sovereigns on the parlor table, Manning rose from his seat and said, "Oh, never mind, old fellow. Why should you and I quarrel?"

On Saturday Manning was out for the day, and on the following morning he asked Mr. Berry where he could go to church. During the course of Sunday he was as talkative as ever, telling the landlord that he had lost all his money in the French Revolution of 1848 and that he must go to Paris to settle his affairs. He asked how much it would cost to cross to Granville, the opposite port on the French coast. When Berry told him that the fare would be about twenty shillings, Manning told him that he would make the crossing and asked Berry to accompany him as an interpreter. The landlord declined and advised Manning that if he wanted to go to Paris, the best way was to return to London and proceed by the usual route to the French capital. Manning pretended to accept the advice, but when he was roused early the next morning for the packet leaving Jersey, he stayed in bed and enjoyed the solitude of his room,

Mr. Turk having left Jersey that day. Berry noted that his guest's appetite was unflagging and that he ate "as much as any three ordinary men."

Manning continued to make it his business to annoy the local populace. On Sunday evening he had entered the parlor of the Bath Hotel, one of the most respectable establishments at St. Helier, and despite the vast quantities of Jersey cookery he had been putting away, he announced that he had had but one good dinner since coming to the island and that was of a conger eel. He should not have been surprised, he added, because before he left London a fellow clerk had told him: "Fred, my boy, you'll find the Jersey people a set of humbugs." While at the Bath Hotel he drank brandy and water steadily, and when the company in the parlor broke up for the night, he was rather drunk. He was not too drunk to lie, for he said he was staying at the Union Hotel. As he left the Bath Hotel, John Heulin, a Jersey resident whom Fred would meet again, observed that he was turning in the wrong direction to go to the Union and attempted to set him right. Manning replied, "I know perfectly well where I have got to go to. Good night."

On the following day, Monday, he treated the barroom at the Bath Hotel to his tactless behavior. He described himself as a traveling salesman for Sir Robert Burnett's British gin. This surprised the landlady, Mrs. Seward, who knew that her husband obtained his gin from Burnett's through an agent named Mr. Mann. Manning threw himself back in his chair and laughing heartily exclaimed: "How very strange! My name is Mann—" and then he stopped short. Mrs. Seward was able to recall some pleasant comments that Manning had made. He spoke of the island as "a most delightful place" and said he must bring "his dear wife" with him on his next visit. He added that his wife "was a very fine woman," that she was passionately fond of him, and that she always addressed him as her "dear Fred."

That night, while walking the streets of St. Helier, Manning met a man whom he had formerly known at Taunton. The man was spending his honeymoon on Jersey. Perhaps the appearance of an old acquaintance from home made Manning feel suddenly uncomfortable at St. Helier, for his landlord at the Navy Arms noticed a remarkable change in his manner after Monday. It could have been that Manning was less affected by the inconvenient honeymooner than he was by a growing worry about his safety and the dwindling proceeds of Mr. Bainbridge's purchase. Certainly he had had no fear of old faces as recently as the day before. On Sunday afternoon Manning had hailed the driver of the St. Aubin's omnibus in St. Helier and enjoyed a ride along the coast in the direction of St. Lawrence. He had talked freely to the driver and praised the beauties of St. Peter's Valley through which the bus passed. On arriving at the hamlet of St. Lawrence, he waved his hand at a man who was walking by the roadside. When his greeting was not returned, Manning asked the driver whether the pedestrian's name was not Ford. The driver replied that it was, and Manning was delighted, exclaiming: "Dear me, how very odd, he is a most particular friend of mine; I knew him most intimately four or five years ago." Learning that Mr. Ford was staying at the British Lion, a small roadside inn nearby, Manning visited him there, chatted in a most pleasant manner, and invited himself to dinner at the inn. After dinner Manning returned to his fantasy about business affairs awaiting him in France. Ascertaining that Ford spoke French, Fred asked him to accompany him to France to help make arrangements for certain property there. Ford began to have some doubts about Manning's honesty and asked why he was traveling in Jersey alone. Manning told him that he had left his wife in London and that he had come over to see how he could invest two or three hundred pounds that he had at his disposal. When he had determined upon an investment, he told Ford, he would return to England and fetch his wife. He claimed that he was presently in negotiations for the purchase of a brewery at St. Helier but told Ford that he was not at liberty to disclose the name of the brewery for the moment. By this point Ford had had enough of his English friend. When Manning expressed a strong wish to see him again the next day, Ford put him off until Wednesday, and when Fred called at the Lion at the agreed hour, he found to his surprise that Ford was out and had left no message.

As he left the British Lion on Wednesday, Manning noticed about three hundred yards away a neat little cottage named Prospect House, whose windows looked directly into the Bay of St. Aubin and provided a fine view of Queen Elizabeth's Castle. The house was owned by an old Jersey couple named Berteau. The old man worked a little land, and his wife supplemented their income by renting rooms in the house. Two rooms were occupied by a Jersey carpenter and his wife, named Weildon, and neither family could speak more than a few words of English. Observing a notice in the window offering apartments for rent, Manning took a large bedroom for four shillings a week and arranged also to take his meals with the landlady, who would also make his bed and do his washing. Manning's limited funds were running low, and perhaps the modest rent overcame the obvious danger of hiding out virtually under the eyes of the unreliable Ford. In any case, Fred was tired of running, his ingenuity as exhausted as his funds, and Prospect House was his last burrow. He returned to St. Helier to inform the landlord at the Navy Arms that he would be leaving on Thursday for a short time to stay with his old friend Mr. Ford at St. Lawrence but that he would leave his trunk at the Navy Arms. He asked that his bedroom not be let and that the door be kept locked.

While Manning was announcing his planned departure from the Navy Arms, Mr. Utermarck, Crown Prosecutor of Guernsey, advised the British Home Secretary and the lieutenant governor of Jersey of the identification of Manning on board the *Despatch* by the young woman passenger. On the same day Commissioner Mayne of Scotland Yard wrote a note to the governor of Jersey stating his belief that Manning was on the island. The governor placed the matter in the hands of Mr. Chevalier, the chief of the Jersey police. Chevalier's first actions were stamped with more energy than success. On Thursday, while Manning was ensconcing himself at Prospect House, Chevalier was tracking two persons who engaged a small steamboat to take them across to Saint-Malo. One of them, he had been informed, bore a strong resemblance to the advertised description of the Bermondsey murderer. Catching up with them at the pier, Chevalier was not satisfied with their statement that they were about to proceed to Saint-Malo to attend the funeral of a relative who had died of cholera, and he requested them to accompany him to the mayor's office for further questioning. That same evening Chevalier received information that Manning had been seen in St. Helier by the honeymooner Trenchard, who had known him formerly at Taunton.

On Saturday morning, 25 August, Detective Sergeant Langley and Constable Lockyer arrived in Jersey by the same steam packet that had brought Manning to the island. Early Sunday morning Chevalier went with them to St. Lawrence and called upon Ford, who told them about his meeting with Manning. As they arrived at the British Lion and as they left, the policemen passed Prospect House, where Manning was in hiding, but he was so well concealed there that neither Ford nor the officers had any reason to believe that he was still on the island. Chevalier, in fact, thought that he must have escaped from the northern coast of the island, so he borrowed a small steamboat belonging to the harbor commissioners to make the crossing to Granville, where they arrived before noon on Sunday. No traces of Manning could be found there, so they returned to Jersey on Monday to look for other possible points from which Manning might have crossed the Channel.

In the meantime, Manning was leading a life of quiet drunkenness with the Berteaus. He was shown to his room by Madame Berteau about eight o'clock on Thursday morning, 23 August, and was told that he might receive friends in her own parlor downstairs. Fred thanked her for her kindness but said that he did not expect any callers since no one knew him in Jersey. He had not been in the house very long before he sent out for his first bottle of brandy, from which he drank frequently during the day. Early Friday morning he sent for a second bottle and repeated the same pattern on Saturday and Sunday without arousing any suspicion on the part of his landlord. Then on Sunday a friend of Madame Berteau called on her, and having heard something of the habits of the lodger, remarked that his conduct seemed very strange. She hoped that he was not the perpetrator of the dreadful murder that had just

been committed in England. Madame Berteau had not heard of
the Bermondsey murder and paid little attention to her friend's
gossip.

However, the sellers of Manning's brandy also had their
suspicions aroused. For Manning Jersey was becoming in every
sense a tight little island, and the circle of the brief acquaintances he had made was closing in on him. The brandy was being
furnished to him from the establishment of a Mr. Heulin, who
happened to be the father of John Heulin, on whom the
doubtful pleasure of Manning's company had been forced at
the Bath Hotel in St. Helier. George Heulin, John's brother,
was in the habit of waiting on the girl who fetched the brandy to
Prospect House, and he was amazed how much liquor was being
consumed at the home of the Berteaus, whom he knew to be
very temperate. He questioned the girl, who told him that the
person drinking the brandy was a lodger who stayed indoors all
day and drank, so he claimed, "to keep the cholera away."
Anticholera diets of the most exotic variety were being published at the time in the *Illustrated London News*, and brandy was
at least as plausible a remedy as any. George Heulin was,
however, a skeptic. He had heard in St. Helier that the
murderer of Patrick O'Connor was holed up in Jersey, and
suspecting that his freely imbibing customer was the man, he set
out to watch daily for the lodger's appearance in the Prospect
House garden, where the girl had told him he generally went in
the evening for a short time. He saw him there on Sunday and
again on Monday, and was strengthened in his suspicions by the
lodger's evident effort to escape recognition by pulling his felt
hat down over his face. Just after dusk on Monday George went
to the back entrance of Berteau's house, determined to ask him
who his lodger was and what name he was using. He found
Manning sitting with Berteau outside the back door in a little
yard, smoking his pipe. Berteau advanced a few steps to greet
Heulin, but Manning quickly retreated into the house. George's
questions to Berteau alarmed the old man, who was in poor
health, but he was unwilling to believe that his lodger was the
suspected fugitive. The man appeared to be a very nice gentleman and had given his name as Jennings. It was true that he did

not go out much, but this might be explained by his being unwell and afraid of the cholera, and no doubt he would get out more when he felt better.

The moment George Heulin had gone, Manning went up to Berteau in the back kitchen, where he had remained during their conversation, and asked him who George was, what he had come for, and why he wanted to know his name. While he asked these questions Manning trembled from head to foot and appeared scarcely able to get his words out. The thought instantly occurred to the old man that he was, in fact, harboring a murderer. As soon as he had satisfied Manning that the visitor was a neighbor and that his motives were only those of curiosity, he rushed to his wife and told her, pointing to Manning: "That's a murderer." In order to prevent the lodger from committing suicide or, still worse, another crime, he hid a hatchet and some pieces of rope that were lying about the house.

George Heulin was as sure as Berteau that the lodger was Manning and proceeded at once to St. Helier to consult with his brother John. When his brother heard him out, he shared George's suspicions, and they went out to look for Sergeant Langley. They found the detective within a few steps of the Bath Hotel, and George told him his story. Langley took the Heulins to Chevalier and urged that they go over to St. Lawrence immediately to arrest the lodger. It was already past nine o'clock P.M., and Chevalier suggested that the man would probably already be in bed and that it perhaps might be just as well to defer the arrest until the morning. However, Langley was not willing to wait, and Chevalier immediately acquiesced in the longer working hours of the London detective.

Chevalier was right at least in predicting Manning's bedtime hour. He was already in bed when the officers arrived at the house at about 9:30 P.M. They got out of their carriage about two hundred yards on the St. Helier side of the cottage and approached on foot. By arrangement Chevalier and George Heulin went around to the back and explained to Berteau that they had come to arrest his lodger on a charge of murder, an announcement that the old couple appeared to receive with relief. It was agreed that Chevalier would return to the front of the house and knock at the door, which Berteau promised to open. The Heulins were to stay outside the cottage and prevent Manning's escape by the windows, of which there were three in his room alone. The plan was followed, Berteau opened the front door and handed Chevalier a lighted candle, and the officers went quickly upstairs prepared to break open Manning's door if it was locked. Unexpectedly they found the door ajar. Chevalier pushed the door fully open, and placing the candle on the table, he rushed to the bed in which Manning lay. At the same instant Langley caught a quick glimpse of Manning's face and immediately recognized him. Manning's arms were pinioned, and Chevalier threw himself on the bed to prevent him from making any resistance.

Manning did not take kindly to these rough measures, crying out: "Hallo, what are you about? Do you mean to murder me?" The moment he saw Langley he became calm and said, "Ah, Sergeant, is that you? I am glad you are come. I know what you are come about. If you had not come I was coming to town to explain all. I am innocent!" He then asked, 'Is the *wretch* taken?" At least that is what the polite Victorian papers said he asked. However, in some accounts the noun is blanked out, and it is likely that the word was "bitch." In any case, Langley supposed that he was referring to his wife. When the detective replied in the affirmative, Manning remarked: "Thank God, I am glad of it; that will save my life. She is the guilty party; I am as innocent as a lamb."

Chevalier commanded him to dress in the presence of the officers and, when he had done so, proceeded to handcuff him despite Manning's protests that it was unnecessary.

Fred remained in the talkative mood that the air of Jersey (and perhaps the brandy) had given him. He said that all the property in the room belonged to him and that the seven sovereigns found in his carpet bag were all that was left of the sum that had been paid to him for his furniture by a man in London. He was led out of Berteau's house and placed in the carriage to be conveyed back to St. Helier. On the way, without any questions being asked of him, he volunteered several comments on the crime. He expressed the hope that his wife would not commit suicide before he got to London for when there he could soon clear himself. Later he said, "I suppose she must have fifteen hundred pounds upon her; at least she ought to have. She has often told me that she would be revenged upon O'Connor." Chevalier asked him what he meant by being revenged, and Manning answered: "Why he induced us to take the house in Minver Place, and to furnish it, on the understanding that he would come and live with us, which he did not do. And my wife got into a great rage, and said she would be revenged. I said, 'Don't be angry, dear'; and advised her to forget and forgive." He also told them that a little before the time of that conversation his wife had gone to O'Connor's apartment, where Patrick had shown her notes and railway coupons and promised that he would leave her the bulk of his estate under his will. He added that Marie had frequently gone to O'Connor's house. About two weeks before the murder she invited O'Connor to come and dine with them, but he did not come. Then

> she wrote him another letter, asking him to dine with us on the fatal day. The dinner was laid upstairs when he arrived. My wife asked him if he would not go downstairs and wash his hands, as was his custom, before dinner. He replied, Yes, and immediately went downstairs followed closely by my wife. As soon as they reached the bottom of the staircase my wife put one of her arms around O'Connor's neck, and with the other hand she fired a pistol at the back part of his head. O'Connor immediately fell dead. I fainted, and do not know what became of the body.

Chevalier asked him whether he had not seen a hole dug in the back kitchen. Manning replied: "Oh! yes, I had seen it and I believed that it was intended for me. I believe my wife intended to murder me." And yet Fred had stayed on living with the murderess of 3 Minver Place.

At seven o'clock A.M. on Friday, 31 August, Chevalier and the London detectives went to St. Helier's Gaol for the purpose of bringing Manning to the packet boat for England. He had made the request that he be allowed to walk through the streets of St. Helier, and since it was so early Chevalier agreed. Fred also asked for a cigar, which was given him. A reporter commented with wonder that "the suspected assassin of Patrick O'Connor actually walked a distance of nearly half a mile from the gaol to the pier through the streets of St. Helier's, smoking a cigar, with all the ease imaginable."

On the voyage to England Fred Manning's words continued to flow. He was sure that his wife, as soon as she came before the magistrate and saw clergymen, would confess at once to having committed the deed. She had threatened to kill O'Connor for the last six months and had said that she would not die happy if she did not do so. He could not help observing to the London detectives that he had been much amused at reading some of the newspaper accounts of the activity of the Jersey police in seeking him out while he had smoked his pipe opposite the chief police office for some days.

Langley and Lockyer kept their ship cabin as private as possible, but they were not able to prevent some passengers from catching a sight of the supposed murderer. Manning was delighted with the attention he was drawing and conversed with one woman for some time, remarking that he had had "two wives, and that was one too many." Captain Childers, the commander of the *Despatch,* recognized him immediately when he came on board and told the detectives that he remembered the night of Manning's first crossing: Manning had come up to him several times and pressed him to drink brandy and, in fact, had become so troublesome that the captain was obliged to ask the steward to get Manning to call it a night.

When the packet steamed into Southampton harbor, Inspector Haynes came on board to receive the prisoner and brought him to London's Vauxhall Station by special train. Manning was taken to Stone's End Police Station to be booked. It was odd, but somehow as soon as Fred returned to London, all his confidence and sangfroid vanished. He would not joke much anymore or lead a silent parade brandishing a cigar.

The reaction of the press to the capture of the Mannings shows that in the public mind there was much more at play than the apprehension of two suspects thought to be plainly responsible for a particularly brutal murder. The circumstances of the arrest of the criminal conspirators in two distant hiding places at opposite points of the compass and beyond England's borders seemed to provide new ground for comfort in the security of modern England life and in the wonders that could be accomplished by technological advance. It was, as in the Tawell case, the marvelous efficacy of the telegraph that was singled out for special praise. An editorial in the *Illustrated London News* opined that "the benefits conferred by science" in the apprehension of great criminals had already been exemplified by the Tawell capture; but that the case of "Mrs. Manning, a woman in comparison with whose blackness of guilt the memory of Tawell appears white, is a still greater warning to future criminals of the folly of crime and the certainty of punishment." The usually cynical *Punch* indulged itself in what is virtually a prose poem in the honor of the telegraph:

God's lightning pursuing murder is become a true and active thing. What was a figure of speech is now a working minister. A phrase in the mouth of poetry, is now a familiar presence—a household retainer, doing hourly errands. We have brought devastation into servitude; we have made a bond-slave of destruction. Thus, Murder has hardly turned from its abomination—scarcely set forth upon its shuddering flight, when the avenging lightning stays the homicide.

Marvellous is the poetry of our daily life! We out-act the dreams of story-books. The Arabian tales are flat, crude gossip against the written activities of our social state. *Sindbad,* with his wonders, so many glories about him, is become a dull fellow, opposed by the electric workman—the Clerk of the Lightning.

Murder, with its black heart beating thick, its brain blood-gorged, reads the history of its damnation. Hundreds of miles away from its ghastly work, Murder in the stupidity of deepest guilt—for the greater the crime the greater the folly that ever as a shadow accompanies, and betrays it—Murder, with forced belief in its impunity, reads its own doings chronicled and commented upon in the newspaper sheet; and—so far away from the victim's grave; the retreat so cunningly assured, the hiding-place so wisely chosen—Murder draws freer breath, and holds itself secure!

—And the while, the inexorable lightning, the electric pulse— thrills in the wires—and in a moment idiot Murder stammers and grows white in the face of Justice. In the marvellousness that sublimates the mind of man, our Electric Tales make poor work of the Arabian. Solomon's Genii may sleep in their brazen kettles. They are, in truth, the veriest smoke compared with the Genii of the Wires.

In the euphoria of retrospect, even the comedy of the *Fire Queen's* pursuit of the *Victoria* seemed to *Punch* to be "another cause of mournful pride," a "noble sermon, preached *extempore* to embryo crime." The warning uttered by the telegraphically ordered sea chase was this, in *Punch's* high-sounding phrases:

> Though the sea encompass you; though you have baulked pursuit, and Justice—like a hound at fault—beats and gropes confounded; though you have begun to count the profits of blood, and how to make the most of them; how, in your new country, to live a life of impunity and ease,—nevertheless, give up the dream; dismiss the vision, and awake to horrid truth. For there, in the horizon miles away, is a thin dark vapour—the man at the mast has seen and reported it—and, with every ten minutes, it becomes more distinct,—and now the distant gun is heard across the water, booming command; and the ship's yards swing round;—she lays to; and—how rapid the ceremony, how brief the time! and Murder, aghast and manacled, is made again to turn its face towards the land it has outraged with the sacrifice of blood.

Several weeks later *Punch* followed up its panegyric to telegraphy with a cartoon showing a fleeing criminal ensnared by telegraph wires at the end of a line of poles, each of which the artist transformed into a scarecrow in the shape of a pursuing policeman swinging a club. Captioning the piece "Swift and Sure" and subtitling the moonlit picture "A vision very like reality," *Punch* concluded its accompanying commentary with a variant of the joke first propagated in the Tawell case: "No wonder the murderer is nervous, when he is, literally, very often 'hung upon wires.'"

The *London Times* shared *Punch's* enthusiasm for the swiftness of the work of the detective force in the Manning case and the vast increase of their powers lent by the science of telegraphy. However, the continuing toll of the cholera cast a shadow over the *Times*'s rejoicing. Its editorial writer could not rid himself of the ironic vision of science enabling police detection to solve one mysterious death but leaving the medical profession powerless to deal with thousands. He noted that on 9 August, the day of the murder, and during the five previous days, the cholera epidemic in Wandsworth had taken the lives of nineteen residents of Albion Terrace, a row of suburban homes much like Minver Place. The "mean intangible instruments" of these deaths "can be invested with no dramatic interest," he concluded, "but fixing our eyes on the victims, it is well worth considering whether substantially it is not as much a part of the sound policy of the country that lives like those in Albion Terrace should be saved as that the murderers of the man in Bermondsey should be hanged."

For other commentators, however, the Manning case was a human drama of absorbing interest, wholly apart from what it might mean for the successes or failures of science and civilization. The crime novelist W. Harrison Ainsworth, who had read of the capture of Fred Manning when he was abroad, put the matter quite simply in a letter he wrote to his daughters from Paris: "So Manning is taken; I am glad of it."

CHAPTER SIX

Homicide Fair

. . . a criminal under sentence of death, or in
great peril of death on the scaffold, becomes,
immediately, the town talk; the great subject;
the hero of the time.

—Charles Dickens, letter to the
Daily News, 28 February 1846

T he special British passion for sensational murder cases cannot easily be explained or explained away. An attractive theory would have it that this law-abiding people (whose total annual murders are fewer than those of many American cities) is fascinated by its murders precisely because they are such rare phenomena. The trouble with this proposition is that the English and the Scots have not always been notably peaceful, and yet for centuries they have continued to read and talk about murders. Gallows sermons and pamphlets on murders, capital trials and executions began to appear in England in the violent seventeenth century, and in the eighteenth century readers avidly read encyclopedic collections of criminal cases, which were named "Newgate Calendars" after London's Newgate Prison. The mild-mannered Londoners who now consume both scholarly and lurid accounts of modern English crimes are inheritors of an old habit.

The great appetite for crime journalism and fiction in nineteenth century England is sometimes blamed on the low level of the public's literary sophistication; it is suggested that simple and bloodcurdling crime narratives were in effect a primitive substitute for literature. There is considerable merit in this theory for not only were the uneducated an eager clientele for crime reports but they found ready means of transmitting their passion to respectable middle-class households. An important agent in this dissemination of popular literary taste was the nursemaid, who fed her young bourgeois charges murder stories along with their milk. Two Victorian murder–fanciers, in entries in the English periodical of literary and historical miscellanies, *Notes and Queries,* trace their first memories of crime sensations to the enthusiasm of nannies. Henry Gibbs recalled (seventy years after the fact) "a nursemaid reading in a winter evening of 1824, from a broadsheet which she had bought from the twopenny postman, a versified account [of the murderer Thurtell]." In 1911, mourning the impending destruction of "The Swiss Cottage," an old London tavern, W. F. Prideaux reminded readers that the Hocker murder was committed within its walls in 1845; one of his earliest recollections, he added, was of being taken by his nurse "to view the scene of the murder on the day following the tragedy." It was the fervor of domestics such as these that Dickens immortalized in his sketch "Nurses' Stories" in *The Uncommercial Traveller,* where the narrator recounts his nurse's diabolical bedtime tale of "Captain Murderer."

Nevertheless, the mass dissemination of crime journalism among the semiliterate cannot fully account for the British preoccupation with violent crime, for the puzzling fact remains that Britain's great writers have always equalled or even surpassed the general population in their attraction to murder cases. The murder obsession of British writers was plain even before Victorian times. In 1828 Sir Walter Scott made a detour on his route from London to Scotland for the express purpose of visiting a tourist attraction that cannot have been in the contemporary guidebooks—the pond where the murderer John Thurtell had thrown his victim four years before. And when William Hazlitt and a circle of literary friends exchanged names of great men from the past whom they would like to have met, Charles Lamb asked for the group's favorites among men who had been hanged.

Britain's history was certainly bloody, but King Henry VIII's beheadings seem small stuff when compared with France's St. Bartholemew's Day Massacre. It will not do, then, to attribute the preoccupation of the British with crime to their history. Yet they have treasured the monuments of historical crimes with the same love Scott had for Thurtell's pond. This odd attachment did not escape the perceptive eye of a French critic, Francis Wey, who paid a number of visits to England in the 1840s and 1850s. He wrote: "The historical monuments of this country, I notice, are popular in proportion to the horrors committed within their walls. Every self-respecting castle has a legend of bloodshed and murder. . . . So inured did we become to these macabre anecdotes that as we entered any building we asked with serene assurance: 'And who was murdered here?'"

The devotion of the British to their crimes must remain as great a mystery as many of the cases they treasure. It is possible, though, that this national trait that struck the Frenchman Wey as so peculiar is related to other more significant aspects of British culture. The appeal of murder cases draws to some extent on violent instincts, but certainly it also responds to the love of drama and exciting and suspenseful narrative. Fascination with murder cases may proceed from the same facet of the British genius that created the Elizabethan drama and gave birth to the eighteenth-century novel of adventure.

The early years of Victoria's reign produced a series of classic murders that suited the most discriminating taste. In 1837, the year of the queen's coronation, James Greenacre was convicted and hanged for the murder of his fiancée, Hannah Brown; and Greenacre's mistress, Sarah Gale, was transported as an accessory after the fact. Mrs. Brown's body had been pieced together by police from portions severed by Greenacre and scattered over outlying districts of London. The torso was discovered first on a building site in Edgeware Road, the head was fished from the floodgate at the tail of a lock in the Regent's Canal, which ran through Stepney Fields, and a laborer came across the legs in a drain in Camberwell. In addition to the clumsy, horrifying dismemberment, the case had a number of features bound to win the fancy of a large public—none more grotesque than Greenacre's story that he had wrapped the head of his victim in a silk handkerchief and calmly carried it on his knee as he rode a London omnibus on his way toward the Regent's Canal.

Greenacre maintained to the end that he had not intention-
ally killed Mrs. Brown, though he finally confessed striking her
in rage over her misrepresentation of her wealth as a marriage
bait. The mutilation and concealment of the body he admitted
and regretted. He also contended ardently that Sarah Gale
knew nothing about the death of Mrs. Brown or the disposition
of her body. It was rumored that Sarah had inspired Greenacre
to do away with her rival, but the prosecution limited the
indictment against her to the charge that she had assisted in the
concealment of the murder. The case against her began with
the conceded fact that she was sent away from Greenacre's
lodgings on 24 December 1836 to make room for Mrs. Brown,
who thought, poor woman, that she was to be married to
Greenacre the day after Christmas. When the house was
vacated two weeks later, neighbors who came in to look (as
neighbors do) found that the floors appeared to have been
carefully scrubbed and that the house had been fumigated. Sex
roles being what they were at the time, everyone assumed that
Sarah Gale had been the housecleaner. Her own loose tongue
may have hurt her, for people came forward who claimed they
had heard her make comments indicating knowledge of the
murder. It was unquestionable that she had at least shared the
fruits of the crime. When Sarah was arrested, earrings belonging to Mrs. Brown were found in her pocket.

Despite this chain of circumstances, at least a slight doubt
about Sarah's guilt seemed to be left in the mind of the judge.
At the time of sentencing he contemplated the possibility that
she might have been at fault only in allowing her "attachment to
the prisoner" to keep her at his side "notwithstanding his
possession of the property of the deceased under circumstances
which I should think must at least have excited suspicion in
[her] mind."

The year 1840 brought a new sensation—the murder of Lord
William Russell in Park Lane, London, by his Swiss valet,
François Bernard Courvoisier, whom his master may have come
upon in the act of taking off with the household plate. Courvoisier's trial produced a legal controversy that was still being
discussed in the newspapers at the end of the decade: the

defendant's counsel, Charles Phillips, in his closing argument to the jury, accused the police of fabricating evidence, and he was understood by some listeners to have expressed a personal belief in Courvoisier's guilt and to have cast suspicion on a housemaid, *even though his client had just confessed the murder to him.*

The next case to startle the early Victorians began as a suspected shoplifting and ended as a torso murder to rival Greenacre's crime. On 26 April 1842 Daniel Good, a philandering coachman known for his violent temper, stopped at a pawnbroker's in Wandsworth, a southwestern suburb of London, and purchased a pair of kneebreeches on credit. After he left, a shopboy told the pawnbroker that Good had also picked up a pair of trousers and had hidden them under his greatcoat. The pawnbroker complained to the nearest policeman, Constable Gardner, who proceeded to the stable at Putney where Good was employed, but was cautious enough to enlist a stableboy for the dangerous task of knocking on the stable door. Good opened the door, with his eleven-year-old son behind, and had his famous temper well under control. When Gardner accused him of the theft, Good pretended to misunderstand. He would pay for the kneebreeches, he said, if the pawnbroker had changed his mind about giving him credit. Gardner persisted in the charge of theft and demanded to search the stable. Good refused, and the constable forced his way through the doorway. However, he overran his quarry, who neatly side-stepped him and fled, locking him inside. At least Gardner could now search to his heart's content, but he did not find the trousers. Instead he discovered, hidden under a bundle of hay, a nude female body without head, arms, or legs.

The victim, it turned out, was Jane Jones, alias Jane "Good," the last in a series of Good's mistresses, whom he had got rid of to clear the way for Susan Butcher, perhaps the only girl he had ever met who insisted on marriage. The hunt for Good was bedeviled by the blunders of his pursuers, none of whom did much better than poor Constable Gardner, and also by shortcomings in the organization of the police force. The authority of each local police division stopped at its territorial boundaries, and even hot pursuit of a fleeing criminal into the next zone was regarded as an intrusion. Training in detective methods was also lacking because the police commissioner, Colonel Charles Rowan, had little use for detective work. Despite the failures of the police, fortune intervened, and Good was ultimately captured due to a tip from a construction laborer in Tonbridge who recognized Good when the fugitive joined the work crew. The laborer, the fates would have it, had once been a police constable at Wandsworth. Good was convicted and hanged. Molly "Good," a former mate of his whose legal status was equivocal (Good's little boy called her "Mother"), was originally charged as an accessory for assisting his flight, but the charge against her was eventually dropped on the ground that as his "wife," lawful or bigamous, she had promised to love, honor, and obey him, presumably even in murder.

The stumbling police efforts in Good's case had a happy outcome: within two months after Good's arrest, Colonel Rowan reluctantly agreed to the foundation of the Detective Department. Daniel Good had become the godfather of Scotland Yard.

It did not take long for 1849 to declare itself a vintage year of crime. On the first night of the year, Poole and Nightingale pulled off their double robberies of the Great Western mail trains. A murder sensation was waiting in the wings—the trial of James Blomfield Rush that opened at Norwich on 29 March for the massacre at Stanfield Hall. On the evening of 28 November 1848, Rush loaded a pistol, left his farmhouse at dreary Potash Farm, and set out on foot for nearby Stanfield Hall, the residence of Isaac Jermy, his creditor and landlord. Rush knew Jermy's habits and waited for him to take his usual walk after dinner. When Jermy came out on the porch, Rush shot him at short range through the heart. He entered the side door of the house and, meeting Jermy's son, shot him in the chest. The young man fell dead in the hall, and Rush continued on his hurricane path into the dining room looking for the rest of the family. He found no one there, but as he left the dining room he came upon the young Jermy's wife and her maid, who in terror was holding her fast by the waist. He fired twice, wounding the servant in the leg and Mrs. Jermy in the arm, and escaped.

The Rush murder case aroused feverish public interest. Why this should have been so is not plain from the turgid trial record. Certainly the multiple shootings lent an element of horror. Rush had not, like Greenacre and Good, contented himself with a single victim whose elimination would benefit him, but had vented his hatred—or perhaps irrational ferocity—on an entire household. It was an added attraction that Rush, who was no fool except in thinking himself wiser than he was, conducted his own defense—a rarity in capital cases. In the vain hope that he could minimize the period of his absence from Potash Farm on the night of the murders, he subjected his mistress Emily Sandford, who appeared for the prosecution, to a rigorous cross-examination that reviewed almost minute by minute how they spent the early part of the evening together at the farmhouse. The case was also spiced by journalistic suggestions that Rush's fierce hatred of the land-owner Jermy had been fired by study of the teachings of radical agitators, and the public, whose memory of the Chartist riots was still fresh, indulged in a special shudder.

Certainly the overt motivation of Rush held no great fascina-tion. Rush feared that his landlord would eject his family from certain farmlands they held under lease. He was also worried that Jermy would foreclose the mortgage he held on Potash Farm. Nobody could have blamed him if he had, for Rush had undertaken to purchase the property for Jermy as agent but treacherously bid it in for himself; then, despite his betrayal of his principal, Rush had the gall to persuade Jermy to finance the purchase price. Always a lover of conspiracy, Rush tried to defend his farms by inserting himself into the midst of a battle within the Jermy family over the ownership of Stanfield Hall and its lands. He made complicated maneuvers intended to provide security whichever party won. He forged contracts with his enemy Jermy that purported to extend his leases and spread out or forgive his mortgage payments. Since Jermy would have denied the authenticity of these documents, they would be worthless to Rush unless Jermy were dead. Rush also signed a genuine contract with Jermy's rivals that also protected his leases, in return for Rush's promise to assist their claims. However, he proved to be a false ally of the claimants, dropping crudely fabricated notes at the scene of the crime that sought to pin the blame on those who were trying to oust Jermy from Stanfield Hall. He persisted at the trial and thereafter in attributing the plot against Jermy to three mythical emissaries of the rival party whom he could never identify by names more precise than "Dick, Joe and the lawyer."

It is hard to think of another murder cause célèbre that is so enmired in complexities of title conveyancing and conflicting rights of inheritance; the trial documents read like a law student's nightmarish memories of lessons in medieval property law. Yet the Rush case closely rivaled the Bermondsey murder in the favor of the murder enthusiasts of 1849. Charles Dickens even paid a special visit to Potash Farm early that year. He found that the search for the murder weapon was in progress but was critical of the lack of professional competence shown by the police: "We arrived between the Hall and Potash farm, as the search was going on for the pistol in a manner so consummately stupid, that there was nothing on earth to prevent any of Rush's labourers from accepting five pounds from Rush junior to find the weapon and give it to him." Dickens found Norwich a disappointment except for its "place of execution," Norwich Castle prison, which he found "fit for a gigantic scoundrel's exit."

Greenacre, Courvoisier, Good, Tawell, Rush. The roll of the "great" murders continued to unfold, and each new case, by varying degrees of intrinsic interest and commercial exploitation, whipped the public into greater preoccupation and frenzy. Thoughtful observers had worried about the phenomenon of murder mania for many years. In 1839 and 1840 the journalist and budding novelist William Makepeace Thackeray had led a critical assault on novels that glamorized crime and the low life and drew their heroes from the Newgate Calendars and other criminal annals. In 1849, however, it appeared that the public had been far from immunized against the lure of murder cases. So it was with good reason that the satirical journal *Punch,* then in its first decade when its social concerns were still strong, mounted an unrelenting campaign against excesses in the commercialization of crime.

Wherever the scornful Mr. Punch turned his eyes, he saw murder cases appealing to profiteers, sensation makers, and, worst of all, victims of their own morbid fancies. Even the celebrated criminal court of London, the Old Bailey, had not lost the opportunity to turn crime into pounds, shillings, and pence. *Punch* took deep offense when the Old Bailey began the "open and undisguised" practice of charging a fixed price for admission to the galleries of the courtroom. This seemed only the latest evidence, if that was needed, that the dignity of the law had fled from the criminal courts and that the Old Bailey had been converted into a place of entertainment and theatrics. In a March article entitled "Theatre Criminal, Old Bailey," *Punch* published a mock program for the coming Old Bailey season in the form of a theatre prospectus. It promised that the judges would include "stars too numerous and too brilliant to number" and that the trial counsel, including Ballantine and Wilkins (later to have leading roles in the Manning trial), would "prosecute and defend with their accustomed ability; and abuse, and tear, and twit, and expose, and badger one another with their usual strength, violence, sharpness, impartiality, and eloquence." A graduated tariff was shown for trials of various offenses, ranging from one shilling for larceny to two shillings for the ordinary murder. However, the entrepreneur could fix no price for a murder "if under extraordinary circumstances, and by an interesting individual of either sex, whose portrait is likely to appear in the newspapers." *Punch* sympathized with the entrepreneur's difficulty, for how was it possible beforehand "to put a price upon a Greenacre?" Later in March *Punch* pursued the same theme in a column headed "Old Bailey Dramas." Now that a charge was being made for admission to the Old Bailey, the writer thought that "the speculators have a right to demand the enjoyment of the usual facilities for going publicly to a place of entertainment open to the public in general." He proposed the use of a poster picturing a vigorous cross-examination and surrounded by claims reading "GREAT HIT, Genuine Pathos,

Legal Jokes, and Real Criminals!!!" An usher should pass through the galleries peddling apples, oranges, nuts, bills of indictment, and ginger beer. If the system worked as it should, the writer would not be surprised to hear of a barrister being called for a curtain speech or "smothered alive in a shower of bouquets."

As for the criminals tried at the Old Bailey, *Punch* found that they had become so popular and the details of their daily life so engrossing that there was no less reason for the newspapers to publish an "Old Bailey Court Circular" than to continue the time-honored chronicling of the doings at Buckingham Palace. In a piece in early October, *Punch* gave a "foretaste" of how the new circular might read: "Yesterday morning Mr. Sikes [the murderer in *Oliver Twist*] rose at 7. Asked if there was anything new in the papers? Wished to write an Ode to Liberty, and desired to be denied to everybody who might call, except to Madame Tussaud or representative."

Punch leveled its heavy guns at the national madness unaccountably inspired by the Rush murder case. Its major piece on Rush, "Homicide Fair," appeared in April 1849 in response to an article in the *Observer* on a remarkable fair that was held outside Norwich Castle, where Rush was held waiting to be hanged. According to the *Observer*, one of London's sensationalist Sunday papers, an "itinerant showman" had engaged an actor to portray Rush. One of the shows was a Punch and Judy pantomime in which Rush appeared in the part of Pantaloon. The *Observer* had expressed great indignation that this exhibition "is one of the most revolting character, but at the same time the most remunerative in the fair" and also deplored its accompaniment of drums and trumpets, and the sounds of revelry proceeding from "the degraded people who are its principal supporters."

To the editorial writer of *Punch*, all England had become a Homicide Fair, and the *Observer* was fully as culpable as "the humble vendor of excitement" whom that paper had rebuked in its article. *Punch* found it no less reprehensible for the *Observer* to drive its vans all day long in the stream of London traffic advertising the latest details of the Rush case together with the "Portrait of the Assassin" than it was for the rustic troupe to raise its din of drum and trumpet against the wall of Rush's prison. *Punch* made a fresh assault on the *Observer* and the other Sunday gossip sheets in a full-page cartoon published in September. The cartoon, captioned "Useful Sunday Literature for the Masses; or Murder Made Familiar," showed a father of a poverty-stricken family reading his wife and children a lurid description of a cutthroat from a newspaper called *The Murder Monger.*

The Norwich exploiters of the Rush case did not stay in their native fields but exported their wares to London. A Mr. John St. Quentin of Norwich built models of Stanfield Hall and Potash Farm (on the scale of three-eighths of an inch to the foot) "for the gratification of the sight-seers and loungers of intellectual, benevolent London," to borrow the words of a *Punch* article from April 1849. Just as there had once been a project espoused to remove Shakespeare's house in its entirety and ship it across the Atlantic, *Punch* had no doubt that if Stanfield Hall and Potash Farm could have been moved to London, the "spirit of the day would have made them a most profitable investment, adapted and laid out as tavern, tap, and tea-gardens." In the meantime, English ladies had to be content with the miniature "murder models" that Mr. St. Quentin had installed on Regent Street where, "'twixt the mercer's and the confectioner's," they "may now step in and see a little murder—take just a preliminary taste of horrors before the cheesecake." In view of Mr. St. Quentin's display in the heart of the metropolis, *Punch* thought it a little too hard that the management of the Eastern Counties Railway had been condemned by some for wanting to turn a shilling by arranging a "railway gibbet trip" to transport tourists to the hanging of Rush.

But beyond its contempt for the exploiters of crime, *Punch* reserved some of its barbs for the public who consumed it. It observed of the national taste for murder: "We are in truth a very domestic people. No sooner is an atrocious murder perpetrated, than the wretch becomes an object of the greatest social interest. His birth, education, early habits, are all a matter of daily import. It is a pity that art is not criticised with the same minuteness as homicide." *Punch* clearly saw that "murder-worship" was not limited to the uneducated but was in fact nondenominational and classless. In November a sonnet composed by "our own Poet-Laureate" asked how the uneducated could be blamed for a passion that writers shared and prompted:

> And who shall blame the unschool'd mob, whilst we,
> The scholars, Law's grim Tragedy allow,
> Nor interest in its actors disavow!
> We chronicle the foul minutiae
> Of their dark deeds of crime;—nay! stop not here,
> But sift their very prison-life, and draw
> The veil from off their hidden histories:
> We crowd to see their waxen effigies;
> We make their portraits household gods, and rear
> Them shrines, where Murder-worship is allowed by Law.

In such a favorable climate the Bermondsey Horror was bound to win a great following. There is no doubt that, bursting on the scene less than four months after the execution of Rush, it inherited the mass audience that the Stanfield Hall massacre had built to unprecedented proportions. But the new case undeniably had its own attractions. The Londoners and their newspapers dearly loved a London murder. It may seem odd to modern readers, who identify murder with metropolitan living, to realize how many of England's most shocking crimes in the nineteenth century took place in provincial towns or rural areas. But when a London murder with a special flavor occurred, whether in the time of Greenacre and Good or during the bloody ten weeks of Jack the Ripper, London knew no other theme for reading or conversation. Though promotion by newsmen of the metropolis played a part in selling these cases to their readers, real emotions were stirred among Londoners. They felt the characteristic urban fear of the "murderers among them," a fear that was most intense when a murderer was still at large but was never wholly dissipated by his capture and conviction. A dreadful new insight was also given them into the violence that might at any moment be erupting without their knowledge on familiar streets or behind the closed windows of the house next door.

Thackeray expressed this mood in an 1861 essay on the "Northumberland Street encounter." The case he described was bizarre. Mr. Roberts, a moneylender, calmly took daily pistol practice in his dusty office in a building a few steps away from the busy Strand. When he was satisfied with the accuracy of his aim, he invited Major Murray in to do business. The unlucky Murray did not know that Roberts was in love with Murray's mistress and was insanely jealous of him, particularly after he caught sight of the major happily visiting the Crystal Palace with his mistress, child, and maid. When Murray called at the Northumberland Street office, a borrowing was quickly arranged, but as he sat waiting for Roberts to bring him the loan proceeds from an inner room, the major received, instead of the cash he hoped for, a bullet in the back of his neck. Despite Roberts's target practice, and his close range, the shot was not fatal. A terrible struggle followed, in which the major dispatched his bewildering enemy with a makeshift arsenal of fire tongs, a bottle, and a vase.

The case destroyed Thackeray's belief in London's peace: "After this, what is not possible? It is possible Hungerford Market is mined, and will explode some day. Mind how you go in for a penny ice unawares. . . . After Northumberland Street, what is improbable? Surely there is no difficulty in crediting Bluebeard. I withdraw my last month's opinions about ogres. Ogres? Why not?"

The Bermondsey Horror was a case worthy of frightening Thackeray. Minver Place was not in the heart of the metropolis like Northumberland Street, but O'Connor was shot, clubbed, and buried on a populous suburban street while the neighbors saw and heard nothing. The burial in quicklime under the kitchen floor gave the case a macabre touch that Londoners had always fancied, and the speed with which the body came to light created a sense of wonder, or even, some were to say, signaled the working of divine providence. The efficiency of the police and their use of the telegraph were widely admired and probably won the Manning case a great following among people who would not ordinarily have paid much attention to the murder headlines.

The relationship of the Mannings with O'Connor must also have sharpened the public's appetite. It is commonplace for a husband or wife to conspire with a lover to dispose of an unwanted spouse, but when a married couple, such as the Mannings, is charged with murdering the wife's reputed lover, the case definitely belongs in the man-bites-dog category. The principal "human interest" of the case, however, was provided by the personality of Marie Manning, who was ready-made for newspaper celebrity. Marie was foreign, and "foreign murderesses" were greatly favored. She was physically impressive, if not handsome, and well dressed, had served the nobility, had often seen the queen herself. There was something else in Marie that caught the public's eye, something that set her apart from what the Victorians expected women (even murderesses) to be: from the moment of her capture Marie was resolute, silent, and "game."

CHAPTER SEVEN

The Inquest at the Tavern

"You expected to identify, I am told, sir?"
"Yes."
"Have you identified?"
"No. It's a horrible sight. O! a horrible, horrible sight!"

—*Our Mutual Friend*

T he Manning case was tried in the newspapers from the moment of the grisly discovery at Minver Place. The news accounts of the "facts" of the murder are much more voluminous than the shorthand renderings of the court proceedings that have come down to us. The crime journalists, enjoying their freedom from the restrictions of hearsay rules, requirements of relevance, and the chastening effect of cross-examination, wrote an enormous amount about the Mannings that was never proved in court. Since their versions of the case were often more vivid than the courtroom records, it is not surprising that many of the traditions about the Manning case can be traced back to newspaper columns but not to the witness stand.

From the beginning there was little doubt in the newspapers that the Mannings, or one of them, had perpetrated the crime. The very first *Times* article on the case (which appeared on 18 August) concluded: "There can hardly be any doubt that Manning or his wife committed the crime, as they sold all their goods to a broker in Bermondsey-street on Tuesday last, and exhibited a great desire to leave the neighborhood. Mrs. Manning was also at the murdered man's lodgings on the day he left and the day after, when she unlocked his drawers." The *Observer,* one of the most popular of London's sensation-mongering Sunday papers, found no difficulty in condemning both the Mannings in its first reports on 19 August: "Since the days of Greenacre and Good this isle has not been frightened from its propriety by a more atrocious murder than that perpetrated about ten days since at Bermondsey upon the person of . . . a Mr. Patrick O'Connor. . . . That Manning and his wife were his murderers there is no present reason to doubt. . . . if his murderers shall pass unpunished it will be a disgrace to civilization."

The *Observer* was a leading propagator of rumor and surmise. It told its readers in its 19 August issue that the crime was long premeditated, for the quicklime that covered the body had been procured three weeks before the murder and the grave "must have been commenced about the same time inasmuch as not a single morsel of the soil is to be traced in the house, in the offices [outbuildings] or in the yard." Neighbors were cited as witnesses of mysterious happenings at 3 Minver Place, though they were never to appear in court. In the words of a "person who resides next door," the Mannings acted suspiciously almost from the week they took possession; they appeared "to be up all night, there was nearly always a light burning, and there always appeared to be something mysterious going on." On the night of the murder, the tenant of an adjoining house, Mr. Truck, was supposedly awakened around midnight by a sound in the lower part of the Mannings' house and roused his wife, telling her he feared a break-in attempt. When she dismissed his worries as nonsense, he pointed out the shadow of a stooping man on the wall opposite the window of the Mannings' back kitchen. But sleep put an end to their fears.

The *Observer* discounted a theory it had learned the police held that O'Connor had been murdered in a bedroom on the upper floor; the staircase was so narrow that O'Connor's large body could only have been dragged with difficulty down to the kitchen two floors below. But in recompense for disposing of the upstairs-downstairs theory, the *Observer* had an explanation of how O'Connor had been overpowered by the Mannings. Reputed to be a teetotaler, he could not have been drunk, but it was reasonable to suppose that a stupefying drug, such as opium, had been infused in his pipe tobacco. The *Observer* noted that O'Connor was a constant smoker and reported that a half-filled bottle of laudanum had been found in the house.

The *Observer* lost no time at all in molding images of O'Connor and the Mannings. It showered the victim with nicknames. When a boy, it reported, he was large for his age, and on account of his size and his somewhat pompous bearing he was given the nickname "the big Nabob." At the docks he had the reputation of being wealthy and was called "the Customs' money lender." Abuse was heaped on the "improper intimacy" between O'Connor and Marie Manning. The *Observer* had been told that O'Connor was in the habit of visiting a Mr. Parker of Bloomsbury in the company of the Mannings and had called with them as late as a week or two before he disappeared. On that occasion the Parkers noticed that Mrs. Manning looked exceedingly pale and "fidgetty." Mrs. Parker, who apparently had a gift of retrospective prophecy, said that she had never liked Mrs. Manning and had wished, because of her suspicions of her affair with O'Connor, to forbid her the house altogether; indeed, Mrs. Parker "had even strong suspicions that something fatal would occur." The *Observer* itself entertained no doubt as to the nature of the relation that existed between O'Connor and "the female Manning," asserting sententiously that "the ascertained knowledge of the sure existence of this abhorrent intimacy will remove, from the breasts of the public, at least all sympathy for the fate of O'Connor."

The *Observer*'s first portrayals of Marie Manning mingled glamor and repulsion. Marie was "an extremely fine woman— handsome and of almost masculine stature. Her manners, at least to the society in which she latterly mixed, appeared those of an accomplished lady." To this portrait a heavy overlay of horrors was applied. The *Observer* reported rumors (soon disavowed) that Marie was a cousin of the Swiss valet Courvoisier, who had murdered Lord Russell. Relative or not, Marie, in the *Observer*'s columns, outdid Courvoisier in nerve and indifference to her crime. To illustrate "the extraordinary nerve of the Mannings, particularly the female," a correspondent of the *Observer* related the famous "goose story," which can be found, without attribution, in many brief accounts of the Manning case: "[Marie] on Sunday prepared her dinner in the back kitchen, where she roasted a goose over the spot where her murdered paramour was lying, and when the police called at the house on the following Monday to inquire after the deceased, she coolly asked them in, bade them take a seat and answered all questions with the greatest composure." The English public might be expected to admire Marie for her good looks and fashionable dress, but nobody was prepared to like a murderess who cooked a goose over the grave of her victim.

The inquest was opened on Saturday afternoon, 18 August, the day after the discovery of the body, at the New Leather Market Tavern, about a block away from Minver Place. The successor of the tavern still stands on Leather Market Street at the corner of Weston Street. Its windows and door are framed by brightly painted blue posts topped by a horizontal beam in the same color, on which the name of the establishment appears in golden letters: "Leather Exchange Tavern." In 1849 it was customary for inquests to be held at the tavern closest to the scene of the crime. Charles Dickens's journal *Household Words* complained about this practice (in its issue of 27 April 1850) as detracting from the dignity due the coroner's inquiry. The scene described in the article must have been appropriate to the inquest at the Leather Market Tavern: "A human being had been prematurely sent into eternity, and the coroner was called upon—amidst several implements of conviviality, the odour of gin and the smell of tobacco-smoke—[to inquire into the cause of death]." Presiding over the inquest was Mr. Carter, one of the coroners for Surrey, and a jury of "thirteen of the most respectable tradesmen in the neighbourhood." It would have been a less unlucky number except that the fourteenth juryman who was sworn was Mr. Coleman, owner of the Mannings' house, and the coroner allowed an objection made by O'Connor's friend Meade to Coleman's service on the ground that he would be required as a witness.

The jury was called upon to view O'Connor's body. It was still naked as found, but the legs and thighs had been tied up to the body with a new rope. The body was partly covered with lime, and such extensive discoloration of the face had taken place that it was only by O'Connor's sharp projecting chin and toothless mouth that identification could be made for the inquest by O'Connor's cousin Flynn. The jury turned away from the body with relief and prepared to hear the testimony.

The first witness sworn was Pierce Walsh, a friend of O'Connor's. Walsh, a former grocer's clerk, presently unemployed, had not the slightest doubt that the body was O'Connor's. He told of his last evening with O'Connor on Wednesday night, 8 August:

"I last saw O'Connor alive at midnight on Wednesday the eighth. We parted after having been at 3 Minver Place. He was then in a good state of health. I spent a great portion of that evening with him at his lodgings and then accompanied him to Minver Place. I had been there with him before, I think four times in all. I know that he and Mrs. Manning were very intimate; he was intimate with both the Mannings. When we arrived at Minver Place, it was about a quarter to ten. The door was opened by Mrs. Manning. I never knew her by any other name for O'Connor had always spoken of her to me as Mrs. Manning. We stayed at her house about an hour and a half."

"What happened then?" the coroner asked.

"We left together."

"During the time you were there did anything particular happen?"

"After we went in and sat down Mrs. Manning said, 'Mr. O'Connor, why did you not come to dinner today? We kept dinner waiting an hour for you.' She then asked, 'Didn't you get my note?' He said, 'No.' Mrs. Manning said, 'I wrote a note to you to the Docks to come to dinner today.' I suggested that it might have been late when she put it into the receiving-office and that it might not have been received at the Docks at 4 o'clock, the time of O'Connor's leaving the office. Mrs. Manning agreed: 'It was 2 o'clock when I mailed it, and he will receive it tomorrow.'"

O'Connor mentioned to Mrs. Manning that Walsh had received that day the balance of a bill of exchange that a Mr. Pitts

Patrick O'Connor,

Late Guager in her Majesty's Customs.

Portrait of Patrick O'Connor, from *The New Wonderful Magazine*.

of Bethnal Green Road owed O'Connor, and for which the witness had taken out execution against Pitts. Walsh was rather surprised that Mrs. Manning appeared to know so much about the transaction, and she went on to speak of three other bills of Mr. Pitts's that O'Connor, the reputed moneylender, held. Marie even gave him legal advice, suggesting that he take proceedings against Pitts for the recovery of the remaining bills, and he replied that he would do so. Walsh then described how the evening wound down:

"O'Connor began to smoke after that, and then growing very weak and faint he laid himself down on the sofa. He smoked a pipe, and Mr. Manning smoked also. Smoking did not lead to drinking—we had nothing to drink. They got some brandy and water for him when he was faint but he refused to take any. While he was on the sofa she had something in a bottle—eau de cologne, I believe—and she kept rubbing his temples with it. We left at about ten minutes past 11 o'clock. He took nothing at the house but water when he was recovering; he was not sick. After he had drunk the water he started smoking again. On leaving the house we passed through Thomas's Street and by Guy's Hospital. It was midnight when we got to the corner of Commercial Street, Whitechapel, and he would not let me go any further with him."

Walsh added that when he had called on O'Connor at his lodging earlier that day, O'Connor was lying on a sofa and seemed to have been drinking, but Mr. Meade, O'Connor's friend, interrupted his testimony, claiming that the witness must be mistaken, for O'Connor had been a teetotaler for upwards of thirteen years.

A juror asked Walsh whether he thought there was any improper connection going on between O'Connor and Mrs. Manning, and he replied, "I do not think it. I have no knowledge of the fact." He also told the coroner that O'Connor had never alluded to any pecuniary transactions with the Mannings.

The coroner announced that it was useless to attempt going further with the case at the present moment without medical testimony. Mr. Odling, the police surgeon who had made a preliminary examination of O'Connor's body at Minver Place, was ordered to perform an autopsy, and the inquest was adjourned until the following Friday, 24 August. In the meantime the public attention was diverted from the legal proceedings by the spectacular news of the capture of Marie Manning.

The first witness heard on the resumption of the inquest was William Keating, who testified as to the circumstances of his meeting O'Connor on London Bridge on the afternoon of his disappearance. Keating was a clerk in the Examiner's Office of the Customs House and had known O'Connor for about ten years. He had last seen O'Connor alive about a quarter to five on the afternoon of 9 August on London Bridge, walking south to the Surrey side. O'Connor appeared well and in good health and spirits. Keating was accompanied by another customs officer named Graham, to whom O'Connor spoke first. The conversation on the bridge lasted less than two minutes. O'Connor had handed Graham a letter. Keating did not see its contents but caught a glimpse of the signature, which he believed was the name "Maria," penned with some flourish. Graham remarked, "I suppose you are going to dine with Maria"; Keating had the impression that O'Connor had replied, "Yes." The witness supposed that by "Maria" the two men meant Mrs. Manning, whom he had met on occasions walking with O'Connor and at O'Connor's house. He said he would know Mrs. Manning if he saw her again.

Keating's testimony was confirmed by Graham. He also took it for granted that the letter shown by O'Connor on London Bridge was from Mrs. Manning. The letter had said: "We shall be glad to see you" or "We expect you to dinner." Graham had seen Manning once about two years ago and did not know him by name. He had met Marie around the same period in O'Connor's house but did not know what their relationship was. He seemed to hesitate on this point, saying that they did not seem more intimate than ordinary friends when he saw them in O'Connor's house but that (presumably on some subsequent occasion) he had seen them arm in arm and considered them to be intimate.

Another witness, John Younghusband, a gauger who knew O'Connor as a brother officer, also saw him last on Thursday, 9 August. Leaving Gracechurch Street on an omnibus at about a quarter to six in the evening, he saw O'Connor on the London side of London Bridge, near the end of Thames Street. O'Connor was walking very slowly northward toward the city and was looking around him. The omnibus was going fast, and O'Connor did not recognize the witness, who never saw him alive again.

The deferred medical testimony was also introduced. Samuel Lockwood testified as to his preliminary examination of the body at Minver Place and his extraction of a large slug from the frontal bone over O'Connor's right eye. George Odling, the police surgeon, reported the results of the autopsy, which he had conducted with Lockwood's assistance. On his external examination on the head, he had found several severe wounds, as many as eighteen altogether, many of them deeper than the others, in the scalp at the back and on the top. Most of the wounds, but not all, appeared to have been inflicted by a blunt instrument such as a "bricklayer's hammer," a large hammer without a division. He could not discover a distinct bullet hole by which the bullet found over the right eye had penetrated. At the back of the head Dr. Odling saw a dark discoloration that was not the result of decomposition but was an extraneous substance like powder. Since the brain was in a fluid state and completely decomposed, he could not trace the course of the bullet but was certain that the bullet could not have entered at the front, there being no aperture.

Odling had opened the abdomen and found nothing unnatural. He had not made any investigation of the contents of the stomach, but had sent his son off to Guy's Hospital to have the stomach analyzed. The witness proceeded to tell an interesting tale of medical economics. When Odling's son delivered the stomach to Mr. Taylor, the chemical lecturer at Guy's Hospital, that gentleman flatly refused to make the requested analysis. He subsequently informed Odling by letter that his refusal was based on the fact that the counties of Surrey and Middlesex had never paid him for his trouble in similar matters in the past. Odling told the court that he had not himself made any analysis of the contents of the stomach because he felt incompetent to do so. The coroner intervened:

"Why did you wish the stomach to be analyzed?"

"Because a policeman brought me a bottle of laudanum partly used, which he had found in the house at Minver Place and I was anxious, therefore, to determine whether any laudanum was present in the stomach of the deceased."

"We have heard nothing yet of the discovery of any such bottle," the coroner complained. "How was it forthcoming?"

At this point a police constable stepped forward and informed the court that, in the search of the house, he had found the bottle and had given it to Dr. Odling, who at once pronounced it to contain laudanum.

"What has become of the stomach and its contents?" the coroner asked Odling.

"Finding no analysis could be made of it, it has been thrown away."

And so it was amid a welter of unpaid medical bills and admissions of professional incompetence that O'Connor's stomach and the speculations about laudanum drugging vanished from the case.

Odling concluded his testimony by stating that he was satisfied that the extensive fractures of the skull were sufficient in themselves to account for O'Connor's death, regardless of whether he had been drugged or shot. Under the scalp over the skull was evidence of ecchymosis (blotching caused by the extravasation of blood under the skin), so it was clear that the fractures had been inflicted while O'Connor was still alive.

James Coleman, a builder and the owner of 3 Minver Place, who had been disqualified as a juror, was then heard. On Tuesday evening of the previous week he heard on his arrival home that a gentleman had called who stated that the Mannings had suddenly left. When he went over to 3 Minver Place about two hours later to make inquiries, he saw a man come out. The man, after refusing to give either his name or address, asked who Coleman was and whether the Mannings owed him any rent. When Coleman replied that they did not, the man replied with satisfaction, "Then you have no claim to the property." His mysterious interlocutor was obviously none other than the dealer, Mr. Bainbridge. Coleman told the jury that he had never been in the Mannings' house since they took occupancy. When they applied for a lease, they gave Mr. O'Connor as a reference.

The next witness to come to the stand produced intriguing testimony. He was William Massey, a medical student who had lodged with the Mannings at 3 Minver Place for about nine or ten weeks and had left about a month before. The Mannings had no servants while he was there, but a woman came in occasionally to assist. He had never seen any visitors there except O'Connor, to whom he had been introduced by Manning. O'Connor had dined there three times during Massey's stay, and Massey had visited him once at his lodgings in the company of the Mannings. It did not appear to the young man that there was any improper intimacy, but the Mannings appeared very friendly with O'Connor. He had heard them mention that O'Connor was a man of property worth twenty thousand pounds.

Manning sometimes talked to Massey about O'Connor, and the conversations seemed to take an uncomfortable medical turn. One evening at about eight o'clock, when the young lodger came upon Manning sitting in his own room, Manning asked him what drug would be most likely to produce stupefaction or partial intoxication so as to cause a person "to put his hand to paper." Manning said that his wife, who was present during the conversation, had been at the docks and had seen the supposed teetotaler O'Connor in a state of intoxication from having taken brandy or port as a preventive against the cholera; when she had gone home with O'Connor, he had shown her his will, in which he made over all or a considerable part of his property to her. Manning proposed to his wife that she lure O'Connor to his house so that the medical student could "frighten him well about the cholera, and persuade him to take large quantities of brandy." Massey thought he was hinting about the possibility of putting a drug in the brandy.

Previous to the conversation about the will, Manning once asked Massey, who was reading a medical work: "Which part of the skull is most dangerous to injure?" Massey said that the most vulnerable place was behind the ear. On another occasion Manning spoke to Massey about the murderer Rush, asking whether the lodger thought a murderer went to heaven. The young man replied, "no," and had pedantically cited a scriptural text in support of his view.

Manning had told Massey that he and O'Connor hated each other and that O'Connor would "pay him off sometime" for having sued him on the claim that O'Connor had failed to honor his agreement to rent a room at 3 Minver Place. Manning, according to the lodger, had sued in the Whitechapel County Court for thirty shillings—three weeks' rent for Massey's room, which O'Connor had allegedly agreed to take before the student moved in. Massey saw the summons lying about the house when he first arrived, and Manning told him that O'Connor had paid the claim rather than have the matter come to trial. Strangely, however, Manning and O'Connor appeared to Massey to be on very good terms when they were together, and he could not believe what Manning had said about their enmity.

But the conversations about weapons and lethal agents did not stop. Once Manning asked him whether air guns made any noise. Massey said he thought not; he had never owned one but had seen one fired off in a course on natural philosophy. During another conversation his landlord asked whether chloroform and laudanum had been employed as stupefying agents. Massey thought little of these questions since they seemed to come up in the natural course of conversation, but he remembered very clearly one pungent maxim of Manning's: "For God's sake never marry a foreigner. She will be the ruin of you." The tenant never noticed any evidence of domestic disharmony between the Mannings, but one morning while he was in bed, he had heard something fall on the floor.

Massey had given up his lodging at Manning's request, and Mrs. Manning also appeared anxious that he should leave. His parents thought it was a great pity that he should have to move so near the end of the school term.

The inquest then heard evidence that tied the Mannings to the preparations for the murder. Richard Welsh, who worked for a Mr. Wells in Russell Street, Bermondsey, took the stand. He recalled that on 23 July a man came into Mr. Wells's yard and asked Miss Mary Wells for sixpence worth of stone lime that he said he wanted for his garden. He wrote out his address in the office and, pointing to the witness, said to Miss Mary: "Here is a lad who will take it up to my house." Welsh could not make the delivery that day because he was busy, but on the twenty-fifth of July he carried a bushel of lime to 3 Minver Place. Miss Mary had given him the directions from the note the customer had left, for Welsh could not read. When he arrived at the house, he saw the customer, who told him to go through the house down to the back kitchen, where Welsh shot the lime into the square basket at the left-hand side of the room near the cupboard. The lime was unslaked (unhydrated) and therefore highly caustic.

Welsh testified that the customer's name was not mentioned either at the time he wrote out his address or afterward, but that he thought he would recognize him if he saw him again. There was nobody else present when the lime was delivered. The man paid him three halfpence, the promised tip for the delivery, and had already paid the sixpence for the lime at the time he gave his order.

The next witness, William Cahill, a shopman to George Langley, of 46 Tooley Street, Bermondsey, was the next to testify. He stated that on Wednesday, 8 August (the day before O'Connor's disappearance), a lady came into the shop at about three o'clock in the afternoon and asked for a coal shovel. Cahill showed her some short-handled dust shovels, which were used for coal. He believed that he had asked her whether she preferred a regular or long-handled shovel and that she had replied that "she would make a short one do." He showed her a shovel priced at a shilling and one at fifteen pence. She said she wanted a "strong" one and therefore settled on the fifteen pence shovel, but not without haggling over the price. The shopman finally conceded a penny, and a deal was struck at fourteen pence. The shovel was of wrought iron without any holes, and the handle was about a foot in length. Although he had never seen the lady before, he would have no difficulty in recognizing her. She wore a rather common-looking black dress with three or four flounces and had a black drawn bonnet. When Cahill asked for her name, she said it was Manning. She spoke with a slight foreign accent. The witness himself made the delivery of the shovel and gave it into Mrs. Manning's hands the same evening at about seven o'clock at the address she had given—3 Minver Place, Weston Street.

A shovel was produced and identified by the witness as the one he had sold to Mrs. Manning; the private mark of the shop and the selling price had been scratched on it with a brad-awl. Cahill's examination then terminated.

Had the evidence of the shovel tied Mrs. Manning to the preparations for the burial? The reporter for the *Observer* was not certain, observing that the shovel identified by Cahill "appeared an implement very unlikely to have been used in digging the pit in which the unfortunate man's body was concealed after the murder."

It was now nearly half past five, and since the jury had been sitting since eleven o'clock, the coroner adjourned the inquest until the following Monday morning. When it resumed, Frederick Manning was still at large, and the *Times* was expressing the concern that "every day that passes diminishes the chance of his arrest, and unless the most strenuous exertions are now made a deed of the most extraordinary atrocity may be suffered to go unpunished."

As the inquest resumed, the jury was given additional testimony about the shovel that Mrs. Manning had purchased. Police Constable William Sopp testified that on 22 August, at Inspector Yates's instructions, he had called on the dealer Bainbridge at his establishment at 14 Bermondsey Square. He knocked at the door and inquired whether Bainbridge was at home. He waited a few minutes outside until Mrs. Bainbridge let him in. He asked her whether among the household goods her husband had bought from Manning there was a shovel. She said there was and brought out an iron shovel for Sopp to inspect. The constable observed some marks of mortar on the shovel and, studying it further, found something that had the appearance of "blood and ashes with human hair attached." Calling Mrs. Bainbridge's attention to it, he asked her: "Did you ever notice this before?"

"No."

"Has anyone used the shovel since your husband purchased it?"

"I don't know for certain that anyone has used it, but I believe someone has done so."

The coroner inquired whether Mr. Bainbridge, who had been asked for at the beginning of the inquest, was now present. The summoning officer said that he was not, but that he had been summoned and had promised to be at the inquest today at half past ten, having been informed that he would be taken as the first witness. The elusive Mr. Bainbridge was finally rounded up late in the session. He said he had received a summons to testify on Saturday and knew that the court was adjourned to this morning, but that he had business that detained him at the west end of town. He apologized for any inconvenience to the court and assured them that he had intended to show no disrespect.

He testified that he had first met the Mannings about seven weeks before (early July), having been introduced to them by another Bermondsey resident, Mrs. Hornby, who said they had some furniture to dispose of. The first time he went with her to call on the Mannings no business was done, but he was told to call again the next morning. When he returned, Manning came to the door and told him that he had already sold the goods. Bainbridge said, "I am sorry for it, as I should have given as good a price as another." The other deal cannot have been firm, for Manning asked Bainbridge to come back again, which he did at noon two days after. This time he saw Mrs. Manning, who showed him around the house. She asked sixteen pounds for everything with the exception of the kitchen things, which he did not see. He offered thirteen pounds and was told to call again. The Mannings seemed to alternate as negotiators, for next time Bainbridge was greeted by Manning, who said he could have the furniture for thirteen pounds fifteen shillings. Bainbridge stuck with his thirteen pound figure, but his persistence did not appear to irritate Manning. He asked the dealer into the back parlor and said: "I have a very respectable young man in my house lodging. He has been rather 'fast' and wants to borrow 10 pounds on his medical certificate in the hospital. Could you lend it to him?" Bainbridge said he did not think the certificate was very good security but that he would ascertain what it was worth.

The coroner was irritated by Bainbridge's ramblings and brought him back to the narrative of the furniture purchase. The long protracted negotiations finally resulted in Bainbridge's concluding a purchase of the goods on the Monday previous to the discovery of the body (13 August). Manning came to see Bainbridge and said he was going to dispose of the furniture. After a little conversation, Bainbridge paid him a fifteen-shilling deposit and was told to remove the goods next morning at five o'clock. Bainbridge cannily responded that he had better not move them so early because it would look bad. Manning left about 10:15 A.M. and returned about a quarter past four the same day. Again, the plans had apparently changed. He told Bainbridge: "My governor says, I am to stop in town another fortnight. I am come to pay the 15 shilling deposit back again." He added abruptly, looking about, "You have apartments to let. I suppose I may come and stop a fortnight here. Do you have a large bedroom upstairs?" Bainbridge agreed to rent him an upstairs bedroom and sent a servant to look for Mrs. Manning so that she could inspect the apartment. However, the girl went to the wrong house, and when she returned for fresh instructions, Manning went home himself. On his return after an absence of twenty minutes, Mrs. Manning was not with him. Manning said cryptically that "he had started her off for the country."

Manning had brought a bottle of brandy with him and he drank a good deal. Bainbridge said that he was out during the greater part of Monday evening. Most of the household goods the dealer had purchased were removed from Minver Place on Tuesday.

Bainbridge described how he picked up the balance of the goods in the company of Constable Burton. Burton handed some of these goods to him. There was an iron shovel in the house which was not a cinder shovel for it had no holes, but a coal shovel. Bainbridge took all these things and put them away. He did not use the shovel. He was shown the shovel that had been produced in court and said that he believed it was the same shovel.

Bainbridge produced the inventory that he had taken of the Mannings' goods. He testified that he had not received a hammer or any similar implement and that he had found nothing like an air gun at the Mannings' house.

Mary Ann Bainbridge followed her husband to the stand. She had gone with him when he picked up the balance of the goods in the presence of Constable Burton. Among the items they took home on that occasion were the shovel, some crockery, and a few old dresses, which she had at home. The previous Wednesday she had given the shovel to a police officer. Among the clothing she had taken was a dress that looked as if it had been washed out in a hurry and put to the fire to be dried. It had not been ironed and appeared to have been put away before it had been thoroughly dry. She had never looked at the dress before last Wednesday, when she gave it with the shovel to the police. The testimony was interrupted for a statement by Constable Burton that there were several stains of blood on the dress.

Continuing her testimony, Mrs. Bainbridge said she had seen Mrs. Manning and had spoken to her but was not acquainted with her. Mr. Manning had slept at the Bainbridges' house on Monday and Tuesday and had left about a quarter to eight or half past seven on Wednesday morning. On Monday evening, Mrs. Bainbridge testified, he went out several times to the Horns Tavern in Bermondsey Square for brandy and soda. Manning had ordered a lobster for his supper, and Mrs. Bainbridge tried to get one. He seemed very tipsy to her; he lay on the sofa and she had to shake him to wake him up for supper. She saw him pour brandy in his tea, one cup after the other. Finding him an unappetizing guest, she asked him, "Will you not sleep in your own house?" He replied, "No; I would not sleep in that house for 20 pounds."

The inquest continued to focus on the shovel. The surgeon, Mr. Lockwood, was recalled and asked to examine the shovel. He testified that there did appear to be human hair on it as well as mortar, but that he was satisfied that the injuries to O'Connor's head could not have been inflicted with the shovel. A juror inquired whether Lockwood had looked at O'Connor's neck in his examination of the body. Lockwood said that since O'Connor's tongue had protruded from the mouth they had thought at first that he had been the victim of strangulation, but that the neck showed no signs of the sort. He was then asked by the coroner to examine the stained dress that Mrs. Bainbridge had received from the Manning house, and he expressed the belief that the stains were, in fact, blood.

Evidence of the flight and arrest of Marie Manning was also introduced. The driver, William Kirk, told of picking up Mrs. Manning and taking her to the Euston Square train station. He got one of the few laughs of the day when he told the court that he thought that Mrs. Manning was a country woman, or a woman who came from Essex or Sussex, for she could not speak the English language. A station porter, William Day, told of placing her boxes addressed to "Mrs. Smith" in the station cloakroom. Being a better judge of accents than Mr. Kirk, he had taken her to be a foreigner. Inspector Haynes told about his examination of Mrs. Manning's boxes at the station. In the small box that contained the will of Frederick George Manning he came upon the skirt and body of a dress. Up to the very top, where the skirt had been cut from the body of the dress, there were several marks of blood on the inner lining, but the stains did not appear to go through. A splash also appeared in one place on the upper part of the skirt where it joined the body. The body of the dress seemed to have been very recently washed. Haynes also found two toilette table covers which had marks of blood upon them and a piece of muslin with blood splashes.

Superintendent Richard Moxey of the Edinburgh police then told the exciting story of the arrest of Mrs. Manning, which must have already been familiar to the coroner and jurymen from the newspaper accounts. Moxey detailed the contents of the luggage and purse taken from Mrs. Manning at the time of her arrest: in addition to the railway securities, banknotes, and coin, he had found a ticket dated 14 August, in the name of Smith, for excess luggage on the Edinburgh train; and a baggage room check, dated the previous day, from the London and Brighton Station. As Moxey then set out to list the articles found on her person by female searchers, the coroner interrupted him. A tone of English chauvinism sounded in his voice: "I do not know in what way evidence is taken in Scotland, but in this country the party who searches the person must be the witness to produce whatever may be found."

Moxey replied that he had personally seen these articles in the prisoner's possession before the search was made, and Mrs. Manning had made no remark when they were delivered to him by the female searchers. The coroner permitted him to proceed with his inventory: a gold watch and chain, a gold seal, three split rings with a watch hook, a brooch with the painting of a woman and child and another set with a Scotch pebble, and a small quantity of black thread to mend Mrs. Manning's persistent black apparel.

Moxey stated that, although Marie had generally protested her innocence at the time of her arrest, it was only during her first evening in jail that his captive first acknowledged that she was Mrs. Manning. Subsequently, despite his repeated cautions to her, she made a number of voluntary statements to the following effect: "I left town suddenly. I came off on Monday when my husband was out. I have left him as I have done before. I was afraid of my life. He has maltreated me for a long time past. His threats generally were that he would cut off my head, all of which can be proved by servants who lived with us in Taunton; and he has pursued me with a knife."

A London stockbroker, Francis Warren Stephens, was then put on the stand to identify certain of the securities that Superintendent Moxey had found in Marie's possession.

Stephens said that he had known O'Connor for about three years in matters of business only. He had purchased railway shares for O'Connor several times. Stephens identified the railway shares Moxey had recovered as securities he had purchased for O'Connor in May and early August. The coroner then asked him: "Do they appear to you to have passed from Mr. O'Connor's possession by sale?"

"I can't say by looking at them. They are not registered shares."

Stephens said that about the first of August a lady called upon him at his office at No. 3 Royal Exchange and asked him a number of questions, after stating that he had been recommended to her by Mr. Patrick O'Connor. She said that she had about two hundred pounds that she wanted to invest. She asked what kinds of securities in which she might invest could be sold abroad. Stephens told her that the word "abroad" was too indefinite a term, and that he could not give her advice unless she told him where she was going. After some hesitation the lady said, "Paris." The broker then showed her a list of foreign railway shares, and she particularly pointed out the Sambre and Meuse. Asked for her name and address, she wrote on a slip of paper "Maria Manning," or some such name. Stephens had lost the paper, but he was certain of the name "Manning." He had never seen the lady again. She was a "stout and rather fine-looking woman." The interview lasted about five minutes, as there was a "female waiting for her outside," but the witness thought that he would know her again "if she were dressed in her bonnet."

Stephens was a little suspicious of Marie. It was strange to him that a married woman would want to have some sort of shares that she could sell abroad without her husband's knowledge. For a moment he had even had the unworthy thought that she might be planning to run off with Patrick O'Connor, but his suspicions were allayed when he "reflected on the steady character of Mr. O'Connor."

As the broker left the stand, Superintendent Moxey expressed a desire to add to his prior testimony. Mrs. Manning had told him that she had money of her own "of which her husband was anxious to obtain possession" and that her refusal to give it to him was the cause of their quarrels. She said that when she asked O'Connor for advice on this matter, he referred her to Stephens. She claimed that the railway securities found in her possession had been purchased for her by O'Connor; the Spanish bond had been "found" by her husband.

The jury was treated to more insight into London stock brokerage practices when John Bassett took the stand. The witness was a clerk in the brokerage firm of Killick & Co. He told the jury that on about 31 July a gentleman came to their office whom he had never seen before. Bassett introduced him to the manager of the firm. Their visitor was considering the sale of some stock, he told them, and wanted to know their terms. He promised to call again the following day but did not appear again until the afternoon of 2 August, when he apologized for missing his appointment. He explained that he would not want to dispose of his stock for a few days, and on Saturday 11 August, he called again in the morning and told Bassett that he had brought the stock with him. Bassett advised him that the manager was home ill but that he could handle he transaction. His customer then produced twenty shares of Eastern Counties Consolidated Stock, and Bassett negotiated him down from an asking price of 120 or 130 pounds to 110 pounds. Bassett paid him with a hundred-pound note, one five-pound note, and five sovereigns in coin. John Hammond, a clerk in the office, wrote down the numbers of the notes.

It is a little hard to believe, but after all the interviews with the new customer, and despite the fact that money had already changed hands, Bassett had never thought of asking the man's name. He only learned this when the customer, as he was departing after receipt of the money, gave him a stock transfer form. The stock transfer was signed "Patrick O'Connor, 21 Greenwood Street, Mile End Road." The incredibly cavalier procedure that Bassett and his firm had used in dealing with a stranger was to draw a tart comment in a letter to the *Daily News* from a broker who was quick to note that Bassett was not, as he was, a member of the Stock Exchange. The writer added: "I am proud to feel that no member of the Stock Exchange would transact business for a stranger at all; our customs uniformly requiring an introduction from a friend accompanying every new client. But here we have evidently Manning himself personating O'Connor days after the murder; walking a perfect stranger into Killick's office, signing a blank transfer, and carrying off the spoil, all in a few minutes."

But was the mysterious customer in fact Manning? Bassett described him as a man of about forty-four or forty-five, tall, stout made and very round faced, about five feet ten inches tall, with rather light small whiskers and "a complexion that was not sallow." He appeared in excellent spirits and was talkative. A juror asked: "What sort of accent had he?"

"I should have thought him to be an Englishman," Bassett stated. "I should not have taken him for an Irishman. I should say he was an Englishman by his talk."

"Did you witness his signature?" the coroner inquired.

"I cannot speak to his signature."

The coroner went on: "Did you see the body of Patrick O'Connor?"

"Yes at six o'clock on Saturday, when the body was lying dead I saw it. I shall never forget its appearance. I could not swear that it was the same person as our customer, though the build was similar. The body very much resembled the man who described himself to me as Mr. Patrick O'Connor. Mr. O'Connor asked me if I was fond of fishing. I answered, 'Yes, I am.' He said, 'I am off for Exeter to fish, and I'll bring you up a salmon peal of my own catching.'"

Mr. Bassett blundered on. He told the court ruefully that after the customer left his office one of his clerks, Mr. Hammond, asked for a memorandum relating to the transaction. Bassett confessed that he had not obtained his customer's signature to a memorandum, and Hammond, warning him that Mr. Killick would be very angry, instructed him to go to O'Connor's house to obtain the signature. He called at the house on 13 August, at the side door, which was opened by a woman, and was told that O'Connor was away from home and that she did not know when he would return. She said that he had not been home since Thursday and was surprised when the innocent Mr. Bassett told her that he had seen him in the city as recently as Saturday.

As he concluded his testimony, Bassett tried to regain some of his composure. He now told the court that he could swear to the identity of his customer if he saw him again. He could not swear that the body he had seen was the body of his customer; it was so mangled and decomposed. One thing at least was plain: the five-pound bank note that was included in the payment Bassett had made to his unknown customer was traced into the possession of Mrs. Manning. It had been produced in court by Superintendent Moxey and was identified by Mr. Hammond, the Killick clerk. Hammond, who also thought O'Connor's body was that of their customer, was shown samples of the handwriting of O'Connor and Manning. He said that the signature on the stock transfer bore no resemblance to O'Connor's but was of the same style as Manning's, though not quite so upright. The coroner thereupon ruled that the evidence had completely exonerated Bassett from any imputation with respect to his role in the transaction; it was clear that he had dealt with someone impersonating O'Connor.

On the basis of Mr. Bassett's testimony, the *London Examiner* struck up a "third man" theme. In an article on 3 September it pointed out that the sale handled by Bassett had taken place on the eleventh of August and that O'Connor must have been murdered by then. It concluded that "the person who sold the stock could not have been Manning, who is 10 years younger than the conjectured age of the man who did business with Bassett, and who is also shorter, and of a very florid complexion; whereas Bassett's account of the self-called Patrick O'Connor is that he was not sallow, which are negative terms that would not be applied to a singularly ruddy man. . . . There is in this case a third criminal implicated, still to be traced out."

On the last day of the inquest, evidence was also heard from Patrick O'Connor's landlady, Ann Armes. She was a single woman and occupied the house in which O'Connor had his lodgings. He had been her lodger for nearly five years and lived on the first floor. His apartment consisted of two adjoining furnished rooms, a sitting room and a bedroom. The bedroom had no entrance from the sitting room but could only be entered from the landing. The doors of both rooms, by his orders, were always left open for airing. Miss Armes had last seen O'Connor alive on Thursday morning, the ninth of August, when she let him out by the door of her shop, which she maintained on the ground floor of the house. He then appeared to be in good health and was dressed in a black coat and plain black satin stock tied with a bow. His trousers were checked and he wore "Albert shoes" and a black hat. The coroner inquired: "Was he a man regular in his habits?"

"Particular," she replied. "He went out at half past seven in the morning and generally returned at five but not with the same certainty."

The witness usually dined at home, but when he intended to do so he left word with his landlady at what hour dinner was to be ready. He had relatives in to see him and male and female acquaintances. Mr. and Mrs. Manning came together to see him. Miss Armes thought that they had been acquainted with him only about a year. Their visits were frequent, but Mrs. Manning came more often than her husband did; she seemed to be on friendly terms with O'Connor and looked in on him when he was ill. She had visited him with great frequency for the last fortnight or month before he was missing. Miss Armes was struck by the fact that Mrs. Manning regularly arrived at an hour when O'Connor was absent on business, but she showed her up to O'Connor's rooms since he had requested that his friends should be admitted there and should await his return. Mrs. Manning came to his room in his absence more times than the landlady could number and sometimes left without seeing him if he did not return from work early enough. When Mrs. Manning called, she walked upstairs into his sitting room.

Miss Armes did not believe that Mrs. Manning had ever dined alone with O'Connor. Once about a month prior to O'Connor's disappearance the Mannings and their lodger, Mr. Massey, took tea with him, but Mr. Massey had only visited on that one occasion. The Mannings had dined with O'Connor before that day but never again afterward. O'Connor had never talked to his landlady about his relationship with Mrs. Manning. They seemed to her to be "on particular friendship" but she did not think they were "so friendly." In fact, both the Mannings appeared particularly attentive to him. Miss Armes had no feeling that there was anything improper going on, but she added: "Might I say this, that they have tried often to borrow money from him. I have heard them attempt to borrow money of him some time back, both Mr. and Mrs. Manning, but I had no knowledge of his having lent them any money. Some time ago, he told me he did not wish to have the 'vagabonds' come up any more—they were too troublesome."

She then described Marie's visit to O'Connor's lodging on Thursday, 9 August. Mrs. Manning called at a quarter to six on Thursday evening. Miss Armes's sister Emily let her in. Miss Armes was standing by and saw Marie go up to O'Connor's room. Marie left at about a quarter after seven or later, and O'Connor had not returned in the meantime. She had no idea what Mrs. Manning might have been doing in O'Connor's room, but she made quite plain her suspicion that Marie was looking for O'Connor's securities. She recalled that on the Friday before, she had gone to O'Connor's room and found him there with Mrs. Manning. Spread out on the table were some papers, and they were talking about railway shares, in which Marie wished to invest some money. The cautious Miss Armes said that she saw the papers but it was her sister Emily who heard the conversation. The sharp-eyed landlady also noticed that O'Connor's cash box was out on a table in the room; it was closed. The cash box had usually been kept in his trunk, which stood on a chest of drawers in his bedroom. The witness had very seldom seen Mrs. Manning in his bedroom, but she must have gone there on occasion "to leave her bonnet."

Miss Armes then told about Mrs. Manning's return to O'Connor's lodgings on Friday the tenth, the day after his disappearance:

"Mrs. Manning came also on the Friday at a quarter to six. She was admitted by my sister in my presence. I saw her go to Mr. O'Connor's room. Until a quarter past seven she was alone there and no other person entered the room during that time.

When she came we still thought that O'Connor would soon follow her. On her leaving she came through the shop, which she dared not do unless she purchased something, as I had forbidden her as well as Mr. Manning to go in or out that way. When she came through the shop I was sitting in the parlour, which is quite open to the front of the shop. Mrs. Manning asked my sister for some kind of plum cake. She had very seldom purchased before and not lately. As I sat I had a view of her face sideways. She seemed all ashake and pale."

The witness then testified as to the inquiries O'Connor's friends had made and confirmed that it was she who spoke to the hapless Bassett when he came in quest of O'Connor's signature. The coroner then asked her: "From the evening of Thursday the 9th until the Monday following, had any person access to this room but you and your sister, and Mrs. Manning?" She replied, "No."

When all the witnesses had been heard, the coroner proceeded to address the jury. He began by calling on them to dismiss from their minds any impression that might have been produced by anything they had heard or read about the case. He asked the jury whether they desired all the evidence to be read over again, and the foreman responded that a summary of the leading points would be sufficient. Nodding his compliance with the jury's wishes, the coroner went on. The first question for them, he explained, was the identification of the corpse; the evidence of Walsh and Flynn was strong in identifying the dead man as O'Connor. The second issue was the means of death. The coroner summed up the medical evidence on O'Connor's death; the jury were to ask themselves whether, although as regards the bullet there was a possibility of a man's inflicting an injury on himself, those wounds on the back side of the head could possibly have been produced without other agency. To the coroner the conclusion seemed inevitable that the head injuries had been caused by some other person or persons; the crucial question for the jury was to name such person or persons. On this point the coroner summarized the evidence pointing to the Mannings. The body was found in their house. O'Connor was seen by two witnesses on London Bridge going, it would appear, to the house of the Mannings. A bank note was found by Mr. Moxey in the possession of Mrs. Manning which had been paid by a stockbroker's clerk to a person under the name of O'Connor. The coroner then came to the question of motive:

> What can have been the inducement leading any party to sacrifice the life of O'Connor? Looking to the circumstances brought out in evidence, it will be for the jury to say whether there can be any doubt that this person's life was sacrificed with the view of obtaining his property. There is reason to believe that the Mannings were acquainted with O'Connor's pecuniary circumstances, and hence a probable motive is suggested for the commission of the crime by these parties, if the jury are satisfied that no others were in the house at the time when the murder was perpetrated.

The coroner addressed himself then to a legal issue that was to become of central importance to the case: to what extent could Mrs. Manning, as a wife, be charged as an active participant in the crime?

> With respect to the position in which Mrs. Manning is placed as a wife, although coverture [marriage] may be pleaded as a bar to a charge of felony, yet it is not so where the wife took a very active part. In that view the jury should put their own construction on the circumstances which have been brought out in evidence; to the statements made by Mr. Massey; and to the purchase by Mrs. Manning of the shovel, which would appear to have been used in placing the lime on the body.

The coroner, it is clear, did not want the jury to overlook the short-handled shovel. Lockwood had testified that the shovel could not have been used to inflict O'Connor's head injuries; and the coroner seems to have agreed with the *Observer*'s reporter that it was not much of a tool for digging graves. By his suggestion that it had been used instead to place lime on the body, the coroner attempted to assign it a more plausible role in the crime. It was curious, though. If the Mannings already possessed a shovel they had used to prepare O'Connor's burial place, why had Mrs. Manning made a last-minute purchase of another shovel?

The jury retired at half past nine in the evening. After an absence of about three-quarters of an hour, they returned to announce a verdict. They found that the deceased was Patrick O'Connor and that he had been willfully murdered by Frederick George Manning and Maria, his wife.

When Fred Manning was informed of the verdict of the coroner's jury during his railway journey from Southampton to London in police custody, he appeared very much surprised and sighed. He was charged at Stone's End Station that evening and was so unwell during the night that a doctor was sent to see him. It was reported that he was still allowed to take brandy occasionally.

CHAPTER EIGHT

A Month in Police Court

The buzz in the Court was awfully hushed. The direction was given to put the Murderer to the bar.

—*The Trial for Murder*

he Mannings were both in the hands of the law, and the verdict of the inquest had cleared the way for further proceedings against them. Anticipation of the public was now riveted on the moment when Fred and Marie would be required to confront each other in Southwark Police Court. Meanwhile, there was great curiosity about the question highlighted by the coroner in his instructions to the jury at the inquest: to what extent could Marie as a married woman be punished for a murder in which she might have participated in collaboration with her husband? The *Observer*, in its 2 September issue, rushed to offer its guidance on this perplexing issue by setting out the governing legal principles and citing certain facts developed at the inquest that appeared relevant; in the newspaper's own comfortable view, its efforts "must have a direct tendency to promote the ends of justice, by setting opinion on the right track in regard to the case at issue."

The *Observer*'s article included a summary of the common-law rules relating to prosecution of married women. In many respects, wives were treated very well under the common law, but the reasoning behind their treatment was not always flattering. When her husband had committed a crime, even murder or treason, a married woman could not be prosecuted as an accessory *after* the fact for harboring him or concealing the crime, since she was regarded as "being bound to receive her husband." No similar privilege was extended to the husband, who was not deemed to have a marital duty to spring to the aid of a guilty wife.

The law not only exempted the wife completely from punishment as accessory after the fact but in many cases treated her kindly when she committed a crime in the presence of her husband, or served as his accessory *before* the fact by aiding his preparations for the crime. In lesser crimes such as theft, the law excused her under these circumstances, on the ground that the mere presence of her lord and master amounted to coercion of the wife's actions. (No relief was given to the wife, though, where she and her husband were tried together for keeping a brothel, for this was an offense "which the law presumes to be generally committed by women.") In serious cases like murder the wife, whether charged as a "principal" (a direct perpetrator of the crime) or an accessory before the fact, did not have the benefit of a presumption of coercion, because society or "nature" was so offended by the crime that it could not in such instances permit wives to obey their husbands' commands.

So it appeared that Marie could face a capital charge either as principal or as accessory before the fact and would not be entitled to acquittal by merely showing that her husband was present during O'Connor's murder. But the same societal feeling that inspired the bar to a wife's treatment as an accessory after the fact—the feeling that a wife often owes a duty of blindly amoral obedience to a husband—could make the Crown uncomfortable in charging Marie merely as an accessory before the fact, who knew of her husband's murder plans and failed to alert the authorities. If, on the other hand, she could be shown to be an active participant in the crime, or even its instigator, all the complicated common-law arguments would fall by the wayside and she could be convicted with the same ease as if she were a single woman.

The *Observer* therefore examined the evidence at the inquest that shed light on the degree of Marie's participation in the crime. First, it grasped the now famous shovel by its short handle. Ignoring the comment of its own reporter and the testimony of Lockwood, the editorial writer proclaimed the shovel to be the implement that dug O'Connor's grave and smashed his head: "It will in all likelihood be discovered that the 'blunt-edged instrument,' with which the medical witnesses believe the fractures on the skull to have been made, is none other than the 'short-handled, strong, iron shovel' wherewith it is presumed the grave the body was found in had been dug." The *Observer* also theorized that, after the murder, Mrs. Manning had taken O'Connor's keys from his pocket and gone to his rooms to steal his property. But why was this theft evidence that she had acted as more than accessory after the fact? The *Observer* came up with an extraordinary explanation, stating that if she had acted solely in that capacity, she would have shared the spoils with her husband:

> If instead of appropriating all to herself and leaving Manning with empty pockets, whilst her own were full, she had manifested even the slightest signs of interest in his fate, she might have laid some foundation for the ingenuity of her counsel to work upon, and have enabled him to give a decent form and shape to the arguments that might be adduced for the purpose of softening the collateral circumstances of the case, and inducing the jury to look upon them, so far as she was concerned, as not going further than proving her knowledge of his guilt after the fact, and therefore entitling her to the excuses allowed by law to a wife in such a case.

While the *Observer* speculated, the detective force pressed its search for the instruments of the crime. Late Saturday night, 1 September, the police made an important discovery. After patient interviews of numerous dealers in the iron trade they called on the ironmongery warehouse of Messrs. Evans, 33 King William Street, London Bridge, and learned from shopman George Stead that on 25 July he had sold a crowbar to a man resembling Fred Manning. His customer had asked to be shown a small crowbar. Stead told him that they did not keep such articles in stock ready-made, but that if his customer pleased, one could be made to his order. The customer agreed but emphasized that he did not want one too large—about seven or eight pounds would do. He left his name and address, Frederick Manning, 3 Minver Place, and asked that the implement be delivered to his home when finished.

The crowbar was made to Manning's instructions, and on the twenty-eighth of July the Evans firm sent one of its porters to make the delivery. A few minutes after the porter had started off, Manning called at the Evans shop to inquire whether the crowbar was ready, and being told that the porter had just left to deliver it, Manning rushed away and overtook him in Tooley Street. The man was carrying the tool unwrapped, and Manning commented sarcastically, "I suppose paper is very scarce at your establishment. One doesn't want everybody to see such things. Come with me." Manning then went into the first stationers' shop they came upon and, buying a sheet of brown paper, took the crowbar from the porter's hands and wrapped it up. He then wrote his name and address on the package and, walking by the porter's side, showed him the way to Minver Place. When they arrived at the corner of Weston Street, Manning told the porter to go on alone and deliver it at his home.

The man proceeded to the house and, knocking at the door, was received by a "tall, well-dressed woman who had a mark on the upper part of her neck." On his presenting the parcel she said, "Oh, you have come from Messrs. Evans in King William Street. What's to pay?" When the porter replied that the price was three shillings sixpence, the woman said that it was sixpence more than she had expected, but without more ado she handed the payment to the porter and he left. The Evans shopman described the crowbar as resembling a large "ripping chisel," with a rather long flat point, tipped with steel, the metal somewhat more than an inch and a quarter in thickness.

The police regarded the crowbar as a more likely candidate for the role of the "blunt instrument" than the little shovel touted by the *Observer*. But the pistol with which O'Connor had been shot still eluded them. Then on 4 September they seemed at last to have a good lead. In the afternoon Inspector Yates, who had been given principal responsibility for the prosection of the Mannings by the coroner, appeared before Magistrate Secker at the Southwark Police Court to apply for permission for a Mr. Yeo to see Manning in Horsemonger Lane Gaol. The inspector told the magistrate that on the afternoon of 6 August a man answering the description of Manning called at the shop of

Messrs. Eastman and Yeo, Stationers, 100 Cheapside, and asked to leave with them overnight a small air gun covered by a cloth wrapper. Yeo observed that the man appeared to be rather excited, but being engaged at the time he accepted the gun without comment and deposited it behind his counter. The stranger did not call again next morning as he had promised; he returned at noon on 9 August (the day of the murder) and asked for the gun. Yeo handed it to him and had not seen him since. Hearing of the Bermondsey murder, Yeo believed that Manning was the person who had left the gun at his shop, and he communicated with the police. Magistrate Secker, after questioning Yeo, granted an immediate order for him to visit the jail so that he might have an opportunity to identify the suspect among the inmates. When Yeo arrived at the jail accompanied by Inspector Yates, the male prisoners from the various wards, including Manning, were brought together, and Yeo was allowed to examine their features closely. However, he was unable to identify any of them as the man who had deposited the air gun with him.

Late in the same day the police, undaunted, tried again. They brought before Magistrate Secker Mr. Adams, of the firm of Adams and Hellstead, pawnbrokers of Bermondsey Street, and produced a pair of pistols that had been pledged at his shop by another person who appeared to meet Manning's description. Adams stated that on the previous evening a police officer had asked him whether he had taken any pistols in pledge during the last month. He recollected that on 14 August a man called and pledged a pair of pistols for one shilling, giving his name as Frederick Jennings and saying he resided at 24 Morgan Square. (The name may have rung a bell with the police, since Manning had called himself Jennings while on Jersey.) On examining the pistols closely, Adams found that one of them had been recently fired.

The magistrate asked him whether he had made any inquiries at Morgan Square. Adams replied that he had, and that the house was occupied by a Mr. Walsh, who denied all knowledge of any man named Jennings or of anyone meeting the description Adams gave of his customer. Secker decided that the discharged pistol should be left with Inspector Yates, who was to make further inquiries.

The next day the police appeared to be making progress. They discovered a dealer in the New Cut, Lambeth, named Mrs. Bliss, who stated that about two months before she had sold a pair of pistols to a man resembling the description of Manning. They were small traveling or pocket pistols of Sheffield manufacture. She added that she had bought two similar pair at the same auction, and she produced the other pair, which were identical to those in the possession of the police.

While some of the police were engaged in these efforts to locate the sellers of the murder weapons, other officers pressed a painstaking search for the weapons themselves. On 4 September the commissioners of police directed that 3 Minver Place, already scoured by detectives, should undergo an even more minute search. At about noon Inspector Haynes led a police team to the house. He found to his surprise and chagrin that the place appeared to have been rented again and that the "new residents" refused to let him enter. Haynes and his fellow officers appealed to landlord Coleman, who turned a deaf ear to their requests. He told them that the house "had been twice nearly demolished" and that he had made up his mind not to permit any further search that might damage the premises unless the commissioners of police undertook to defray the cost of any necessary repairs. Not having the authority to give that guarantee, Haynes and his associates left disappointed, cheated of their fond hope of examining the water closet at the rear of the house where they thought the pistol and crowbar might have been thrown. They had previously probed the toilet for O'Connor's clothes, but a thorough search would have required them to follow the outlet from the toilet to the common sewer sixteen feet below.

The dogged Haynes applied the next day for an order from the busy Magistrate Secker to require Coleman to permit the further search. Coleman came before Secker in far from the best of humor, irritated by the "unjust remarks" the morning papers had made about his refusal to cooperate with the police. He told the magistrate that to make the search of the course to the sewer, the whole of the garden and the lower part of the house must be pulled to pieces, and that if the police wished to do so, they must employ their own laborers and put the place in proper order. He said that the previous searches had already resulted in extensive injury to the property, which he had to repair at his own expense. Brandishing the unfavorable newspaper reports, he reminded the magistrate that when the body was discovered by the police, he had sent two of his own laborers to assist them, and all the way along he had done all he could to aid them in finding any evidence that might be concealed. Coleman also denied the assertion by the newspapers that the house had been relet. This was not the case; he had placed one of his workmen in it until "the horrid affair had blown over."

The magistrate told the contending parties that he could not be troubled with any further observations on the matter. He had no doubt that the commissioners of police would consider the propriety of again searching the house, and that if they decided on the search, they would certainly put it in proper order.

On other fronts the investigation moved relentlessly forward. Checked in their plan to search the sewer, the police hunted for O'Connor's clothing among London's old clothes dealers. The devotion of their efforts is indicated by the fact that they made their laborious way through the teeming Petticoat Lane Market in London's East End, following up on reports that a man resembling Fred Manning offered various articles of clothing of a superior quality for sale to several of the market's dealers on the Monday after the murder. The fatal crowbar was pursued by inquiries of most of the marine store dealers in the metropolis. Then, on 11 September, a letter was mailed from Bolton in Lancashire to Inspector Yates offering the services of a locally prominent clairvoyante:

> SIR: In a cellar underneath the house where the body of O'Connor was found is concealed the pistol with which the murder was committed. Should the information be correct, publish it immediately, and I will send you more information

detailing the particulars of the affair, which I am enabled to do by the aid of a "clairvoyante."—Your obedient servant, W.

P.S. The clairvoyante says that there are three cellars underneath the house; she could not see the end of the one in which the pistol is hid. Search, and you will find it.

According to the *Observer,* the clairvoyante was worth listening to, because she had earlier been successful in discovering certain lost banknotes that had been sent to a Bolton firm and had by some mistake been thrown among some other documents and laid aside. On being mesmerized, the clairvoyante had minutely described the hiding place of the notes, so that they were instantly discovered.

As a consequence of the clairvoyante's intervention, Constable Burton was sent to Minver Place the following day to make a further search. The clairvoyante was right about one thing: there were three cellars underneath the house, and one of them had not been closely searched. Burton had the good fortune, or the wisdom, to obtain permission for the search from the younger Mr. Coleman rather than his irascible father. The constable did not find the pistol, but he did notice some spots and streaks of blood on the wall opposite the back kitchen door. The marks were very thick, and Burton supposed that O'Connor, after being shot, must have fallen against the wall, and that he had then been struck by some heavy instrument. The newspapers regarded it as "very strange" that the marks had not been discovered before, as they were very prominent. While this new evidence was being tardily discovered, some old evidence was evaporating. It was determined that one of the two bottles of laudanum supposed to be the property of the Mannings in fact belonged to Mr. John Packer, a surgeon, who assisted in lifting O'Connor's body from the grave.

A missing witness was also sought by the police. They had learned that a girl had been employed by Mrs. Manning to clean up the back kitchen after the body had been buried and the flagstones relaid. Mrs. Manning was known not to keep a servant, and the appearance of a "strange female" cleaning about the house on the Saturday after the murder attracted the notice of neighbors. They were particularly struck by the sight of Mrs. Manning sweeping the steps in front of the house attired in a black satin dress, while the servant was busy washing the passage. The girl at the end of her day's work remarked to a servant next door that she had had a "filthy job" in cleaning out the back kitchen. It was in a "beastly state": the flagstones were covered with lime and dirt, and she wondered what the Mannings had been doing to put them in such a condition.

After inquiries in the neighborhood, Constable Burton finally learned of a young girl who was in the habit of coming to several of the houses in the vicinity for the purpose of washing the steps and assisting the regular servants. He was able to trace her to the home of relatives in Bermondsey with whom she lived. The girl, Hannah Firman, told Burton that at about nine o'clock Saturday morning, 11 August, Mrs. Manning engaged her to clean the house. She cleaned the upper part and found several spots "like blood" on the wall of the passage leading to the kitchen, which she tried to wash off. Then she proceeded to the back kitchen and was about to start cleaning it when Mrs. Manning came up to her and pulled her away exclaiming, "I cleaned this place yesterday, and it don't want scrubbing any more." Hannah saw a square basket in the back kitchen covered with lime, which Mrs. Manning told her to wash. During the time she was in the house Mrs. Manning went out two or three times, and at about noon Manning came downstairs and stamped his foot violently as if in a passion. He shouted to his wife, "Give it to me directly," and Mrs. Manning replied, "Yes I will directly" and went upstairs to him.

The girl said that the back kitchen was extremely wet and that the stones in the passage appeared to have been recently rubbed with a brick or stone.

There was a point in the inquest testimony that the police particularly wanted to patch up with further evidence. Bainbridge's recollection of Manning's words after his discovery of Marie's flight indicated that Fred had claimed credit for having sent her away. If this story stuck, there would be some basis (as the *Observer* had noted) for her counsel's arguing that Marie had acted only as her husband's accessory. There were some reports that Marie had foreshadowed this defense by recent statements in Horsemonger Lane Gaol that Fred in fact had ordered her to leave London. It would therefore be an important link in the prosecution's increasingly strong case to bring forward new witnesses who could testify that Fred was genuinely surprised by Marie's disappearance.

On 14 September the *Times* reported that the police had come up with a helpful witness on this thorny issue—Matilda Weldon, the Bainbridges' servant. It was understood that she had told the police that Manning seemed very excited when he returned to the Bainbridges' after finding his wife flown and had said that she had "cut into the country." The thorough questioning of the Mannings' neighbors was also fruitful. Mrs. Mary Anne Schofield of 12 Weston Steet, opposite the murder house, told the police that at about 5:00 P.M. on Monday, 13 August, Manning went to his house and knocked at the door without any response. He then came over to Mrs. Schofield's house and asked after his wife. Mrs. Schofield told him that Marie had left in a cab at about three o'clock with several boxes. As soon as he heard this, he went to 2 Minver Place, passed through that house, and climbed over the back wall into his own. Sophia Payne, who resided at No. 2, confirmed that she had permitted Manning to pass through her house.

Mrs. Payne was also able to give the police an account of a conversation she had had with Manning on the night of O'Connor's disappearance. On Thursday, 9 August, she saw Manning sitting on his garden wall at about a quarter to seven in the evening, smoking a pipe and drinking some half-and-half. He struck up a conversation with her and an old gentleman who lived in her house. The conversation turned to railway shares. After about twenty minutes Manning jumped down rather abruptly and said that he had an appointment to meet and that he must go and dress. He then went into his house, and Mrs. Payne saw no more of him that night.

The news of these developments in the police investigation was punctuated by reports of a long series of hearings in the Southwark police court. Time and again for a period of over a month the Mannings were hauled into the public gaze in Magistrate Secker's courtroom while the Crown trotted out the witnesses whose testimony had been heard at the inquest and introduced the new witnesses that were being turned up by the police. The proceedings were formally described as "examinations" of the Mannings, but they said nothing during the courtroom sessions while their lawyers probed for possible weaknesses in the prosecution's case.

On 31 August and 1 September the Mannings faced separate hearings that preceded their long-awaited reunion in court. When it became known that Marie Manning would be brought up on Friday morning, 31 August, the day of Fred Manning's return to London, the various routes to the courthouse were "besieged long before the time for opening the court at ten o'clock, by a crowd of persons of both sexes, anxious to obtain a sight of the culprit." The democratic writer for the *Daily News* rejoiced that the wealthy who sought admission into the body of the court by means of money were "invariably unsuccessful," but noted the presence of "a crowd of ladies and others whose influence was sufficient to enable them to gratify their curiosity." Such a large number of onlookers were accommodated in a small courtroom that it was rendered "about as agreeable as a residence of equal duration in the celebrated Calcutta dungeon." Sometime prior to the entrance of the prisoner into the courtroom, Magistrate Secker directed a passage to be cleared from the cells to the dock in order that she might not be embarrassed by the crowd pressing on her.

It was a few minutes after one o'clock when Marie was finally placed in the dock. Her dress was much the same as when she appeared for her first hearing the week before. Over her bonnet she wore a thick black veil, which concealed her features except when she had to raise it up to give the witnesses an opportunity of identifying her; at such moments the *News* reporter observed that "though she bore herself with amazing coolness and self-possession, her eye was bloodshot, and her features bore the marks of bodily fatigue or mental suffering." This description is confirmed by the visual impression of Marie that has been recorded for posterity by the genre painter William Mulready, who sketched both the Mannings in the police court proceedings.

Marie stood during the entire hearing, occasionally commenting on the evidence to her solicitor, Joseph Solomon, who was at her side. As soon as she entered the dock, Mr. Hayward, assistant to the solicitor for the Treasury, rose and said that, as prosecutor for the Crown, he intended only to examine a few witnesses whose testimony would be sufficient to support a remand of Mrs. Manning to prison pending further proceedings. He brought to the stand William Kirk, the cab driver who had taken Mrs. Manning away from Minver Place, and William Day, the railway porter at the London Bridge Station who had taken charge of her boxes. Both of them recognized Mrs. Manning, but William Dyne, the clerk of the London Bridge Station cloakroom, who followed them, could not say whether she was the person who had deposited the boxes with him.

The principal witness was Superintendent Moxey, who detailed again the circumstances of Mrs. Manning's arrest and recounted her voluntary declarations to him. Expanding his inquest testimony, he now told the court that on the afternoon of her arrest or the following morning Marie had said that "O'Connor had acted like a kind friend to her; in fact, he had acted the part of a father." She had expected him to dinner on Wednesday but he came in the evening under the influence of liquor. She invited him again on Thursday, she told Moxey, and was surprised at his not coming; she went to his lodgings to find out why he had not come but he was not at home.

Only Kirk was cross-examined, and Mrs. Manning was remanded to Horsemonger Lane Gaol. When Fred Manning was told that his wife had been examined that day, he made no observation other than, "Oh, was she." He asked where she had been taken after the examination and, told that she had been removed to Horsemonger Lane Gaol, he said, "Then it's likely I shall see her there and confront her, and it will be seen that she will exculpate me from all participation in the murder."

But his court appearance the next morning at ten o'clock was a solo performance. He walked into the courtroom with a firm step but appeared to be downcast. The *News* reporter said that he seemed some years older than the thirty years set down in the charge sheet and described him as follows: "He is a stout man, of fair complexion, sandy hair and whiskers, the latter appearing to have been recently shaven closely. His neck, which is short, is of unusual thickness. He wore a blue frock coat buttoned up in front, and a red silk handkerchief around his neck. During the examination, which lasted but a very short time, the prisoner seemed extremely nervous and scarcely lifted up his eyes." Frederick Binns, a solicitor, stepped forward and advised Magistrate Secker that he had been retained by the prisoner. Inspector Yates, who had charged Manning the night before, began the presentation of the Crown evidence by testifying as to his observation of the disinterment of Patrick O'Connor. William Massey, the Mannings' lodger, was then brought to the stand for the purpose of identifying Manning, and the proceedings terminated with the remand of Manning until the following Thursday, when he would be recalled for his first joint appearance with his wife.

On Thursday the crowd, eager for the family reunion, massed in front of the police court as early as eight o'clock, and by ten o'clock the whole of Stone's End, from Trinity Street to the Borough Road, was stopped up by thousands anxious to catch a glimpse of the Mannings. The *Observer* said that the street resembled a fair, with "numerous vendors of all sorts of eatables disposing of their wares, and ginger beer merchants doing a roaring trade to a hungry and thirsty mob. The light-fingered gentry were also occupied in 'diving' into their neighbours' pockets, and generally met with success."

The circumspect Magistrate Secker, fearing the occurrence of a "scene" in court if the Mannings had their first meeting there, asked Mr. Keene, the governor of Horsemonger Lane Gaol, to permit them to have a five-minute interview at the prison if they desired it. Carrying out his suggestion, Keene had Manning brought first into the hall of his residence, and Marie was shortly afterward led in to join him. As she entered, Manning "raised his hand somewhat theatrically, and frowned upon her." A heavy silence followed, and when Mr. Keene asked Mrs. Manning whether she had anything to say to her husband, she replied firmly, "No," and Manning gave the same answer.

While this disappointing rendezvous took its course, the body

Frederick George Manning. **Manning's Solicitor.** **Mrs. Manning's Solicitor.** **Maria Manning.**

(Drawn in Court by Mr. Robert Cruikshank.)

Robert Cruikshank's drawing of the Mannings and their solicitors in court, from *The New Wonderful Magazine.*

Sketches of the Mannings made by William Mulready, R. A., during the police court hearings. By permission of the Victoria & Albert Museum.

of the court was becoming so crowded that several women fainted and had to be carried out. The spectators' benches were heavily dotted with celebrities, including Prince Richard Metternich and the secretary of the Austrian Embassy, Baron Koller. Precisely at noon, Fred Manning, trembling slightly and appearing somewhat alarmed, was brought into court and placed at one end of the dock; when "relieved from the pressure of the spectators" he regained his composure. After the solicitors Binns and Solomon took their places in the dock, Mrs. Manning was introduced as the star attraction. The crush and noise of the courtroom appeared to disconcert her, and while the clerk, Mr. Edwin, was endeavoring to quiet the crowd, Marie sat down and conversed with the female turnkey, resting her head upon her hand and endeavoring to avoid the earnest glance of her husband, who sat at the opposite corner of the dock. Throughout the days of the hearings their eyes never met.

Mr. Edwin requested the prisoners to stand on chairs provided for them at either side of a table in the dock. Manning complied immediately but, instead of standing erect, took a slouching attitude. Marie rose from her seat but seemed unwilling to mount her chair, and she still objected even when Edwin directed an officer to assist her. As the prisoners were put upon their pedestals, the *Observer* reporter sketched his impressions of their appearance: Manning's red checked silk handkerchief, worn around his neck as at the previous hearing, was tied in a "flash" or underworld style, and the absence of a collar emphasized the malformation of his neck and chin. Mrs. Manning was "genteelly attired" in her ubiquitous black satin dress, a white straw bonnet, and a black lace veil. The reporter thought that her appearance was "decidedly improved" since the preceding week. Maintaining the same degree of poise that had been remarkable in her earlier appearances, she seemed to show great attention to the evidence and occasionally suggested questions to her solicitor.

William Henry Bodkin, Q.C., informed Magistrate Secker that he had been engaged by Mr. Hayward to present the prosecution's case. He then brought to the stand a number of the inquest witnesses who repeated the substance of their earlier testimony: Constables Barnes and Burton, surgeons Lockwood and Odling, and O'Connor's friends. O'Connor's landlady, Ann Armes, ran into some difficulty when she failed to recognize Fred Manning, but her problem was repaired by her more observant sister Emily, who identified him without hesitation.

The cross-examination was perfunctory until Fred Manning's solicitor, Binns, faced the lodger Massey. Binns brought out the fact that Massey had served equivocally as the Mannings' messenger to O'Connor:

"Did you ever write any letters to Mr. O'Connor?"

"Yes, I did."

"How many?"

"Two or three. They were written at the request of the Mannings, who appeared very anxious that I should have him to dinner frequently."

"How long before the ninth of August did you write to O'Connor?"

"About a fortnight before."

"That is the first letter?"

"I thought it was the last. I don't know when the first was written. The second was written about the middle of July. But that may have been the first."

"Do you know whether, after any of those letters were written, O'Connor came to the house of the Mannings?"

"Yes."

"How often did you see him after those letters were written?"

"I have seen him there twice."

"Was he not there three times after you had written the letters?"

"He was there twice, but I won't swear as to his having been there three times, or to my having written three letters."

"When did you see O'Connor after you wrote the last letter?"

"I don't believe I ever saw him after writing the last letter."

As the usual hour for adjournment approached, Bodkin proposed that the proceedings be resumed at eleven o'clock the next morning. Secker agreed and the prisoners were removed to Horsemonger Lane Gaol. Their first appearance together in the proceedings stirred feverish activity among the artists in the press corps; the reporter for the *Observer* noticed that several artists were sketching in court during the day and that "one ingenious photographist contrived to smuggle in a miniature camera inside his hat, with which he hit off several facsimiles of the scene, including portraits of the prisoners."

The next morning, Friday, 7 September, the Mannings took their places in the dock as before. At the beginning of the hearing Marie stood up, but Fred, having complained of illness, was permitted to sit all day.

Bodkin began by stating that the Crown would not oppose the application one of the prisoners had made with the assent of the other that the case should not be tried at the next sessions of the Central Criminal Court (Old Bailey), to begin on 17 September, on the ground that there would not be sufficient time by then to make the necessary preparations for the defense. He then called as his first witness Richard Welsh, who had delivered the lime to the Mannings' house. The boy had changed his story since the inquest. He now testified that Manning did not pay him when he delivered the lime, so he returned the next day. When he knocked, Mrs. Manning opened the door a crack, handed him the promised three halfpence, and closed the door. On cross-examination, Solomon was able to shake his identification of Mrs. Manning; Welsh said that he could not swear who the woman was who gave him the money. Bodkin could not induce him to change his mind on this point. All he was willing to say was that the woman was "rather tall, but not quite so tall as Mr. Manning." But Cahill, the seller of the shovel, and Danby, who had delivered the crowbar, both recognized Mrs. Manning with assurance. Danby, who also identified Fred Manning as the purchaser of the crowbar, admitted, on cross-examination by Solomon, that he had seen Marie at her door only two or three minutes and had never seen her before or since, but asserted that he could still solemnly swear that the female prisoner was the woman to whom he had delivered the tool. Lockwood was recalled to clinch the significance of the crowbar purchase. He was shown another crowbar and testified that if it were five inches longer, it could have inflicted the wounds he had found on the skull. The sharp end of the crowbar would have made the incised wound, and the blunt end the other injuries. But he still did not have much to say for the shovel; he had seen "a single hair" on the shovel at the inquest, but thought that the hair was too long to belong to a male.

Then came a dramatic moment, the testimony of the pawnbroker, Thomas Adams, who had taken in pledge for a loan the two pistols delivered to the police. Unfortunately, his testimony was disappointing. After scrutinizing the Mannings in court for two days, he could not recognize either of them.

Charles Bainbridge, the furniture dealer, repeated the substance of his inquest testimony about his purchase of the Mannings' household goods and Manning's stay at the Bainbridge house. On the question of Manning's words about Marie's departure he remained firm. He recollected that when Manning returned to the Bainbridges' after searching for Marie, he stated that he "had started his wife into the country." The Crown was obviously not happy with Bainbridge's testimony, and his would not be the last word on the matter.

On cross-examination Solomon hoped to establish that there were other shovels at 3 Minver Place besides the small one purchased by Mrs. Manning. But the witness said that he had only seen two shovels in the house while the property was being removed. One was a "parlor shovel."

As Inspector John Haynes took the stand, Solomon watched him intently, for he knew that Haynes and his colleagues Langley and Lockyer would testify as to statements of Manning that incriminated his wife. Solomon's expectations were sound. Haynes testified that, on the train back to London from Southampton, Manning asked him whether he had seen Marie. Haynes said he had not but cautioned him against further conversation: "This is a serious affair, Manning. I'm an officer; don't say anything to me that would prejudice yourself." Haynes quoted Fred as saying, after dismissing the warning: "If I can see her in the presence of a magistrate and clergyman, she will confess all. It was her that shot O'Connor."

Solomon jumped to his feet, objecting to this evidence. Under common-law rules of evidence, a husband's statements could not be used against his wife.

Bodkin for the Crown maintained that the testimony was strictly legal evidence. It was not intended to use Manning's statements against his wife. At the trial the jury would be instructed that what the husband said in the absence of his wife was not to prejudice her.

Mr. Secker agreed: "It appears to prejudice Manning himself, and we are bound to hear all that he said to prejudice himself."

Solomon replied: "Yes, but it prejudices the wife also."

But Secker was unmoved: "It has no weight whatever as against her, but I must say that what he said affects himself, showing that he had a knowledge of what transpired."

Solomon knew he was defeated but could not resist a parting shot: "The course taken is at variance with all that I have seen in my experience."

With the attempted exclusion of the evidence denied, Inspector Haynes's damaging summary of Manning's statement continued: "It was she that shot him. She had invited him to dinner, and laid the cloth and shot him as she was walking downstairs behind him. She would not care any more about killing a man than she would about killing a cat."

Binns, on cross-examination in behalf of Manning, attempted to obtain the witness's admission that, by referring to the case as "a serious affair," he had intended to draw Manning out. When Haynes denied this charge, Binns seemed to lose his aplomb. Inquiring about the seating arrangement on the train, he asked a bewildering question: "Did Manning sit next to you, or did you sit next to him?" When the courtroom laughter died down, Binns recovered his lost composure and tried another tack; he asked whether Haynes had shown his written statement to officers Langley and Lockyer, who were also due to testify. Haynes would admit only that he had spoken to Langley on the subject of the conversation with Manning on the train. Binns promptly inquired of the court clerk whether Langley or Lockyer was in court and was informed that Langley was present. He requested that Langley be removed, and Magistrate

Secker so ordered, stating that he thought that he had made arrangements that the witnesses were to be kept apart and not to communicate with each other until after they had testified.

After Haynes left the stand, Bodkin called Sergeant Langley, who testified again as to Manning's already celebrated greeting to him at the time of his arrest in Jersey: "Oh, Sergeant, I am glad you're come. I was coming to London to explain it all. Is the wretch taken?" As he left for St. Helier's prison in hand-cuffs, Manning had added, "I am perfectly innocent—she committed the murder herself." It was obvious from Langley's account that Manning's version of the murder was far from complete. Fred had described very circumstantially how Marie invited O'Connor downstairs to wash his hands and shot him in the back of the head when he reached the bottom of the stairs. But he had had nothing to say about the head wounds inflicted by the "blunt instrument," and he was very vague about the preparation of the grave, telling Captain Chevalier merely: "she had a grave dug for him."

Constable Lockyer was the next witness. He had not over-heard Manning's conversation with Langley, but he had heard the prisoner comment while on board the packet returning him to England: "She certainly did it, but the Duchess of Sutherland will intercede for her, to get her off, and she will not be hanged." And on the train from Southampton, the witness had heard Manning tell Inspector Haynes that "she did it, because she could not die happy until she had done it, for he had deceived her twice."

A critical point in the day's proceedings then arrived, as the stockbroker Bassett took the stand and was promptly asked whether he could identify Manning as the customer who had impersonated O'Connor. Despite the fact that the description he had given of his customer at the inquest did not fit Manning well, Bassett was ready with his response: "The male prisoner at the bar is the same man. I have no doubt of it." And so, to the sound of zithers, the "third man" about whom the newspapers had been speculating passed into oblivion.

The Crown then led on evidence that buttoned up Manning's involvement in the stock sale handled by Bassett. Archibald

Griffith, of the Exchange Office of the Bank of England, testified that on Saturday, 11 August, the day of the stock transaction, a man had come into the bank to exchange the hundred-pound note that had been identified as the one given to Manning by Bassett. Griffith had no recollection of the appearance of the man, but he recalled that on the back of the note, under another name, appeared the name "Fred. Manning, 7, Weston Street, Bermondsey." Joseph Adams, another clerk of the Exchange Office, identified by number five ten-pound banknotes that he had issued on the exchange of the hundred-pound note. These numbers corresponded to those of the banknotes discovered in Marie Manning's possession at the time of her arrest in Edinburgh. Bodkin completed this line of evidence with the testimony of Henry Webb Shillibeer, a solicitor who had had business dealings with Manning, that the name and address on the back of the hundred-pound note produced by Griffith were in Fred's handwriting.

A strange picture was beginning to emerge of the Mannings as partners in crime. Fred must have combined a clumsy instinct for craftiness with a high degree of stupidity, if indeed he thought to disguise his identity by endorsing his true name on the note and merely making a slight change in his address. The *Observer* thought it plain that both the Mannings had participated in the stock transaction, since Marie had presumably stolen the securities from O'Connor's room and Manning had then handled their sale and the exchange of the hundred-pound note. What was far from clear was how the five ten-pound notes received in exchange had ended up in Mrs. Manning's possession. Of course, Fred might have given them to her. The *Observer,* however, preferred to assume that Marie had taken advantage of him in some brandy-sodden moment and had stolen the proceeds of sale from him before she left town. This theory may have been inspired in part by an increasingly unfavorable view of Marie, but the *Observer* put forward other grounds. The newspaper was searching for the roots of the mutual hostility that had led the prisoners to hurt their cause by failing to concert their defense. Although Marie had ample reason for irritation with her husband in view of his accusing statements to the police, there was no similar basis for alienation on his part, since Marie had said nothing to incriminate him. The *Observer* thought that Manning's disaffection might have originated in her absconding with the spoils of the crime.

After Shillibeer's testimony was concluded, the stockbroker Stephens was called to the stand to identify Mrs. Manning as the woman who had consulted him about the sale of railway securities, and the second day of the joint examination of the Mannings drew to a close. The Mannings were remanded again to Horsemonger Lane Gaol until Saturday, 15 September, when the Crown proposed to introduce the balance of its witnesses. But the cholera would not have it so; a number of witnesses were stricken ill. On Tuesday, 11 September, it was reported that the stockbroker Bassett, who had testified the previous Friday, was suddenly attacked by cholera that night and died the following morning. His colleague Mr. Hammond also fell ill on Sunday and was not expected to live. The grim progress of the epidemic did not, however, diminish the crowds at the hearing on the following Saturday, and "from the curiosity and excitement which prevailed the whole scene reminded one of the pit of one of the minor theatres during some attractive performance." For a while the Manning case was put off while the police court dealt with a health emergency. The parish authorities of St. Saviour's, Southwark, appeared before Magistrate Secker to answer for their disobedience to an order of the Board of Health "forbidding them any longer to poison the air by burying the dead in their already over-crowded graveyard." Mr. Bodkin, the prosecutor of the Mannings, had been retained by the Board of Health, and his late arrival led to an agreement that the burial dispute should be put over to another day so that the Manning hearing could proceed.

At two o'clock, as the prisoners were led in, the reporters had an opportunity for a fresh appraisal of their appearance. Manning was dressed more respectably, in a black suit; his step and bearing were firm, but his face was "overspread with a deadly pallor." His flabby lower jaw seemed monstrous, "being clothed all round with folds of fat, which terminate in a huge double chin in front, and extend beneath the ears in lumps of flesh, more like swellings than natural formations." The thin lips of his unusually small mouth were often compressed in an expression of obstinacy, and his eyes, stern and watchful, made a man, without knowing why, "feel uncomfortable when they are turned upon [him]." But the eyes were generally cast down. He was ill at ease, and Binns again obtained the permission of the Court that he be permitted to sit. Mrs. Manning's black satin dress was relieved by a straw bonnet trimmed with a gray ribbon. She had dispensed with her cloak, and her figure was commented on favorably: "Whatever may be the character of Mrs. Manning's countenance, her figure is decidedly good and she is remarkable for what the French would term 'une svelte ceinture.'" The *Times* thought she looked unusually strong for a woman. When she raised her veil from her face, she "looked about her with a fearless and unembarrassed expression." She was sufficiently self-possessed to show anxiety not to crease her dress while she was seated. And the *Times* found something to like in her face, where "amidst all the coarseness and sensuality of her expression, there is something almost approaching to goodnature about her irregular features, which certainly makes her less unprepossessing than Manning."

When the hearing began, the depositions of all the witnesses who had given previous testimony were first read out. When the clerk read Lockyer's evidence and came to the statement that Manning said his wife would never be hanged because the Duchess of Sutherland would intervene, it was observed that Mrs. Manning "doubtingly shook her head." Reporters continued to subject the prisoners to close scrutiny when the surgeon's evidence describing O'Connor's head wounds was being read. The *Observer*'s man thought that he had discovered "by the movements of Mrs. Manning's lips and throat that she labored under something like a choking sensation" and that at intervals during the proceedings as the days went by she cleared her throat in a peculiar manner. An amateur scientist on the *Observer*'s editorial staff provided a footnote venturing the opinion that the writer was referring to the *globus hystericus,* or "ball in the throat," which he referred to as "a well-known feminine symptom." Perhaps the courtroom onlookers searched for signs of emotion in Marie's throat because they could see none on her face. No one could help being struck by the contrast between the stamina and impassivity of Marie—who stood motionless and bolt upright in the dock—with the apparent weakness of her husband, who looked ill and had been permitted to remain seated for two days of the hearings.

During the session of 15 September the maladroitness of Manning's solicitor, Binns, was becoming so painfully apparent that it could only be relieved by laughter: in examining Mary Wells, who identified Manning as the purchaser of the lime, Binns irrelevantly inquired into the extent of her familiarity with the case from newspaper reading. She said defensively: "I read it in the *Patriot* newspaper, which we take in. I have not read the whole of the evidence in the *Patriot*."

Binns then asked her: "Well, now, what part is it that you have not read?"

The court was convulsed with laughter over this unanswerable question.

The Crown brought on its new witness, Hannah Firman, to tell of her cleaning of the Minver Place residence, and then turned back to a point that was becoming the prosecution's obsession, the question whether Manning had claimed, as the Bainbridges had testified, to have sent Marie Manning into the country. Matilda Weldon, the Bainbridges' little servant, was questioned about the words Manning had used. She stated that she could not remember whether he had said, "I sent her into the country" or "She is gone into the country."

The last two witnesses brought on by the Crown gave evidence that was intended to help pin down the likely time of O'Connor's arrival at Minver Place on 9 August. But the difficulty of this crucial point was becoming apparent. Young-husband, who told the inquest he had seen Patrick from the top of a bus at about 5:45, now testified in police court that "it was about a quarter-past five, or rather more, I judge, as far as my memory serves me." He said that O'Connor "was just on the move, like a man undecided which way to go." The final witness, James Coleman, a locker at the Customs, stated that he had last seen O'Connor on 9 August, between 5:00 and 5:10 P.M., or thereabouts, walking south on Weston Street toward Minver Place; O'Connor was at the time about a three-minute walk away from the Mannings' house. Coleman was sure the man he saw was Patrick, but he did not speak to him.

Bodkin then told the court that he had originally intended to ask for a deferment of the next session of the hearings for eight days, but he now proposed they be resumed next Wednesday because of "the mortality by which we are surrounded." He had already lost one witness to the epidemic, and did not want to risk losing more.

As the proceedings in the police court dragged on, the Manning case submerged in news of the cholera. Wednesday, 19 September, the date of the next police court hearing, had been set apart by the deanery as a day for "humiliation and prayer" because of the ravages of the plague. All the shops in Southwark were closed and the streets were generally deserted, but still the usual crowd gathered in front of the police court, clamoring for admission and oblivious to fear of contagion and the mandated religious observance. The clerk Hammond had recovered and took the stand on that morning, but other witnesses were unavailable, and again the Mannings were remanded to prison.

Both the Mannings appeared to bear up reasonably well under the delays, and some of Marie's confidence seemed to have communicated itself to her husband. At the hearing on 28 September, which was expected to be the final hearing, Fred entered the court first with a firm step and seemed "wonderfully improved" in appearance. His style of dress continued to follow the direction of his wife's austere fashion; he was appareled in a "handsome suit of black." His downcast look was gone, and he seemed positively cheerful. Marie entered the courtroom "with the manifestation of the same cool self-possession which has characterized her deportment throughout the whole of the trying ordeal through which she has, so far, passed unmoved." She had altered somewhat the style of her costume, without losing her characteristic nicety and taste, by wearing over her black satin dress a rich silk blue plaid shawl, with a lace collar, and a neat straw bonnet with a white lace veil. She seemed to the reporter for the *Observer* to be "the picture of health." The hearing proved disappointing to the Mannings, for once again some of the witnesses had produced certificates explaining that they could not appear that day. Mr. Secker was upset with these delays, and, concurring in Bodkin's view that "no public good could accrue from these continued exhibitions of the prisoners," he announced that, if the witnesses were not forthcoming on the next day fixed for continuation of the hearing, he would go to the prison to authorize a further period of detention without requiring the Mannings' attendance in court.

The final session of the police court proceeding took place at last on Friday, 5 October, with technical testimony showing that the shares in Eastern Counties Railway Company sold by Manning were in fact the property of O'Connor and recorded as such on the books of the railroad. And Bodkin brought Mrs. Bainbridge back to the stand to testify further about his favorite issue, the exact words Manning had used when he found that Marie had left 3 Minver Place. Mrs. Bainbridge remained certain that he had said, "I have sent her to the country." Bodkin then told the magistrate that his evidence was complete, and he argued that it sufficiently made out the case against both the Mannings to warrant their being committed for trial. Secker than addressed the prisoners:

"Frederick George Manning, having heard the evidence, do you wish to say anything to the charge?"

"I have nothing to say, sir," Manning replied in a firm, clear voice.

Secker continued: "Then I need not read the usual caution. Maria Manning, have you anything to say?"

Marie replied in a low tone: "I leave all in the hands of my attorney." These were Marie's first public words, and they were spoken so quietly that the first impressions of the court reporters were understandably mixed. The *Daily News* writer said that "the ear could not catch any foreign accent," whereas the *Observer* found her accent to be "distinctly perceptible."

Secker then formally committed the prisoners for trial at the next Old Bailey sessions and ordered the prisoners to be committed to Horsemonger Lane Gaol, from which they would be removed to Newgate Prison, adjacent to the Old Bailey Courthouse, six days before commencement of the trial session.

Before the police court hearing adjourned, Binns rose to pursue a matter that he had been pressing for weeks. He asked for an order directing that all property found on the prisoners, other than that claimed by the prosecutors to belong to O'Connor, should be handed over to the prisoners for purposes of their defense. He noted that counsel for the government had stated that he had laid before the court an abundance of evidence to make out a case against both prisoners. The "greatest knowledge and eminence in law were arrayed against the prisoners, and it was to meet these, and the strong case which was made," that they desired to have the property restored.

From the time of his appearance in behalf of Manning, Binns had argued that, under the common law, all the property recovered from the Mannings belonged to the husband alone, for every contract made by a married woman and every gift or legacy given to her vested all property interests in her husband. Binns's argument had presented a strange anomaly: Manning was more than willing to concede his wife's legal independence as a criminal; indeed, he insisted on her sole responsibility for the crime. But when it come to making claims against family property, Manning, through his solicitor, was ready to assert the primacy of the husband. Binns was prepared to be generous, though; he told Secker that Manning proposed to have Marie receive defense funds equal to his own.

Secker would not rule on Binns's application, saying that the title to the property was uncertain and could only be decided by a jury. The commissioners of police, however, stepped in and reached a practical solution: they granted Binns defense funds totaling 33 pounds 10 shillings, the same amount that had been awarded to Solomon for Marie.

CHAPTER NINE

The Mannings in Prison

*Round what other punishment does the like
interest gather? . . . persons who have rendered
themselves liable to transportation for
life . . . are never followed into their cells, and
tracked from day to day, and night to night;
they are never reproduced in their false letters,
flippant conversations.*

—Charles Dickens, letter to the
Daily News, 28 February 1846

n September *Punch* published a satire on the
Murder of Mr. Cock Robin describing the
capture and imprisonment of suspects for that
infamous crime, as they might have been
reported in successive editions of a sensational journal given the
lugubrious name "St. Sepulchre's Bell." The fourth edition of
the imaginary tabloid includes an account of "the meals which
[the murderer] took on the road from the place of his capture
and afterwards at Newgate, of the numbers of hours of sleep
which he had, of the shop at which he bought the last pair of
trousers which he ever wore."

If the author of this lampoon intended to outdo the excesses
of crime journalism, his efforts actually paled before the
contemporary reality of newspaper reports devoted to the
Mannings. Any Londoner who could read knew how Marie
Manning had been arrested by telegraph and Fred had been
taken in his bed in Jersey, and now the daily theme of the
penny-a-liners was the life of the Mannings in Horsemonger
Lane Gaol, their reactions to each other and to news of the case,
and what they did to occupy their time until the police van came

around again to haul them off to the next hearing at the Southwark police court.

It was reported that Marie Manning, after learning of her husband's capture, lost the composure and firmness she had displayed while he remained at large. During much of the Saturday after his arrest she was seen pacing the ward where she was confined "evidently in a state of great mental excitement." In the course of the day a police inspector came to see her to ask for a receipt for an advance of twenty pounds, which Secker had allowed her to prepare her defense out of the money found in her possession by Superintendent Moxey. Shaking the inspector's hand in a "hearty and fervent manner," she said, "I thank you and the worthy Magistrate for this assistance; I am much obliged." She then wrote the receipt on a slip of paper. Her style of writing, however, proved one of the early disappointments of her observers among the press; it was "certainly not in keeping with her reported accomplishments." When Marie was informed of Fred's arrival at Horsemonger Lane Gaol, she remarked that it was very annoying that they were to be brought up together at the next examination at the police court. She frequently asked the prison guards what the newspapers were saying about the case, and their reports did not seem to relieve her anxiety. When she heard that Manning, at his arrest, had accused her of committing the crime by shooting O'Connor at the bottom of the staircase, she declared, "The villain, it was him that did it, not me."

Marie's agitation seemed to be short-lived; indeed, observers were soon surprised by the "coolness and general levity of her conduct." She often voiced concern about Manning and would say, "Ah, poor boy, he ought not to have been taken." Some had the impression that she had lost interest in the case and that all her thoughts were devoted to dress. Marie had, in fact, obtained Secker's permission for some satin dresses and bonnets found in her luggage to be given back to her; but the journalists, dissatisfied with this modest show of vanity, widely propagated a story that she was employing much of her time making a new dress for her first joint police court appearance with her husband. She was also said to have been very busy in adding a double fall to her bonnet so as to screen herself from the eyes of the courtroom audience. The restrictions of the prison regimen did not weigh on her spirits; she ate heartily, and her sleep was undisturbed. Often she would express her satisfaction with what the prison authorities had done for her, saying, "I have plenty of room, air and food, and am not without society." Marie's odd attachment to Superintendent Moxey also surfaced again for, upon being told that that officer had left London to attend to duties in Scotland, she seemed rather disappointed and observed: "I wished particularly to have thanked him for his gentlemanly conduct. But I intend to go again to Scotland as soon as I have got over this difficulty, and I will call and see him." Conversing freely with her guards, Marie told them about her early life and the comfort and happiness that had been hers in the service of the Duchess of Sutherland and other families. She radiated assurance that she would succeed in dispelling all suspicion of her being involved in the murder. On Sunday, 2 September, she attended religious services in the chapel at Horsemonger Lane Gaol both in the morning and in the afternoon; her husband was not present on either occasion.

The impression that Marie had turned her mind away from the case was misleading. In prison, as in court, she seems to have taken a more active role than did her husband in instructing her solicitor as to lines of inquiry. At her behest Mr. Solomon applied to Magistrate Secker for the restoration of a letter that his client had received from Patrick O'Connor in July 1847. Marie had stated that the letter was of great consequence to her since it was sent to her while she was in the service of Lady Blantyre at Stafford House and related to her purchase of railway stock and other securities out of the considerable sums of money she then owned. On 3 October Inspector Yates, as a result of the application, called on Mrs. Manning at Horse-monger Lane Gaol for the purpose of obtaining better identification of the letter. She told him that the letter was one she had received from O'Connor shortly after they became acquainted and that it contained her request for the purchase of some Eastern Railway shares and foreign stock. Yates told her that her parcels had been closely examined and that no such letter could be found. Marie maintained that the letter was taken from her by Superintendent Moxey and that if it was produced it would prove how she came into the possession of the property that had been found on her. Yates reported the conversation to Secker, who ordered him to give Mrs. Manning copies of any letters that could be found.

Fred Manning's prison moods, like his wife's, were closely watched by the press. He had an air of dejection, of profound despondency combined at times with considerable nervousness. Late on his first day at Horsemonger Lane Gaol he asked to be furnished with ink and paper and on its being supplied to him he wrote and addressed a letter to Marie. The terms of his communication never came to light, and it was suspected that the governor of the jail had intercepted its delivery. Having nothing to show for the one effort to which he had roused himself, Fred relapsed into depression and panic. Opinions were divided as to whether his sorry state was due to the effects of dissipation while he was in Jersey or to the turmoil of his mind.

After his first month in prison, Fred eventually found a way to shore up his spirits; it was reported that he had taken to writing poems, which he was regularly delivering to his solicitor, Mr. Binns, whose own courtroom prose was none too steady. One poem published in Manning's name was a dirge entitled "The Prison Bell," which attained some popularity. But the merciless *Observer* declared that there was not a "shadow of truth" in the attribution of the piece to Manning and that in fact "it was written by a convict in Pentonville Prison and possesses a far higher degree of merit than anything Manning could possibly compose." As an example of Manning's more pedestrian efforts, the *Observer* publshed four lines Fred had written for one of the turnkeys of Horsemonger Lane Gaol:

> I heard the toll
> of the great, solemn Newgate bell;
>
> I said, a soul
> is gone to Heaven or Hell.

The *Morning Herald* also reported that while at Horsemonger

Lane Manning "made some excellent drawings," which he sold to the artist and publisher Robert Cruikshank, who himself drew the Mannings in court. The *Morning Herald* continued: "In fact the whole of Manning's time has been occupied in writing and drawing. He seemed so confident of his success . . . that he told Mr. Keene the Governor that as soon as he was discharged from custody he should go to the West indies, but should call upon him before he started, to thank him for his kindness."

All this loving attention to the domestic life of jailbirds was more than the perpetually indignant *Punch* could pass by without comment. It pronounced the discovery by the penny-a-liners that Manning was occupying his time principally in writing poetry to be good news for the music publishers, "who were beginning to want a new sensation after the decline of the Merry Sunshine which the poet has 'loved not wisely,' but rather 'too well.'" *Punch* was sure that a new song by Manning would be a great hit and would replace the present-day favorites of boarding-school classes. There was no doubt that "we shall soon have the Bermondsey Ballads in the hands and mouth of every sentimental Miss." And, of course, *Punch* predicted, there would be an end to all further applications by Mr. Binns for defense funds "with such valuable property as the poetical manuscript of a suspected murderer in his possession."

Punch had also obviously had its fill of the tidbits about the supposed preoccupation of Mrs. Manning, the genteel ladies' maid and failed dressmaker, with her courtroom fashions. Its columnist ended by stating his expectation "to hear in a day or so that Mrs. Manning has taken to crochet work."

CHAPTER TEN

King Edward III's Jury

Mr. Sapsea expressed his opinion that the case had a dark look; in short . . . an un-English complexion.

—The Mystery of Edwin Drood

he trial of the Mannings opened at the Old Bailey on Thursday, 25 October, with all the appearances of a gala premiere, providing further proof of the accuracy of *Punch*'s prophecy that the venerable criminal court would soon be converted into a "Theatre Criminal." None of the trappings of a "first night" was missing. Admission could only be obtained by tickets from the sheriffs and, much as *Punch* had mourned this commercialization of justice, the regulation at least had the beneficial effect of preventing the overcrowding of the court. The sheriffs may have misjudged their market, since the gallery seats, for which a high charge had been fixed, were only sparsely occupied early in the day. But the main floor was full from the beginning of the session. Among the distinguished visitors in attendance, according to newspaper accounts, were several members of the foreign diplomatic community including the Swedish minister, the first secretary of the Prussian legation, Sardinia's chargé d'affaires, and Baron Koller, who had obviously become an aficionado of the case and now brought with him the Austrian ambassador, Count Colloredo. Preoccupied with these glittering public figures, the reporters did not pause to identify other celebrities in the crowd. However, Sheriff Donald Nicoll, in a book written decades later, recalled that one of the onlookers was Charles Dickens.

The judges and lawyers at the trial included stellar personalities that lent additional glamor to the long-awaited day. Sir

Frederick Pollock, the Lord Chief Baron of the Court of Exchequer, presided, and he was assisted by two judges of the Court of Common Pleas, Sir William Henry Maule and a nobleman with the insistent name of Sir Cresswell Cresswell. Pollock, who had been attorney general in the first administration of Sir Robert Peel, had acquired an enviable reputation as a result of his natural brilliance, retentive memory, and profound legal knowledge. He had a lifelong interest in mathematics and in 1846 had been elected to the Royal Society. Mr. Justice Maule had made his name as a commercial lawyer, and after his elevation to the bench in 1839 became known as an excellent judge who combined knowledge with courtesy and had the practical man's impatience with technicalities. Sir Cresswell Cresswell had served in Parliament, where he "spoke little, but always supported Sir Robert Peel." Peel rewarded Cresswell for his silent votes by appointing him to the Court of Common Pleas. He became a strong, somewhat overbearing judge noted for the clarity of his summations.

The attorney general, Sir John Jervis, appeared for the prosecution together with William Clarkson and William Henry Bodkin, who had handled the police court hearings. On the defense side, Serjeant Charles Wilkins led for Frederick Manning and William Ballantine, assisted by John Humffreys Parry, represented Mrs. Manning. The personalities of these men come alive in the candid descriptions Ballantine gives us in his memoirs published in 1882. Sir John Jervis was a kind man who later became Lord Chief Justice of the Court of Common Pleas; Ballantine recalled an instance when Jervis had assured a dying lawyer who was appearing before him that he would find employment for the lawyer's clerk. Ballantine recalled Bodkin as "acute and clear-headed, . . . a pleasant companion and extremely popular." Clarkson he gave lower marks, writing that, "loud-voiced and swaggering, with one undeviating form of cross-examination, whatever might be the position or character of the witness, and that the very reverse of gentle or refined, he did much to maintain the opprobrium attaching to those who practiced at the court."

Ballantine made a mixed appraisal of Manning's counsel,

Lord Chief Baron Pollock.

Charles Wilkins. At the time of the Manning trial Wilkins was already a member of the order of the Serjeants-at-law, to which Ballantine and Parry were later admitted. The Serjeants (whose company took its name "the Order of the Coif" from the close-fitting cap that was a distinctive feature of their costume) were the most honored rank of English barristers and drew their origin from medieval times when they furnished law officers to the Crown. Ballantine wrote of Serjeant Wilkins: "An imposing person and a deep sonorous voice controlled the audience. He was a fluent speaker, and arranged the matter he had to deal with very clearly. His experiences in many walks of life must have furnished him with extensive knowledge of human nature; his mind, however, was incapable of grasping the niceties of law, and he possessed no readiness in dealing with any matter suddenly started. A successful repartee threw him upon his back, and ridicule drove him frantic." The reference to the "many walks of life" Wilkins had known was a polite reflection of gossip rampant in legal circles about Wilkins's early life. Ballantine had heard that Wilkins was at one time in the medical profession and at another an actor in the provinces. The twentieth-century crime writer Horace Wyndham asserts more boldly that Wilkins "had begun life as a clown in a circus; and his forensic methods were always a little suggestive of the sawdust."

Ballantine himself came to the Manning case shortly after his first great success; in 1848 he had defeated the suit of the heiress Esther Field in the House of Lords for the annulment of her marriage by subjecting Miss Field to a devastating cross-examination. He went on to acquire the reputation of being the greatest cross-examiner of his era. His younger colleague Montagu Williams wrote of him: "The Serjeant was a very extraordinary man. He was the best cross-examiner of his kind that I have ever heard, and the quickest at swallowing facts. It was not necessary for him to read his brief; he had a marvelous faculty for picking up a case as it went along, or learning all the essentials in a hurried colloquy with his junior." Ballantine in his memoirs noted some of the classic errors of less skillful advocates, the "reckless asking of a number of questions in the chance of getting at something" and the mistaking of noise for energy. He liked to quote the comment of a judge to a lawyer of this type, "Mr. _____, you seem to think that the art of cross-examination is to examine crossly."

In his book Ballantine had high praise for his assistant in the Manning case, John Parry, "a man of great knowledge, power and ability." Montagu Williams also had favorable recollections of Parry: "Remarkably solid in appearance, his countenance was broad and expansive, beaming with honesty and frankness. His cross-examination was of a quieter kind than that of Serjeant Ballantine. It was, however, almost as effective. He drew the witness on, in a smooth, good-humoured, artful, and apparently magnetic fashion. His attitude towards his adversary also was peculiar. He never indulged in bickering, was always perfectly polite, and was most to be feared when he seemed to be making a concession."

The first session of the Manning trial began shortly after ten o'clock with the entry of the judges, accompanied by the Lord Mayor and other officials. The two prisoners were then led in. Fred Manning, escorted by the governor of Newgate prison, was the first to enter the dock and took his place at the right-hand corner. Marie, who followed, walked to the other end of the dock, still avoiding his eyes. The costumes of the prisoners were familiar from the most recent police court hearings; Manning was dressed in a black suit with a black neckerchief, and Marie in a black dress fitting closely at the neck, which she brightened with a shawl of gaudy colors in which blue predominated, and primrose gloves. As a headdress she wore a handsome white lace veil. Manning appeared to be "in better health and spirits" than at the police court, but observers still detected a "nervous restlessness." Marie seemed to have lost her earlier appearance of robust health and buoyant spirits but remained an impressive figure in the dock, standing throughout the day "as motionless as a statue."

Mr. Streight, the Clerk of Arraigns, read the indictment that had been returned by the Grand Jury a few days before. Frederick George Manning was charged in the first count with having, on 9 August 1849 at Bermondsey, feloniously discharged a pistol loaded with a bullet at Patrick O'Connor and inflicted upon him a mortal wound, of which he then and there died. The second count charged him with having caused the death of O'Connor by striking, cutting, and wounding him on the back part of the head with a crowbar. Other counts alleged that Manning had caused O'Connor's death both by shooting and beating, and transformed the pistol into an air gun.

Then the charge against Marie was read: she had been indicted for having been present and aiding and abetting her husband in the commission of the murder. It was obvious that the Crown stopped far short of placing full reliance on Manning's accusation that Marie had fired the gun.

Both the defendants pleaded "not guilty." The clerk was proceeding to swear the jury when he was interrupted by Ballantine, who rose to present a motion: "Mrs. Manning desires to be tried by a jury *de medietate linguae,* and prays your Lordships to award it."

The words of the motion were burdened with the fustiness and obscurity of law Latin, but heavy stakes rode on its success. In his recent triumph in the Esther Field case, Ballantine had outbattled singlehanded an opposing array of eminent counsel, but never had he undertaken a case in the face of greater odds. The prospects would have been gloomy enough if the Mannings were coordinating their defenses and jointly proclaiming their innocence, but here was Manning heaping the blame on Marie from the moment of his very first words to the police on Jersey. It would help little for the learned Chief Baron to explain to the jury that the statements made by Manning were admissible only against him and could not be taken as incriminating his wife. The rules of evidence were notoriously blind and deaf to psychology. No juror had the hermetic mental compartments in which, as the law assumed, he could keep Manning's statements sealed away from doing injury to Marie.

If only there were a way to sever Marie's trial from her husband's, so that Manning's statement could be completely excluded from evidence in her case. Ballantine had reflected on the problem and thought he had an answer. The criminal law of England was a seamless web that had been spun for centuries, and to find a solution Marie's barrister placed his hopes on a remarkable statute enacted in 1355 in the reign of Edward III. This law provided that in cases between English citizens or the Crown on the one side and aliens on the other, the jury must be "equally divided as to language" *(de medietate linguae),* that is, one-half of the jurymen must be English and the other half aliens, if enough aliens could be found in the "town or place" where the trial was to be held. It is a tribute to the fair-mindedness of the English that, in the very era when they were sweeping from victory to victory in France under King Edward and the Black Prince, they could still recognize that foreign litigants deserved protection from the insularity of an all-English jury. However, the statute was not free of a parochial flavor: all aliens were lumped together as a single group regardless of nationality, and a Frenchman could be legally tried by a jury consisting of none of his countrymen, but of six Englishmen and six Russians. The world, of course, was smaller then, and only the residents of a few nations were likely to end up with any frequency in English courts.

In 1849 the statute of Edward III was still on the books, and if Ballantine's argument was accepted by the court, he would achieve his aim of a separate trial for Marie; for the case precedents were clear that where an alien and a citizen were charged together, only the alien could be tried by the mixed jury provided by King Edward's law.

But Attorney General Jervis now rose to cite a legal "Catch 22." A Victorian law enacted in 1848 provided that "any woman married . . . to a natural-born subject . . . shall be deemed and taken to be herself naturalized, and have all the rights and privileges of a natural-born subject." The attorney general said that, under these provisions, Marie, by her marriage to Manning, had become a naturalized Englishwoman for all purposes and therefore lost the right only aliens had to be tried by King Edward's mixed jury.

Ballantine had anticipated this counterargument and was ready with a response. The statute of Edward III had granted foreigners a right to exemption from usual criminal procedures. A law containing so important a right, Ballantine argued, could "only be abrogated by express terms, and there was nothing in the terms of the act cited by the learned gentleman to take away that right." His colleague Parry buttressed his position by pointing out that the Victorian statute conferred certain privileges on alien women who married Englishmen but did not take away any privileges previously granted by Parliament.

None of the lawyers on either side addressed themselves to the social purpose of the ancient statute, to the insight of Edward III's ministers that jurors unduly impressed by a defendant's foreignness or otherness could be distracted from fair appraisal of the facts presented to them. Was this an antiquated concern in 1849? It would not seem so if one were to judge from the reactions of journalists to the police court proceedings in the Manning case; each reporter had strained to assess the exact degree of accent in Marie's few words. The new Victorian law cited by the attorney general could change Marie's citizenship in a stroke, but it could not take away her accent or her un-English mannerisms.

After a brief response by the attorney general to the arguments of Marie's counsel, the judges retired to consider their ruling. After a consultation of about a half hour, Chief Baron Pollock announced the decision: Marie Manning, as a result of her marriage, had lost her previous right to be tried as a foreigner by a mixed jury. The Chief Baron said that the privilege of being tried by a jury composed half of foreigners was not an individual privilege belonging to Marie but a privilege of the alien status that she had held. The Victorian law had changed her status, and therefore this privilege and all other alien rights fell away; it was not necessary to revoke them by express words. The Court therefore ordered that the joint trial of the Mannings by an English jury must proceed.

Ballantine's plan had gone awry. His failure was due to a legal irony that had worked its strange will: a general enactment intended to advance the lot of a large class of women had put his client in mortal peril.

CHAPTER ELEVEN

The Case for the Crown

*"But recollect from this time that all good
things perverted to evil purposes, are worse
than those which are naturally bad. A thoroughly wicked woman, is wicked indeed."*

—*Barnaby Rudge*

ttorney General Sir John Jervis made the
opening statement of the Crown's case. He was
well known to the judges, who listened to his
words with interest and respect. Only the year
before he had introduced into the House of Commons three
important bills for the regulation of the duties of England's
justices of the peace, and they had been enacted under the
popular name of Jervis's Acts. Now this eminent legal official
had decided to accept responsibility for the Manning case. The
attorney general began his address by telling the jury why he
had done so. He told them that the great importance of the
investigation they were to enter upon and the excitement that it
had created in the mind of the public had induced him, as the
public prosecutor, to assume the conduct of the case. He was
quite certain that, on a charge of this serious nature, it was
unnecessary for him to caution the jury, as he implored them to
do, to dismiss altogether from their minds everything they had
heard or read on the subject of the case and to confine their
attention solely to the evidence that would be put before them.

Briefly Jervis described the personal backgrounds of the
Mannings. He was careful to avoid any mention of the criminal
suspicions that had fallen upon Manning in connection with the
train robberies, but he did permit himself a reference to
Manning's service as a guard for the Great Western Railway, an

allusion that might have awakened the jury's recollections of the robberies and the stories that had implicated Manning.

Jervis then took up the matter of O'Connor's disappearance. On Thursday, 9 August, O'Connor had left his residence in Greenwood Street about half past seven in the morning. He was present at the London Docks at the ordinary time, eight o'clock, and had signed the appearance book. He remained on duty until four, when he signed the departure book as having left his duty. About a quarter before five he was seen by two friends, Graham and Keating, on London Bridge and had shown one or both of them a letter of invitation to dinner signed "Maria." About five on the same day he was seen in Weston Street about three minutes' walk from Minver Place, and a little later was again seen by another person on London Bridge, apparently hesitating about which way to go. That was the last occasion on which he was seen alive. Detailing the discovery and identification of O'Connor's body, the attorney general noted that the police searches of the premises had not discovered O'Connor's clothes, any letter of invitation to dinner, or any instruments likely to have inflicted his wounds. The finding of O'Connor's body in the house occupied alone by the Mannings was not to be taken as "conclusive of the guilt of both or either of the prisoners." However, Jervis continued, there could be no doubt that O'Connor had been murdered between the ninth of August, when he was last seen alive, and the seventeenth of that month, when his body was found. He thought that his learned friends who were acting for the prisoners would have no right to complain if he started with the assumption that O'Connor had been murdered on the Mannings' premises, and he thought also that it was no unfair presumption to conclude that one or other of the Mannings had taken part in the dreadful act. When the jury heard the evidence, he feared that they would be of the opinion that the death of O'Connor "was the result of a deep-laid plot" and the question for them was whether both or either of the prisoners had been concerned in that plot.

The attorney general then explained the legal meaning of the indictment. Frederick George Manning had been charged with having actually committed the murder and his wife with being present and aiding and abetting in its commission. But he pointed out that under the law the proof did not have to conform to the language of the indictment. If the jury found that Marie Manning's hand had committed the fatal deed and that the husband had aided and assisted her—or even that he had aided and assisted some other person not mentioned in the indictment—then Manning must be found guilty. The jury, in other words, "would not be encumbered by any technical inquiry as to whether it was the hand of the man or the woman that inflicted the deadly wound upon the deceased." If either of them committed the act, and the other was present and participated in the murder, both would be guilty of the murder. Further broadening the scope of the charge, the attorney general told the jury that under the law they were free to find either defendant guilty of the murder even if such defendant was not physically present during the murder but had had previous knowledge of the act.

Jervis stressed the legal responsibilities of married women, which many of the jurors had undoubtedly already read about in the *Observer*. In some cases, he told them, the humanity of the law presumed that married women were under the coercion and constraint of their husbands, but that rule had never applied to treason or murder. He then attempted to anticipate arguments that Ballantine might put forward for Mrs. Manning. It might be alleged for the defense, he said, that the murder was committed by the man, and that the woman could be regarded only as an accessory after the fact. But Jervis emphasized that she was not so charged, nor could she be so charged, for the law did not allow a married woman to be charged as an accessory after the fact for comforting and harboring her husband; and he did not believe that the evidence in the case would warrant any such conclusion with regard to Mrs. Manning.

Taking the jury back to the facts of the case, Jervis began chronologically with a history of the relations of the Mannings and O'Connor. The origin of the intimacy between O'Connor and the Mannings he had been unable to trace, but he had reason to believe that at some time prior to 1847 O'Connor had paid his addresses to Marie and recently, and for some time past, they had been upon terms of intimacy. Marie was in the constant habit of visiting him, and she was on such terms of intimacy with him as not only to be acquainted with all his pecuniary affairs (he being a man of considerable property) but to have free access, by his direction, to his apartments, where she remained frequently in his absence for a substantial period of time. After summarizing Manning's odd conversations with the lodger Massey, Jervis turned to the evidence of purchase of the lime, crowbar and shovel. He said that when Manning was asked whether he required gray lime or white lime, he had responded that he wanted the lime that would burn the quickest, and accordingly gray, unslaked lime was sent. Jervis told the jury that the purchases of the implements of the crime were completed on 8 August with the purchase of the shovel and that it was on this very day that Mrs. Manning wrote a letter to O'Connor asking him to dine at the house that day in these words:

> Wednesday morning.
>
> Dear O'Connor,—We shall be happy to see you to dine with us today, at half-past five.
>
> Yours, affectionately,
> Maria Manning.

The note was posted on 8 August at three o'clock in the afternoon and was addressed to O'Connor at the London Docks, but because of its late mailing it would not be delivered until the following day, and was evidently not the letter that O'Connor had shown to his friends on the bridge. In fact, the note of 8 August was delivered to O'Connor's house the following day by a porter from the Docks. O'Connor, having left home at half past seven in the morning, never saw it. On the evening of 8 August O'Connor had gone to the house of the Mannings, Jervis stated, "happily, in company with a gentleman named Walsh." Mrs. Manning said she had written a letter to ask him to dinner and was surprised he had not come; O'Connor replied that he had not received the letter.

The attorney general referred again to the evidence placing O'Connor on London Bridge and in the neighborhood of Minver Place on the evening of 9 August. He told them that at about a quarter to six on the ninth Mrs. Manning "went to" O'Connor's lodgings in Greenwood Street. The attorney general had instructed the police to ascertain the period of time it would have taken her to go from Minver Place to Greenwood Street and found that it would take about forty-two minutes on foot, thirty-five minutes by omnibus, and about twenty-five minutes by cab. Mrs. Manning stayed at Greenwood Street until about a quarter past seven. Her husband was certainly at Minver Place that evening, for about a quarter past seven he was seen smoking and chatting on his garden wall. On the next day, Mrs. Manning had returned to O'Connor's lodgings about a quarter to six and had stayed there about the same length of time as on the previous evening; and Jervis thought it was not unfair to presume that on this occasion she had gone there for the purpose of removing part of O'Connor's property.

Jervis then gave the jury a preview of the evidence about the cleaning of the Minver Place kitchen on 11 August; the sale of O'Connor's Eastern Counties Railway shares; and the disposition of the household furniture to the Bainbridges. He also told them of the flight and arrest of the Mannings. When he came to summarize Manning's statements incriminating Marie, the attorney general paused to caution the jury: "At this point of the case it is necessary that I should do what will be afterwards done by their Lordships—caution you against using adversely to the female prisoner any declarations made by the male prisoner upon his apprehension. It is necessary that the whole case should be detailed in evidence before you, but the rules of law preclude the statements made by Manning from being used adversely against his wife." He pointed out the gaps in statements of Frederick Manning, who had never told the police "how it was that O'Connor's head had been so cruelly and frightfully mutilated—indeed, knocked to pieces—by some blunt instrument, probably the crowbar."

As he reached the conclusion of his statement, Attorney General Jervis turned again to the implements of the crime.

The jury would find, he suggested, that, before the murder was committed, the lime, which was undoubtedly used for the purpose of obliterating, if possible, all traces of O'Connor, had been purchased by Manning, and the delivery boy had been paid by his wife; and that the crowbar, "which was well calculated to loosen the hard ground under which the unfortunate man was buried, and to raise the flag which it was hoped would cover him from observation" had been purchased by the male prisoner on the twenty-fifth of July, delivered to the female prisoner on the twenty-eighth, and paid for by her. Jervis was less confident on the role of the shovel, stating that on 8 August Mrs. Manning herself purchased a shovel which "although it might be used for ordinary purposes" was handy and convenient for the removal of the earth. As he closed his address, Jervis expressed his confidence that the jury would draw its conclusions from the evidence calmly and fairly, patiently and honestly.

The first Crown witness called was Police Constable Henry Barnes, who told how Constable Burton and he had pried up two flagstones in the back kitchen of 3 Minver Place and discovered O'Connor's body. The cross-examination by Wilkins was ineffective, but as he sat down Attorney General Jervis saw an opportunity. If he could emphasize how Barnes and Burton had worked together to remove the stones, perhaps the jury in their mind's eye could see the two Mannings performing that same task jointly when O'Connor's body was interred. He asked Barnes: "You say you removed the stones with a crowbar, could you move them yourself?"

Barnes was evasive: "I used the crowbar, and after that the shovel."

Jervis was dissatisfied with his answer. "Was it necessary to have more than one person to lift the stone?" he asked.

But Barnes remained unresponsive. He said: "I held the crowbar, and Burton held the stone up with the boat hook while I raised it with the crowbar, so that the two tools held it up."

Jervis decided to leave well enough alone, but Ballantine was determined to let in more light on the issue. In one question and answer the picture Jervis had hoped to paint faded: "You say, in point of fact, that you and Burton acted together in removing the flagstone. Could you have removed the flagstone yourself?"

"Yes, quite easily," Barnes said.

Burton's testimony produced no surprise, and the surgeon Lockwood followed to describe the results of the medical examinations. The summoning officer, Mr. Slow, then produced the set of false teeth that Lockwood had taken from the body, and Mr. Comley, a dentist, testified that he had sold the teeth to O'Connor.

No challenge was mounted by counsel for the defendants to the testimony of Pierce Walsh about O'Connor's visit to the Mannings' on the evening of 8 August. In fact, his testimony was not wholly unfavorable to the Mannings, who he said "appeared to be as friendly as brothers with the deceased." Pursuing this theme on cross-examination, Ballantine underscored the kindness Marie showed O'Connor by bathing his temples with eau de cologne in a vain effort to bring him out of the faint condition into which he fell during the visit.

The first conflict over the prosecution's evidence came during the testimony of William Keating about the letter O'Connor had shown him and Graham on London Bridge on 9 August. When Bodkin asked the witness whether he noticed the name on the letter, Ballantine leaped to his feet with an objection. He said that since there had been no proof that the letter was in Marie's handwriting or that it had been destroyed, testimony as to its contents was inadmissible. The Chief Baron said he was inclined to agree with Ballantine, and the attorney general did not press the matter further; accordingly, the famous last letter of Marie to O'Connor was heard of no more, either in the testimony of Keating or of David Graham, who followed him to the stand. In their cross-examinations of these two witnesses, Ballantine and Parry attempted to reinforce their testimony that Marie Manning and Patrick O'Connor appeared to be on friendly terms. Another important point in their testimony was left in apparent ambiguity: in their interview with Marie at Minver Place on the Sunday after the crime, she had told them the hour at which she had visited his lodgings, but their recollections differed as to the hour she had mentioned, and they were not very clear as to whether she was referring to the time of her departure from home or arrival at Greenwood Street. According to Keating's testmony on direct examination, Marie had stated that she "went to" Greenwood Street at seven, but on cross-examination by Ballantine he appeared to quote her as having stated that she was at O'Connor's place at seven. Graham rather vaguely recalled her telling them that "she went to his lodgings at a quarter to 6 or a quarter to 7 on Thursday."

It now being close to two o'clock, the court adjourned for a few minutes. When the trial resumed, the attorney general brought on his two other witnesses who placed O'Connor near the Mannings' home on the evening of his disappearance. The Customs "locker," James Coleman, said that he had seen him about five or ten minutes after five only about 150 yards from Minver Place. John Younghusband, who thought he had seen O'Connor from the top of a bus on London Bridge, now placed the time of that encounter at about a quarter past five. On cross-examination by Serjeant Wilkins, Younghusband repeated his previous testimony that O'Connor was walking north toward the city at the moment he saw him.

Sophia Payne, examined by William Clarkson for the Crown, testified as to her conversation with Manning on the garden wall. On cross-examination, Serjeant Wilkins changed the subject; he wanted to know whether the Paynes could hear any noises next door at 3 Minver Place. Mrs. Payne said that when people were bustling about next door, she and her husband could hear them if they were quiet. The Paynes took tea at about five o'clock, and during that time they were rather quiet. They did some lithograph printing in their house, but it did not begin until seven in the evening. She said that there was nothing else in the Payne house likely to make noise.

This testimony did not please Clarkson at all. If he left it undisturbed, the obvious implication would be that the Paynes would have heard the sounds of the murder had it taken place at 3 Minver Place at the early evening hour suggested by the Crown. Therefore, on redirect examination he inquired about another possible source of distracting noise in the Payne household: "Do you have children?"

Mrs. Payne was unflustered in her reply: "Yes, I have children, but I always keep them very quiet."

Then O'Connor's cousin Flynn was examined by Bodkin. He recounted his interview with Marie on Monday, 13 August, in which she had said of the missing man: "Poor Mr. O'Connor; he was my best friend in London." When Flynn asked her what time she had left her own place on the ninth to search out O'Connor at his lodgings, she had at first said six o'clock but then said it might be a quarter past. She had added that she had met one or two friends on her way, and as Flynn left her she had said, "You gentlemen are very susceptible." Bodkin asked whether she had given any explanation for this puzzling expression, and Flynn said that she did not. A juryman, obviously struck by Mrs. Manning's use of the words "Poor Mr. O'Connor," asked whether the witness had said anything to elicit the expression. Flynn said that he had not done so.

The next witness was Ann Armes, O'Connor's landlady, who told of Marie's visits on the evening of O'Connor's disappearance and the following evening. According to Miss Armes, Marie arrived at Greenwood Street on both evenings at about a quarter to six.* The cross-examination by Serjeant Wilkins was an important turning point in the day. In his questions of the witness he revealed his intention to continue in the courtroom the effort Fred Manning had made since his arrest to throw the full blame for the crime on Marie. He interrogated Miss Armes closely about O'Connor's keys. She stated that he always carried his keys on his own person. When Marie came to visit him, she usually had tea. The key of the tea caddy, from which O'Connor took the tea, was in the same bunch with his other

---

*I have followed the account of the *Daily News* as to this hour. The *Times* quoted the Armes sisters as testifying that the time of arrival was a "quarter *past* six." However, the *News* seems clearly correct, since the Armes sisters had consistently testified to the earlier hour at the previous hearings and, as will be seen, Serjeant Ballantine, without challenge, referred in his closing argument to the sisters' having fixed Marie's arrival at a quarter to six.

keys. Miss Armes also said that she had seen the cash box lying on a table in Mrs. Manning's presence on the Friday evening previous to O'Connor's disappearance. The drift of the questioning was clear. Marie knew that O'Connor carried all his keys (including the key to the cash box) in his pocket; she must have taken the keys from his dead body and used them to open the cash box.

Ballantine brought out on cross-examination that when the cash box was on the table, O'Connor seemed to be pointing out certain papers to Marie and recommending the purchase of particular securities. He then shifted to an attack on the probity of the witness by suggesting that Miss Armes had been paid by O'Connor to permit Mrs. Manning to sleep in his room overnight. In fact, he suggested that the specific sum was nine shillings, but she denied his charges.

Emily Armes confirmed her sister Ann's testimony that on the Friday prior to O'Connor's disappearance he had been with Mrs. Manning in his room and had advised her to purchase certain railway shares. She also agreed with Ann in placing the time of Marie's arrival on Thursday, 9 August, at a quarter to six. Describing Marie's appearance when she passed through the Armes shop after her visits to O'Connor's lodgings on 9 and 10 August, Emily observed a difference between the two occasions; on Friday, 10 August, she was "more shaky" and her left hand trembled very much. Serjeant Wilkins, pursuing his assault on Marie, had Emily repeat on his cross-examination that Mrs. Manning was also paler than usual. Ballantine did his best to retrieve some ground. He asked: "Could not Mrs. Manning, on going out, have passed through the private door and not come near the shop at all?" Emily conceded that on previous occasions Mrs. Manning had done so when O'Connor let her out, and that Emily had sometimes also let her out by the private door, but she insisted that Mrs. Manning had never left by herself through the private door.

Before the witness left the stand, she identified at the attorney general's request Marie's invitation letter of 8 August which had been brought to the house the following Friday by a person from the docks. She believed that the writing was that of

Mrs. Manning. But Ballantine would not let her go without a final salvo: had Mr. O'Connor ever paid nine shillings on account of Mrs. Manning having slept overnight in the house? Emily Armes, like her sister, said no.

The medical student William Massey was then called to testify. He related Manning's questions about drugs, air guns, and the fate of murderers. To emphasize the triviality of the conversations, Serjeant Wilkins asked a single question: "You being a medical student, questions connected with your profession sometimes became the topic of conversation?" Massey agreed that they did.

After Massey was excused, Mary Wells told of Manning's purchase of the lime "to kill slugs in the garden." She asked him which he would have, white or gray, and he replied that "he would have that kind which burned quickest." On cross-examination by Serjeant Wilkins she said that the lime was sent home two days after his order and that no inquiry had been made after it in the meantime. The Wells employee who delivered the lime to 3 Minver Place, Richard Welsh, had been unable at the police court hearing to identify Mrs. Manning as the woman who had paid him for the delivery. But today, when he followed Mary Wells to the stand, he appeared to have no doubt that it was Mrs. Manning who had paid him, and Ballantine for the moment did not challenge the identification.

William Danby, who then testified about his delivery of the crowbar, came under heavier fire. Addressing himself to the testimony about Manning's insistence on the wrapping of the tool, Wilkins submitted to the witness that Manning had said that "it was not a respectable way of doing business, for a shop to send goods out without wrapping them in paper." But the witness maintained that Manning had said only that they might have wrapped it up; this demand made no sense to Danby, for no one wrapped crowbars in paper. Ballantine tried to establish whether Manning had stated his purpose for buying the tool: "When he ordered the crowbar, did he say for what he wanted it?"

"No."

"How was the tool described in the bill of sale?"

"I do not know whether it was called a crowbar or a ripping chisel. Some people call them one thing and some the other, but it would not be called a chisel."

Bodkin then recalled Lockwood for a repetition of his police court testimony about the capacity of a crowbar to inflict O'Connor's head injuries. Showing the witness a crowbar, he asked: "Look at this crowbar, would an instrument four or five inches longer than that, of that sort, be such as would inflict the wounds you saw on the head of O'Connor?" Lockwood said that it might have done so, both the cuts and the fractures. But Serjeant Wilkins was puzzled by the precision with which the length of the murder weapon had been postulated: "Would the length have anything to do with it?" he asked. Lockwood was a careful man and felt impelled to qualify his earlier testimony. He replied to Wilkins: "The length would make it easier—I cannot say but what the fractures might have been inflicted with a short one."

The Chief Baron asked him whether he could tell from the appearance of the head wounds how long before the disinterment they had been inflicted. Lockwood said he could not, but judging from the decomposition of the body, he thought that the body must have been underground for a week, and perhaps a little more. He had taken into account the use of the quicklime, which must certainly have hastened decomposition. The effect of the lime would be to destroy the facial features very rapidly if there was a sufficient quantity, and yet O'Connor's features were not so far obliterated as to prevent identification by his friends. The witness thought that the lime might also have been absorbed through the fractures and so have caused the decomposition of the brain that was noted, for the examination of the intestines showed that they were not as much decomposed as one might have thought from the external state of the body.

Completing the evidence on the purchase of tools, William Cahill testified as to the sale and delivery of a short-handled dust shovel to Mrs. Manning on Wednesday, 8 August. Cahill had recommended that she buy a regular long wood-handled shovel, but she said she would make a short one do. On cross-examination by Ballantine, the witness said that in addition to the dust shovel priced at fifteen pence, his firm sold spades for two shillings and a variety of other prices. Marie's counsel had scored the point he was seeking to make: if she was looking for a digging tool, she could have made a better purchase from Cahill. At Ballantine's request Constable Henry Barnes was then recalled to the stand. Ballantine asked him whether he had found any shovel in Manning's house. He replied, somewhat pompously: "I cannot charge my memory that I saw any."

"Can you tell whether this shovel produced in court today was there when you searched?"

Barnes was a little vague; he said: "I am sure that there was no shovel there the day the body was found, but it might have been there when I first searched the house."

Serjeant Wilkins had his own avenue of attack. He appeared to be pursuing the possibility that the purchased tools might have been used to build the parlor chimneypiece. When Wilkins asked him whether he had noticed a new chimneypiece in the front parlor, Barnes replied that there was a chimneypiece, either of marble or imitation, but he did not notice whether it was new. Wilkins went on undeterred: "Weren't the houses in Minver Place quite new?"

"They are nearly new."

"Was the front parlor papered?"

"It was papered nearly to the bottom, I believe," Barnes replied.

"Well, didn't you notice whether the chimneypiece lacked the paper round the top of it, as if it had been put in new?"

Barnes had not noticed this, and Wilkins let him go. Later in the day, when the Mannings' landlord, Coleman, was on the stand, Wilkins again inquired whether the Mannings had put up a marble chimneypiece. Coleman was sure that they had not, and that in fact there was no marble chimneypiece in the house.

Having presented its witnesses on the tools acquired by the Mannings, the prosecution turned to the aftermath of the crime. Hannah Firman, the little twelve-year-old cleaning girl, was brought to the stand and bravely faced the attorney general of England. In reply to his gentle questioning, she told how she had cleaned 3 Minver Place on the Saturday after O'Connor's disappearance, and identified Mrs. Manning as the woman who had hired her.

Ballantine then rose to cross-examine:

"Did Mrs. Manning pay you for your work?"

"They gave me sixpence.'

"And did she scold you?"

Hannah began to squirm a bit as she responded: "No, they gave me no scolding."

"Then were they angry with you?"

Hannah did not recollect that they were angry with her for anything. Ballantine assumed one of his most confidential expressions and said: "Now tell me, did you take anything away with you from the house?"

Poor Hannah showed some hesitation, but when he repeated the question, she exclaimed, "Yes sir. I will tell the truth, for it will go furthest."

"That's right," he agreed. "Now tell us what you did take away."

"I cannot tell everything," she said. "I took an egg from the larder."

"And a razor?" The former lady's maid, Marie Manning, had evidently made a careful inventory.

"Yes sir," Hannah answered.

"Where from?"

"From a box."

"You took an egg from the larder and a razor from the box. Was there anything more?"

The list of Hannah's perquisites grew. "Yes sir," she answered, "a purse out of the drawer."

"Anything besides the purse?" Ballantine persisted.

"I do not remember."

"Did you not take some stockings, two pairs of stockings?"

"No sir," said Hannah, finding at least a little relief in being able to deny one of his charges. "I only took one pair out of the cupboard."

"Then you took some clothes belonging to Mrs. Manning, a dress and petticoat, did you not?"

But Hannah was clearly exhausted. "I don't recollect any more, sir."

"Nor a smelling bottle?"

"I don't remember about the smelling bottle."

Dismissing the child harshly, Ballantine exclaimed: "Oh, you can't recollect any more. You may go."

Hannah immediately fled the courtroom. A reporter noted that by her confession of the thefts she left an impression on the minds of the audience very different from that she had created during her direct testimony, which she gave "with much clearness and appearance of simplicity."

The furniture dealer Charles Bainbridge, after his testimony about the purchase of the Mannings' furniture, was cross-examined by Serjeant Wilkins. Wilkins threw himself into the breach of the battle over Manning's description of Marie's departure. Like the prosecution, he wanted to show that Manning was surprised by his wife's disappearance so that it would appear that she was acting independently in the crime. He submitted to the witness that Manning had said that "his wife had started into the country" but Bainbridge would have none of it; he swore that Manning had told him he had sent her there himself. The serjeant then questioned Bainbridge about the items he had purchased from the Mannings, hoping to find that they included tools that could have served as well as the purchased crowbar to raise the kitchen flagstones. Bainbridge said he was sure that there had not been a pickax among the articles he had purchased or an ax of any kind. But he had received a pair of secondhand tongs, which were part of a very common set of fire irons. The tongs stirred Bodkin into action for the Crown. "Was there a crowbar among the articles?" he asked Bainbridge. Bainbridge said, "No," and left the stand.

Mrs. Bainbridge followed with her testimony on Marie's apparently blood-stained dress, which was produced in court by Constable Burton for the witness's identification. On cross-examination Ballantine had some success in limiting the alleged blood stains to the cape of the dress. He asked Mrs. Bainbridge: "Were the marks, that you now suppose to be blood, on the cape only, or on any other part of the dress?"

"On the cape only," she replied. "That drew my attention. I examined the rest of the dress very minutely, but I took more notice of the cape. I discovered other marks on the dress which I considered to be scorches—not from too hot an iron being used but from being dried in a hurry."

If the blood stains were only on the cape, it was not likely that they were the result of Marie's being bespattered in the act of murder. Attorney General Jervis, therefore, rushed in to repair the damage to his witness's testimony: "Explain what you mean," he said to the witness. "You say you first saw what you thought were marks of blood on the cape?"

"Yes. I think from the appearance of it that there had also been blood on the dress. These stains would not be got out with washing alone, unless they were boiled. I think that some of the dress was washed and scorched from being dried in a hurry."

A juryman seemed somewhat skeptical and inquired of her, "Did you examine that by daylight?"

She answered, "Yes," but the Court inquired further: "Have you any particular acquaintance with the mark which blood would make upon such a dress?"

Mrs. Bainbridge avoided the challenge to her expertise. She replied: "I am quite sure there has been blood upon the dress. When I first saw it, I said: 'It looks to me more like blood upon it than anything else.'"

Wilkins, who would be pleased to have the jury find the dress to be soaked in blood, did not touch upon this subject when his turn for cross-examination came, but instead took up again the question of Manning's report of Marie's disappearance. Mrs. Bainbridge, as her husband had done, held fast. Manning had said, "I have sent my wife into the country." She was sure those were his words.

As the afternoon drew on, Detective Sergeant Langley, Superintendent Haynes (who had recently been promoted from Inspector), and Superintendent Moxey testified about the arrests of the Mannings. Moxey and Haynes left the stand largely unscathed by cross-examination, but Langley's testimony about the discovery of gunpowder in the pocket of Manning's shooting jacket piqued the curiosity of a juryman.

"How long after you had the coat did you find the gunpowder?" he inquired of the witness. Langley replied that it was after he got it to Scotland Yard. Serjeant Wilkins cross-examined on the point: "This is a shooting coat, is it not?"

"Yes, it is."

"Do you know whether Manning was a sportsman when he was at Taunton?"

"No."

"Isn't it true that he often went out shooting?"

"I do not know whether he used to shoot a good deal. I only knew him a little when he lived at Taunton."

"Did you ever see him out with his dogs?"

"No."

At the conclusion of the police testimony, the attorney general put in evidence Marie's letter to O'Connor of Wednesday, 8 August, inviting him to dinner that evening, which he had identified by Emily Armes, and the court adjourned until the next morning at ten o'clock. The Mannings left the dock without taking the slightest notice of each other. Marie, before leaving, curtsied slightly in the direction of the Bench.

When Friday morning's session opened, Superintendent Haynes, who had been the last witness examined on the previous day, was recalled to the stand to identify some dresses and a piece of muslin he had found in the boxes left by Mrs. Manning at the London Bridge railway station. He said that he had delivered one of those dresses and the muslin collar to Mr. William Odling. This testimony cleared the way for the appearance of Odling, who was the twenty-year-old son of the police surgeon who had participated in the postmortem. Young Odling stated that he had examined a portion of a dress of Mrs. Manning's that had been delivered to him by Superintendent Haynes. He submitted the stains that were on the dress fabric to the usual chemical tests and arrived at the conclusion that they were blood. On cross-examination by Ballantine he said that he had made the experiments last Wednesday and had not given any evidence before Magistrate Secker. He had cut a piece out of the dress for the purpose of the experiment and had since destroyed the piece. Pointing to the dress which Haynes had produced in court, the witness said that the piece on which he had experimented was cut from the left side of the skirt; its stains resembled others to which he pointed on the skirt but were rather thicker and that was the reason he had chosen them. Ballantine asked him whether the stains on the collar of the dress were blood, but Odling said he could not say.

On redirect examination, Bodkin attempted to reinforce the witness's credentials. Odling said that he had studied chemistry for five years, had obtained prizes at Guy's Hospital and at the College of Chemistry, and had received a certificate from a Dr. Hoffman. Taking comfort from his own recital of his honors, he was now prepared to say that the stain on the white collar of the dress was not iron mold or any coloring matter with which he was acquainted; that he could not say what it was positively but that it was more like blood than anything else.

The court wanted a clearer explanation of the basis of the witness's examination of the stains, so the Chief Baron intervened in the questioning: "You say the stains on the dress are stains of blood; state how you've come to that conclusion."

Odling's candid answer revealed the primitive state of the forensic sciences. He told the court that the experiments he conducted excluded the opinion that the stains were anything else than blood, for there was no direct or positive test to ascertain the presence of blood. He had cut out the stained portion of the dress and sliced it into several slips, which he suspended one after another in a small quantity of distilled water. They had imparted a smoky red color to the water, from which he afterwards obtained a precipitate indicating albumen, one of the constituents of blood. His chemical experiments had ruled out a very large number of sources of stains, but he could not swear positively that the stains were blood. He also told the court that he had not examined the stains by microscope, because "it did not appear to me to be a case suitable for microscopic observation."

After Mr. Odling was excused, the Crown introduced its stockbroker witnesses Francis Stephens and Alexander Lamond, who testified as to O'Connor's purchase of Sambre and Meuse Railway, and Eastern Counties Railway, securities, and Mr. Griffin, the clerk from the Bank of England, who described Manning's exchange of the hundred-pound note he had received from the sale of the Eastern Counties shares. Their testimony was unshaken on cross-examination. But a temporary shock was suffered by the prosecution when the solicitor Shillibeer was called to the stand. As he had done in police court, he testified that the endorsement of Manning's name and address on the back of the hundred-pound banknote was definitely in Manning's handwriting, but he now added that the signature "Patrick O'Connor" on the stock transfer given to the stockbroker Bassett did not bear the slightest resemblance to Manning's writing. Still, it appeared clear that the man who had impersonated O'Connor in the stock transaction with Bassett had signed the transfer. Bassett's colleague, the clerk Hammond, testified that he had not seen the transfer signed but that Bassett had brought the signature to him wet and he had had to dry it with a blotter; he had no doubt that Manning was Bassett's customer. The Crown attempted to bolster Hammond's testimony with that of George Linthorn, a share-dealer who was in the Killick offices at the time of the transaction. Linthorn had seen the stranger sign the stock transfer, but being an outsider, had taken no particular notice of him and could not say that he was Manning. He explained that he had not testified at the police court because he had been exceedingly ill.

After these witnesses had done, Richard Welsh, who had delivered the lime to the Manning's house, was recalled to the stand at the request of Ballantine. He was asked to look again at Marie Manning and then Ballantine said: "You told the Court that, on the day after you left the lime at Manning's house, you called, and received three halfpence. Have you a distinct recollection of the person from whom you received it, or may you be mistaken?" Welsh's confidence was shaken, and he answered: "I may be mistaken about it; it was a female."

Ballantine would have been happy to have the prosecution's case end on this note of doubt, but the attorney general tried to shore up his faltering witness. "Who do you believe it was?" he asked Welsh.

"I believe it was the female prisoner," Welsh said, recovering some of his courage. With his testimony the evidence for the Crown was concluded.

Neither of the Mannings offered any witnesses, and they relied for their defense on the speeches of their counsel.

CHAPTER TWELVE

The Arguments for the Defense

*"You're a handsome woman, . . . but good
looks won't save us. And you're a proud
woman; but pride won't save us."*

— *Dombey and Son*

 erjeant Wilkins now rose to address the jury in
behalf of Fred Manning. He began with traditional ingratiating comments, seeking sympathy for the difficulty of his task. Not only did
the mere accusation itself against any man "argue a foregone
conclusion in nine cases out of ten," but Wilkins was required to
answer the case presented by the attorney general, "the first
counsel of the land." When this brief prelude was done, Wilkins
put aside diplomacy in favor of attack. The first object of his
offensive was the press, whom he accused of irresponsibility in
creating prejudice against his client. He cautioned the jury
"against the efforts of those who set themselves up as the
defenders of our liberties, but who, in such cases, do all they can
to prejudice your minds, to pervert your path, to dam up the
streams of justice, and prejudge the case by urging upon the
public topics and circumstances which ought never to weigh
with you for a moment, but which, nevertheless, have an effect
upon your minds, whether you will or no." Wilkins reminded
the jury that the attorney general (who, he was happy to say in
passing, had conducted the case in a manner reflecting the
greatest credit on him) had urged them to forget all they had
read on the case and to come to their decision with their minds
unprejudiced and unbiased. But, Wilkins asked:

> Who are they that render these precautions necessary? Who are
> the rebels against justice? Who are they that transgress the law?

Who are the men who dare to dictate to a Court and Jury, and who seek to intimidate you into a particular verdict, because it squares with prejudices resulting from an imperfect knowledge of the whole history of the case? I have read with deep interest of that frightful event, the French revolution—an event that did more at once to ennoble and to debase, to dignify and to degrade the human race, than any other event with which I am acquainted; and I have found that what adds to the horrors of each stage of cruelty, as it presents itself to our view, is, that a depraved press prejudged every case before its investigation, making the trial a meaningless form and an empty pageant.

Having now blamed the newspapers not only for his client's plight but for the worst excesses of the French Revolution, Wilkins sufficiently calmed himself to address himself at last to the substance of his defense. He would not dispute, he said, that Patrick O'Connor had been murdered, though he observed parenthetically that O'Connor was no great loss to mankind, and "excites our sympathy only because he was hurried in so awful a manner from time into eternity." Wilkins thought that the means of death had been proved beyond a doubt by the medical evidence and that the prosecution was probably correct in theorizing that the murder took place on the afternoon of Thursday, 9 August; but he argued that it was by no means clear that O'Connor was murdered in the house of the two prisoners.

Then came the most important question: Was O'Connor murdered by both defendants? Serjeant Wilkins lost no time in making it clear that, as had been indicated so strongly by his cross-examinations, he would follow Manning's lead in placing the sole blame on Marie, who was now to join the English press as the target of his invective:

My hypothesis is one which at first sight may appear shocking and unmanly; but we must not allow the usual urbanities of life to interfere with our judgment on questions like the present. We are all in the habit of associating the female character with the idea of mildness and obedience, and that of the male with the idea of power and strength. It is not necessary, however, to come to the conclusion that this rule is an universal one. History teaches us that the female is capable of reaching higher in point of virtue than the male, but that when once she gives way to vice, she sinks far lower than our sex. My hypothesis, then, is, that the female prisoner Manning premeditated, planned, and concocted the murder, and that she made her husband her dupe and instrument for that purpose. . . . It might be said, as it has been said, that Manning is crowning himself with infamy in throwing the blame upon his wife. That is easily said, but if the blame is justly due to his wife—if it was she alone who committed the murder, has not the husband suffered enough from her already, without standing coolly and allowing himself to be sacrificed by the wicked woman who entrapped him?

Serjeant Wilkins then gave the jury his interpretation of the facts of the case. Taking up the purchase of the lime, he argued that Mrs. Manning had suggested to her husband that the lime was necessary to destroy slugs in the garden and had got him to purchase it for that purpose. Manning had made no secret of the purchase as he might have done had he had any criminal intention. He could have bought it in a remote district and carried it home himself. It was worth noticing that although it was not delivered for two days, he showed no impatience to receive it.

Having emphasized Manning's nonchalance about the lime purchase, Wilkins had to dispose of contrary evidence relating to the crowbar, namely, Danby's account of Manning's annoyance that it was being carried unwrapped through the streets. In this instance Wilkins was happy to call on the newspaper gossip that he had condemned so roundly at the beginning of his address. The press "by way of amusing the public, had described Manning as a conceited, consequential sort of man." Wilkins conceded that "it might be so" and that it was this same feeling of conceit that had prompted his client to insist on the wrapping of the crowbar. In any event, he pointed out that Mrs. Manning knew the crowbar was coming and had received it at the house. Then, changing the direction of his argument, he expressed doubt that the implement was purchased for use in the murder or burial since there were a poker and pistol in the house to deprive O'Connor of life, and the flagstones could have been lifted with a meat chopper or a pair of tongs.

Having dealt with the evidence of preparation for the crime, Serjeant Wilkins turned to the murder itself. He told the jury that there was nothing to show that the murder had been done by both prisoners and the circumstances indicated the contrary. There was no evidence of concert between the Mannings beforehand, and "there was everything to show the opposite of concert after" when they went off in different directions and never spoke to each other again. The murder and burial were physically capable of commission by one person. After O'Connor was shot, anyone "with the strength of childhood" could have inflicted the headwounds. And, taking a leaf from Ballantine's book, Wilkins claimed that the burial could with equal ease have been accomplished by the murderer acting alone.

Wilkins then came to the question of motive for the murder. The suggestion of counsel for the prosecution that Manning was jealous was not persuasive, for "no man who had read the history of the case could doubt that Manning was only too easy about his honour as a husband." And it could not be said that Manning was influenced by love of money, for it did not appear that Manning "possessed himself of a shilling that belonged to O'Connor, or the slightest tittle of his property." Wilkins would show presently, he promised, that in the transaction involving the sale of O'Connor's Eastern County Railway shares Manning had again been the victim of his wife's deception.

Swinging back to his attack on Marie, Wilkins called the jury's attention to the fact that it was Mrs. Manning who wrote the notes inviting O'Connor to dinner, was constantly with him at his lodgings, and had access to his secrets about his property. He recalled to the jury Marie's odd behavior when Keating called on her on the Sunday after O'Connor's disappearance:

> On Sunday, the 12th of August, Keating called at Manning's house. At that time O'Connor was dead. Whom did Keating see? Mark that. He saw Mrs. Manning. Observe her hypocrisy—her falsehood—her consummate wickedness. Keating asked Mrs. Manning if she had seen O'Connor. She replied that she had not seen him since Wednesday night. Keating said it was a very

strange thing. "Very strange," repeated the female prisoner, "for I invited him to dinner on the Thursday, and Mr. Manning thought it a most ungentlemanly thing that he did not come at the appointed time. I went to his lodgings to ascertain the reason why he did not come."

On that occasion—the only time when her lip was noticed to quiver and her cheek to blanch—she made use of an expression which struck me, as I saw it did some of you. She said, "Poor Mr. O'Connor! he was the best friend I had in the world."

"Poor Mr. O'Connor!" repeated Serjeant Wilkins. "Why 'Poor Mr. O'Connor'?" He whirled around to face Marie in the dock: "You knew his body was mouldering in your kitchen. You knew you were at that moment in possession of his property. You knew his voice would never be heard again. You knew that he had been hurried out of time into eternity. Well might you say, 'Poor Mr. O'Connor,' thrown off your guard at the moment. If you believed merely that he had gone out of town in some freak of fancy—for you describe him as a fitful and fanciful person— why exclaim 'Poor Mr. O'Connor?'"

Wilkins suggested that Marie had taken O'Connor's keys from his pocket after the murder and used them to remove his property from his lodgings. He disagreed with the attorney general's suggestion that she had not taken any of the property on her Thursday visit. Why would she have spent an hour in his rooms that day and why did she come down pale and trembling? Wilkins thought it most likely that she took a portion of the property on Thursday and the balance the next day. The serjeant took care to place Marie at 3 Minver Place at the probable hour of the murder. The evidence of Graham and Keating seemed to him to concur with that of James Coleman in spotting O'Connor on his way to the house around 5:00 P.M. on 9 August; he thought that the witness Younghusband must have been mistaken in his testimony that he saw O'Connor at a quarter past five on London Bridge going in the opposite direction toward the city. Where were the Mannings at this time? If Mrs. Manning, as she claimed, had gone to O'Connor's lodgings to fetch him, she would have had to leave her own house before five o'clock when he was almost at her door, and yet Mrs. Manning had admitted in her own statement to Flynn that she was still at home at six o'clock.

While trying to thrust upon Marie the role of receiving O'Connor on his arrival at 3 Minver Place, Wilkins separated his client from the scene. He noted that it was only a quarter to seven when Manning was seen by his neighbor Sophia Payne sitting on the garden wall of his house. Wilkins would not go so far as to rule out the possibility that Manning might "partly from fear, and partly, perhaps from some regard for the woman," have assisted her in disposing of O'Connor's body, but here Fred was as early as seven sitting on the wall in his ordinary dress with no bloodstains seen upon his clothing.

Serjeant Wilkins thought it clear that Marie's flight from London was not prearranged by the Mannings and that it came as a great shock to Fred. Not only had Manning questioned his neighbor after he was unable to obtain any answer when he went to his house looking for Marie, but Marie herself, when arrested in Edinburgh, had told Superintendent Moxey that she did not know where her husband was and had left London suddenly without his knowledge. The Bainbridges must have clearly been wrong in their recollection of Manning's words, for he had not "started his wife into the country."

Wilkins then dwelt at some length on the evidence of the lodger Massey. The attorney general and the community, he said, seemed to have been led to suppose that Massey was to prove something very wonderful, but Wilkins thought that his evidence really amounted to nothing. His testimony had revealed that the statements that the attorney general had mentioned as the subject of one conversation "turned out to have been scraps and fragments of different conversations held at various times; and those observations naturally and necessarily arose out of topics which happened to be the subjects of conversation." Singling out Manning's question of Massey whether he thought murderers went to heaven, Wilkins agreed that the question was odd but noted that the conversation had related to the exhibition of a wax figure of Rush at Madame Tussaud's, which had suggested the inquiry. Wilkins could not help thinking, he told the jury, though he had no wish to injure Madame Tussaud, that her "exhibition, in immortalising such villains as Rush, was a great nuisance." Dismissing the rest of Manning's conversations with the medical student, Wilkins said: "When a man is accused of crimes of this nature, it would really be amusing—but for the seriousness of the investigation—to mark the ingenuity which has been displayed in raking up every trifling act as evidence of his guilt. Why, every one of these observations was just as likely to be made by any man in Manning's situation as by Manning himself, and that with the most innocent intentions."

Wilkins alternated his attacks on Marie Manning with fresh praise for the public authorities. In commenting on the evidence of Superintendent Moxey of Edinburgh, he said that "he might congratulate that city upon possessing so excellent an officer." He had never heard a man in his capacity give evidence in so intelligent a manner, and so creditably to himself. But Wilkins was not merely currying favor; he had a deadlier purpose. In Moxey's testimony as to Mrs. Manning's behavior on her arrest, Wilkins found further proof of her guilt. That woman, he said, certainly must have the most extraordinary control over herself of any person of whom he had heard. She treated Moxey "with all the courtesy of the drawing room" and had retained her self-possession even when Moxey had told her of his impression that she was Mrs. Manning. Wilkins contrasted Marie's cool evasions of Moxey's questions with Fred's very different response to his arrest on Jersey by Sergeant Langley. He reminded the jury how Manning had protested his innocence and told Langley that his wife had shot O'Connor. Wilkins had now crowned his assault on Marie by using against her in argument the very same incriminating statements that the common-law rules barred from use against her in evidence.

Wilkins then dealt briefly with Fred's shooting coat, in which some tissue paper and loose gunpowder had been found. He pointed out that it was not known how long it might have been since he had worn the coat, and if, at the time he kept a hotel at Taunton, he had been a sportsman, it was not at all surprising that he should have a few grains of gunpowder in his pocket.

As he had promised, he then turned to the evidence concerning stock transactions. Referring first to Marie's inquiries of Mr. Stephens as to the possibility of selling Sambre and Meuse securities without the knowledge of her husband, he felt justified in saying that even then she was seeking to cheat her husband "as well as everybody else." Could there be any doubt, he added, that at that very time she was contemplating stealing the railway securities belonging to O'Connor and that she had formed the intention of leaving England and abandoning her husband? It was his opinion that throughout these securities transactions Mrs. Manning had sought to avoid the vigilance of her husband and to use him as her dupe. He asked the jury whether, looking at the male prisoner, they thought any person who had ever seen him was likely to forget him. Well, it had been proved that some person had gone to the office of the stockbrokers Messrs. Killick and Co. and had disposed of the Eastern County Railway securities that had belonged to O'Connor. But Mr. Shillibeer, who knew Manning's handwriting well, had said that the signature on the transfer paper did not resemble it at all, and the clerk Hammond would not swear that it was Manning who had signed the transfer. Wilkins thought it clear that it was not Manning who had signed the transfer or sold the securities, but that after the transaction Marie induced him to exchange the hundred-pound note at the Bank of England. If Manning had impersonated O'Connor in the stock transaction, Wilkins argued, he would not have gone to the bank or written his name on the note as he did "with all the fearlessness of a man who had nothing to dread." And the final proof of Manning's innocence in the stock transaction, Wilkins said, was the fact that he did not end up with the proceeds, which were found in the possession of Mrs. Manning when she was arrested at Edinburgh.

Wilkins ended with a burst of oratory:

> I have been called upon to discharge a duty from which, had I consulted my own feelings, I would have shrunk. Not that I am oppressed by a consciousness of the guilt of my client, or bowed down by the real difficulties of the case, but I feel I have had to fight against a mass of prejudice which has been created by those

who ought to have known better. I know the interest which attaches to the case from the manner in which it has been written up. I feel it most lacerating and agonizing to stand here as a representative of the husband, criminating and seeking to convict his wife. This is to me such a task that it almost unfitted me for the important duties which devolved upon me.

I call upon you not to allow those common impulses—good, divine, as they are—which influence you in private life, and induce you to yield affection, protection, and respect to woman, to step in between you and truth, but to treat the matter as a pure abstract question of reasoning, as between two human beings.

At the end of Serjeant Wilkins's address, the court took a twenty-minute adjournment for lunch and then was reconvened to hear the arguments of Ballantine for Marie Manning.

Ballantine opened by complimenting the attorney general on the fair and temperate manner in which he had presented the case for the prosecution. He then took up the problem of the extensive pretrial publicity but, unlike Wilkins, spoke in tones of moderation. He could not ask the jury to dismiss from their minds all they had heard or read with reference to the case, but he was sure that, when the evidence presented by the prosecution was concluded, they must have wondered how it was that many allegations relating to "this unhappy woman" that had found their way into public print had not been proved. But Ballantine reserved his contempt, not for the exaggeration and calumnies of the press, but for the incriminating statements of Fred Manning, for "the attempts which had been made, even before [his] client came into a court of justice, on the part of one who ought to have cherished and protected her, to place her in such a position as to render it impossible that she could be rescued from the tomb prophesied for her by many." In view of these statements, Ballantine was certain that the jury was not surprised at his attempt to obtain a separate trial for Marie.

Ballantine then moved to a round condemnation of the line of defense pursued by Serjeant Wilkins:

I would have been glad if you could have escaped the spectacle, unparalleled in a criminal court, of finding an advocate, either for the prosecution or for the defense, in the presence of a person who is undergoing a trial for her life, denouncing her in terms that, to say the least, were utterly unnecessary—terms which I can hardly help calling somewhat coarse. I consider that the presence of the person against whom those observations were made, ought, at all events, to have prevented my learned friend from using them, whatever might be the necessities of his case. Far be it from me to say that my learned friend did not exercise the best judgment that he could apply to this matter— that he did not conscientiously follow the instructions he had received; for I will do my learned friend the credit to believe that he acted contrary to his own taste and feeling in performing what he believed to be his duty to his client.

My learned friend appeared to anticipate that I would follow his example, and endeavour to throw upon the male prisoner the burden of this miserable, this unhappy transaction. God forbid that I should pursue that course! I would far rather never enter this court, or any other, than, in the presence of a fellow-creature awaiting his doom—who might be led from this court to the scaffold, and might soon have to appear before his Creator—I would use such terms as were applied by my learned friend to the female prisoner. I will do that which is my duty as an advocate; but, if my duty as an advocate required that I should cast upon the male prisoner the sort of observations and accusations which have been made against the woman, I would feel that my profession was a disgrace, and that the sooner I abandoned it for one somewhat more creditable, the sooner I would be a respected, an honest, an honorable and an upright man, and placed in a position better to respect myself.

Passing then to his analysis of the case, Ballantine recalled the attorney general's position that Mrs. Manning could be found guilty either as a principal or as an accessory before the fact. Ballantine suggested that the jury should hesitate before finding her guilty as an accessory, since acts of assistance rendered between husband and wife were "extremely vague." He could not help thinking that it would be almost impossible to find her guilty as an accessory before the fact unless the jury formed the clear opinion that Marie was present at the murder.

He promised to consider later whether the facts did not show that at the time of the murder, the female prisoner was absent from the house. But he first wished to dispose of the charges that the woman had actually committed the murder herself or had actively aided and abetted its commission. He began by urging upon the jury the proposition that "this woman did not forget her sex, and do that which few women were recorded to have done—commit a cold-blooded and atrocious murder, under circumstances of cold-blooded and atrocious violence." No one could entertain any doubt, he conceded, of the nature of Mrs. Manning's relations with O'Connor, and it appeared from her own statements that her husband had mistreated her in a way "not likely to strengthen any feelings of virtue she might possess." Under these circumstances, why would she have been impelled to the murder? O'Connor was past middle age and had reached the time of life when it was "almost proverbial" that men were weak enough to yield anything to their mistresses. The jury then had a right to assume either that Mrs. Manning was a woman of abandoned character who could have possessed herself of O'Connor's property without murder by being taken into "comparatively wealthy keeping" or that she was a woman of kindly feeling, which would have made it most unlikely that she would terminate a love affair with violence.

Ballantine then supported his contention that Marie had been away from Minver Place at the time of the murder. The crux of his chronological reconstruction was the testimony of Younghusband and the Armes sisters. Unlike Wilkins, he accepted the testimony of Younghusband that placed O'Connor back on London Bridge at a quarter past five heading north and apparently vacillating as to whether he should go to the Mannings' or not; it was reasonable to suppose that his hesitation was resolved by a decision to turn back and go to Minver Place, where he must have arrived later than expected. The Armes sisters, who, Ballantine noted, were evidently not favorably disposed to Marie, testified that she had arrived at their house that evening at a quarter before six and had remained there until after seven. Since the distance from Minver Place to Greenwood Street was about three miles, it must have taken Marie nearly three-quarters of an hour to walk from her home to O'Connor's lodgings, and therefore she must have left home about the time O'Connor was still hesitating on London Bridge. Was the murder committed while she was away? He thought it must be so, since the prosecution's case permitted no hypothesis other than that the crime was completed before Manning was seen on the garden wall smoking his pipe at a quarter past seven o'clock. But the evidence of the Misses Armes tended to show that Marie, who had stayed at Greenwood Street until a quarter past seven, could not have returned home much before a quarter to eight.

Ballantine then came to the three points put forward by the Crown as showing that Marie was an accessory before the fact; namely, that she had been involved in the purchase of the crowbar, the lime, and the shovel. He noted that the shovel was an ordinary coal shovel entirely unfit for the purpose of digging the grave; and, since the prisoners had a garden, "why should not Mrs. Manning at once have purchased a spade, which would have been much more serviceable in digging a hole, had she required it for such a purpose?" As for the lime, Mrs. Manning might have supposed that it was in fact intended for the destruction of the garden slugs, and in any event the woman who paid the delivery boy who brought it to the house was not identified by him as the female prisoner. There was no doubt that the crowbar, which had been ordered by her husband, had been paid for by Mrs. Manning at his directions, but "what was a more usual occurrence than for such a payment to be made by the wife in any family in ordinary life?"

Ballantine brushed aside the prosecution's evidence of bloodstains. The only marks found on the dress acquired by Mrs. Bainbridge were on the back of the cape, an unlikely location if they had been received during the commission of a murder; but in fact these marks were not shown to be blood at all, and he was inclined to believe that they were iron-mold. As for Marie's toilette-table covers (which he noted in passing were so handsome that she had probably obtained possession of them in houses where she was employed as an upper servant, "houses which indicated that she had been highly respected, and considered as a person altogether unlikely to be mixed up in a transaction of this kind"), there were a hundred ways in which

they might get drops of blood on them. Then it was said that
there was blood on the inside of another dress examined by
Odling, but he commented discreetly that the jury "would have
no difficulty in finding an explanation of the fact of there being
marks of blood inside the dress of a woman."

The testimony of Massey as to his conversation with Manning
was not of significance to the case against Marie, Ballantine
argued. The talk about drugs and the vulnerable parts of the
skull and the like did not take place when Marie was present,
since it would have excited her attention. Ballantine would not
say whether the conversations ought to have moved Massey to
make inquiry, but "it would at least have been discreet on his
part to mention them, and then probably this awful tragedy
would not have occurred, and you would not have been this day
sitting to make inquiry into the fate of poor Patrick O'Connor."

There was one "remarkable circumstance" to which Ballantine then briefly called the jury's attention: that was the evening
of Wednesday, 8 August, when O'Connor had visited the
Mannings in the company of Walsh. What was Marie Manning's
conduct on that day? O'Connor had been invited to dinner, and
a letter of invitation was found in Marie's handwriting. Ballantine mentioned in passing that "if Manning had intended any
evil to O'Connor that night, you could quite understand that he
might get another person to write a letter asking him to dinner,
and that just in the way she had been made to pay for the
crowbar, Mrs. Manning might have been led to write the letter."
But if Mrs. Manning had made up her mind by that evening to
commit a murder, Ballantine urged the jury to consider
whether her demeanor would have been as it was: "I would ask
if even the worst prostitute could have bathed the temples of a
man suffering from giddiness after smoking, with a murderous intent in her heart? At such a moment the heart of even the
basest woman would speak out, and she would shrink from
going near the man whose murder she had contemplated, and
with whom she had lived on terms of the closest intimacy."

Ballantine was willing to assume that Marie had learned of
the murder before she left London. If she had heard of the
murder first from her husband, his criminality would have

operated powerfully upon her, she might have believed that
jealousy was the groundwork of the murder, and she would
have shrunk from making known a crime that she had good
reason to believe her own course of life had motivated. With
respect to the property of O'Connor found in her possession,
he thought it probable that O'Connor had purchased shares for
her in the Sambre and Meuse Railway; that she thought herself
justified in taking them away and, while doing so, took other
property to which "perhaps she thought she was entitled."
Placed in such circumstances, what was a woman likely to do?
Whether a woman were the most innocent and virtuous in the
world, or the most profligate and abandoned, the course she
would take on finding that a husband had murdered her friend
would depend very much on the temperament of the two
spouses. In the present case, Marie had decided to escape from
her husband, and while doing so she possessed herself of a
considerable amount of property. Ballantine was not putting
her forward to the jury as a person of pure mind or pure habits,
and he did not regard her as a person guided by high moral
feelings. Knowing that O'Connor was murdered, it was not
improbable that she immediately reacted by going to
O'Connor's house to recover her property and take other
property, without knowing whether it belonged to her or not.

Ballantine closed quietly. He thanked the jury for its attention
and expressed the fullest confidence that his client, though a
foreigner, would receive from an English jury the most patient,
careful, and impartial consideration.

When Attorney General Jervis was about to reply to the
speeches for the defense, Mr. Parry interposed an objection
for Mrs. Manning. Perhaps, he said, the attorney general
technically had a right of reply, but it was not customary to
exercise this power in a case where no evidence had been put
forward by the prisoners. Chief Baron Pollock ruled that the
attorney general clearly was entitled to reply, but Parry persisted: "Will the Attorney General exercise the right in a case
where the lives of two of his fellow creatures are at stake?"

The attorney general, unmoved by Parry's appeal, said that
he undoubtedly had the right as a representative of the Crown

to have the last word; it was a right that had usually been exercised with great caution, and he should not have exercised it in this case except that he thought it his duty "to endeavour to hold as evenly as possible the scales of justice between the parties whose interests were now before the Court." He proceeded to state his belief that Mr. Ballantine had not been justified in complaining of the course that had been adopted by Serjeant Wilkins. He considered that the learned serjeant had only done his duty as an advocate to his client; and, in an allusion to Ballantine's subtler attempt to place the sole blame on Manning, he added that it appeared to him "to be the more manly course boldly to state a charge against a party and the grounds upon which the charge was supported, than to insinuate it, and not have the boldness to openly make the accusation."

Jervis took issue with a proposition that was common to the arguments of counsel for both defendants, namely, that the murder had been committed by one person only. He thought this highly improbable. He did not think that one person could have raised the stones in the kitchen, dug the grave, covered it over, and, above all, thrust the body into the grave in the manner that had been described. He saw no reason why Manning should have committed the murder alone because, unless he perpetrated it with the concurrence of his wife, who would not create suspicion by her presence in O'Connor's room and could thereby obtain the property he sought, he would have no motive for the crime.

Obviously concerned about the possible impact of Ballantine's effort to bracket the hour of commission of the crime within the period of Marie's absence from the house, the attorney general urged a flexible position on the jury. There was no evidence as to when the crime was actually committed, he said, and it was very possible that O'Connor had been murdered after the return of the female prisoner from his lodgings. He suggested this explanation for O'Connor's being seen by Younghusband apparently in a hesitating and uncertain mood heading north across London Bridge: the probability was that, not finding Marie at home, O'Connor had left Minver

Place soon after five o'clock but had afterward returned. When Manning jumped from his garden wall after 7:00 P.M., he may have gone to open his door to O'Connor, perhaps accompanied by Marie.

Ballantine interrupted him to comment (apparently erroneously) that it was half past seven when Manning was seen smoking on the wall. But Jervis went on, hammering again at his trinity: the chisel, the lime, and the shovel. The shovel had been purchased on the day before the murder, he reminded the jury. Why would the Mannings purchase a shovel on that day when they were already in discussion with Mr. Bainbridge over the price for their household goods? He said that he had no doubt the shovel was used for the removal of the earth from the floor. Perhaps this was the best that could be done to reconcile the last-minute shovel purchase with the notion of the long-premeditated murder plot. Jervis's suggestion appeared to be that the grave had been prepared earlier but that the new shovel had been used to take away a heap of earth from the kitchen floor. It was a delicate point in the Crown's case, and Jervis hurried on. After making a few additional points, he told the jury that he did not intend to trouble them with any minute examination of the different parts of the evidence; he would now leave the distressing case in the hands of the Bench and in theirs.

The Chief Baron then delivered his charge to the jury. He told them that there did not appear to be any doubt that Patrick O'Connor had been murdered on the ninth of August. The question then very naturally arose: "Who were the parties living in the house, in the back kitchen of which the body was found, and what was the history of those parties during the days that elapsed between the time when O'Connor was last seen and the time when his body was found?" The only two persons living in the house at the time were the prisoners at the bar, and it had not been suggested by either of the learned counsel for the prisoners that the murder could have been committed by any person other than the inmates of the house, nor had they claimed that anybody from outside had committed the murder and brought the body inside and deposited it in the kitchen. Grave suspicion, then, must attach to the Mannings.

The judge reminded them how the two prisoners, by their counsel, had attempted to throw the guilt upon each other, but he advised the jury to attend to the evidence as well as to the observations of the lawyers and to reach a conclusion by means of their own good sense, experience, and sound judgment. They ought to take a "broad, general, and comprehensive view of the case," not stopping to inquire what expressions a man or a woman, under certain circumstances, would use, but trying to see what were the natural and inevitable results of all the circumstances brought out in the evidence. It was, for example, of no importance to his mind that a few grains of gunpowder should be found in the pocket of a shooting jacket or that mention should have been made of poisons in conversation with a young surgeon and so forth, but there were circumstances as to the intentions of the two prisoners that were worthy of the jury's notice and to those he would call their attention.

As for the male prisoner, the Chief Baron continued, he had said he was present at the murder, for he saw his wife shoot O'Connor. He instructed the jury that although this statement had no force against his wife, it was conclusive evidence that Manning was present at the crime. The jury naturally should inquire whether Manning knew anything of the crime before-hand—whether it was a sudden occurrence of which he had not the slightest expectation or whether he had reason to antici-pate it even though he could not have predicted its exact moment. The judge pointed out that Manning's "explanation" of the crime was incomplete. He had given no explanation of the head wounds inflicted by the blunt instrument and had also failed to give any account of the burial. Assuming then that Manning was present when somebody else fired the pistol—and the judge emphasized the word "somebody" because Manning's statement was no evidence against his wife—what course did Manning take? Did he endeavor to prevent further violence? These were the questions the jury should ask themselves.

As evidence of premeditation of the crime, his lordship

pointed to the abandonment of 3 Minver Place by the Mannings. Massey's evidence on that point was important, for he had testified that they had got rid of him as a lodger on the pretext that they were leaving for the country on 30 July but they did not go until the following month. They had also had conversations with Bainbridge about selling their goods as early as 20 July.

It was the province of the jury, and theirs alone, to decide how far the Mannings' intention to leave was conceived in connection with the fatal day when Patrick O'Connor was murdered. Reviewing the testimony of Walsh and O'Connor's other friends who had seen him on the day of his disappearance, the judge said it was difficult to avoid the conclusion that the murder was committed on the night of 9 August. It might be uncertain at what hour, but the jury must decide on the period that was the most probable.

Turning to deal with the evidence against Marie Manning, the judge left no doubt as to his view on her involvement in the crime. It seemed to him that the weight of the stones and the condition and position of the body made it difficult to suppose that one person only was concerned in the burial. Moreover, if Frederick Manning had committed the murder, he said, it remained quite clear that Mrs. Manning had obtained the keys from the person of the murdered man, either directly or from her husband. The whole of this part of the transaction "strongly argues a preconceived plan of operation; a surmise amply borne out by Manning's disposal of the property, and the proceeds being found upon his wife." The judge then threw the jury the ultimate question: did they find that the Mannings were so mixed up with the affair as not to be able to separate them? That was a point of importance, and whatever quarrel might have ensued afterward between them was a matter of no moment.

After referring to the testimony of several other witnesses, he invited the jury again to look at the whole case. Here was a murder committed in a house in which two persons lived, and it was for the jury to consider whether it was possible to believe that either of the parties, without the knowledge of the other, could be the perpetrator. If they believed that could happen "in the ordinary course of events," if they could believe that one alone of these parties was guilty and that the other had no previous knowledge of the transaction, they should give their verdict against that one only. He cautioned them against an insistence on relieving themselves of all doubt: "That degree of certainty on which you would act in your own private affairs is the degree of certainty you are now called to act upon. It is not necessary that the crime should be established positively beyond the possibility of doubt. Crimes committed in darkness and secrecy can only be brought to light by a comparison of circumstances pressing on the mind more and more as they increase in number."

The Chief Baron concluded with an exhortation to the jury to consider that they had on the one hand a duty to the public to take care that the guilty should not escape; and on the other, a duty to the prisoners to take care that they should not be convicted upon mere surmise or suspicion, upon rash or light grounds, but only upon grave and solid reasons leading the jury to the satsifactory conclusion that one or both were guilty of the crime.

The jury retired at six o'clock and was absent for three-quarters of an hour. At a quarter to seven the jury returned and the prisoners were again placed at the bar. Mr. Streight, Clerk of the Arraigns, addressed the jury: "Gentlemen of the jury, do you find the prisoner Frederick George Manning guilty or not guilty?"

The foreman replied: "Guilty."

"Do you find the prisoner Maria Manning guilty or not guilty?"

"Guilty."

CHAPTER THIRTEEN

Rue in the Dock

*Turn your eyes to the dock. . . . Mark how
restlessly he has been engaged for the last ten
minutes, in forming all sorts of fantastic figures with the herbs which are strewed upon the
ledge before him.*

—*Sketches by Boz*

In the eighteenth century inmates of Newgate
Prison, which was adjacent to the Old Bailey,
suffered from repeated outbreaks of so-called
gaol fever, a form of typhus that grew on the
crowded conditions and lack of sanitation in the prison. The
public was not terribly concerned about the loss of life among its
prison population, but during the celebrated "Black Assizes" of
1750 it was proved that so far as the typhus germ is concerned
"stone walls do not a prison make." An epidemic of gaol fever in
Newgate spread to the Old Bailey courtroom and took the lives
of two judges, the lord mayor, and over forty officials, lawyers,
and jurymen. The public and Parliament were finally stirred
into action by this calamity, and an extensive rebuilding both of
Newgate and the Old Bailey was undertaken in 1770.

In memory of the Black Assizes, nineteeth-century legal
officials still celebrated traditions of symbolic purification of the
Old Bailey's air. At the beginning of the Manning trial the
judges, sheriffs, and undersheriffs all carried into the courtroom bouquets of old English garden flowers that had once
warded off the stench of the prison. Along the ledges of the
dock in each courtroom attendants scattered rue, an herb to
which medicinal properties had long been attributed.

As she listened to the jury's verdict, Marie Manning saw
sprigs of rue lying on the dock before her. Since she was not

English, she may not have known that for centuries the name of the herb had been called upon in punning allusion to regret or remorse. But when the clerk, Mr. Streight, asked the prisoners whether they had anything to say why sentence of death should not be passed upon them, Marie, following Ophelia's injunction in *Hamlet,* decided to "wear her rue with a difference." In great excitement she addressed the court. The reporter for the *Times* noted that she spoke with a strong foreign accent and with remarkable vehemence, but that her emotion appeared to supply her with fluency of speech. Marie said:

> There is no justice and no right for a foreign subject in this country. There is no law for me. I have had no protection—neither from the Judges, nor from the prosecutors, nor from my husband.
>
> I am unjustly condemned by this Court. If I were in my own country I could prove that I had money sent from abroad, which is now in the Bank of England. My solicitors and counsel could have called witnesses to identify shares that were bought with my own money.
>
> Mr. O'Connor was more to me than my husband. He was a friend and brother to me ever since I came to this country. I knew him for seven years. He wanted to marry me, and I ought to have been married to him. I have letters which would prove his respect and regard for me; and I think, considering that I am a woman and alone, that I have to fight against my husband's statements, that I have to fight against the prosecutors, and that even the Judge himself is against me—I think that I am not treated like a Christian, but like a wild beast of the forest; and the Judges and Jury will have it upon their consciences for giving a verdict against me.
>
> I am not guilty of the murder of Mr. O'Connor. If I had wished to commit murder, I would not have attempted the life of the only friend I had in the world—a man who would have made me his wife in a week, if I had been a widow. I have lived in respectable families, and can produce testimonials of character for probity in every respect, if inquiry is made. I can account for more money than was equal to the trifling shares that were found upon me. If my husband, through jealousy and a revengeful feeling against O'Connor, chose to murder him, I don't see why I should be punished for it. I wish I could have

expressed myself better in the English language. That is all I
have to say.

Fred Manning having nothing to say, Mr. Justice Cresswell (in
the absence of the Chief Baron) proceeded to deliver judgment.
He first laid cornerwise on top of his wig a square cap of limp
black cloth, the traditional "black cap" dating from Tudor
times, which tokened the judge's sorrow and the authority with
which he performed a solemn duty. The judge began to address
the prisoners: "Frederick George Manning and Maria
Manning, you have been convicted of the crime of murder," but
he could get no further, for Marie interrupted him in an angry
outburst: "No, no. I won't stand it. You are to be ashamed of
yourselves. There is neither law nor justice here." She then
turned around as if to leave the dock, but was stopped by Mr.
Cope, the prison governor. Mr. Justice Cresswell continued,
unruffled by the interruption: "You have been defended by
able counsel."

Marie protested: "They didn't call any witnesses for me," but
Cresswell did not pause. He said:

> Every topic which ingenuity or experience taught them would
> be at all available for your defense has been urged by them. You
> have been found guilty by a jury upon evidence which, I will
> venture to say could leave no rational doubt upon the mind of
> any human being who heard it.

The judge ignored a new attempt by Marie to speak and went
on:

> Murder is the highest crime that one individual can commit
> against another in this country. It is at all times a horrible
> offense; but the present murder was one of the most cold-
> blooded and deliberately calculated I ever remember to have
> heard or read of. Under the pretense of friendship, or rather
> affection—for such was the description of the invitation of the
> 8th—under that pretense you unhappily deluded him to a place
> where his grave was probably then prepared, and where the
> deed was afterwards committed which had, no doubt, been for
> days contemplated. It is one of the most appalling instances of
> human wickedness which the annals of this court can furnish.
> It has been suggested that the deceased led a vicious course of

life with one of you prisoners; but, whether that was or was not I profess not to judge; that rests with your own conscience. But, whatever was his course of life, without a moment's warning or preparation, without the slightest opportunity of thinking of futurity, or endeavouring to seek pardon for any offenses he had committed, that unhappy man was hurried into eternity.

The law, more merciful, allows to you a space of time for preparation. It appears that on a former occasion a conversation passed between one of you and the witness Massey as to where the soul of a person who had committed a murder would go. The time has arrived when you should ask that question again. As I cannot hold out the slightest hope of a commutation of the sentence which I am about to pronounce I am bound to tell you that, as far as my judgment goes, your doom is irretrievably fixed when that sentence is passed. I advise you, therefore, to resort with all humility, and all contrition to the advice and counsel of the minister of the Gospel appointed to attend you. From him you will receive all the consolation which, in your unhappy condition, he can, in the faithful discharge of his duties, afford you. From him you will learn what you have to fear. He will no doubt point out to you, in strong terms, the full extent of your guilt; and I am sure he will rejoice if he can conscientiously hold out to you any hope of that pardon hereafter which, in this world, is impossible. I consign you to his advice, and pray you to profit by it.

Mr. Justice Cresswell then made an apparent allusion to Marie's impassioned address:

Whatever sorrow, or even indignation, you may really feel, or affect to feel, as to the course of proceeding this day, depend upon it that others will judge differently; and I doubt whether everyone who has heard the trial will not be as well satisfied as I am that the result is the only one consistent with justice.

The judge then proceeded to pronounce sentence in the routine dread of the time-honored formula:

That you be taken hence to Her Majesty's gaol for the county of Surrey, and thence to the place of execution, and there to be severally hanged by the neck until you be dead; and that afterwards your dead bodies be buried within the precincts of the gaol in which you shall be confined after this sentence; and may the Lord have mercy upon your souls!

Mrs. Manning made a new effort to address the court, but Mr. Justice Cresswell's patience was exhausted, and he ordered her removed from the courtroom. As the turnkeys began to lead her away, her eyes fell again on the rue that lay at the front of the dock. Giving final vent to her indignation, Marie picked up some pieces of the rue and threw them into the well of the court. She accompanied this gesture with a last scornful outburst and was led away.

The reporter for the *Times* was not well placed in the courtroom and he could not hear Marie's parting words. A colleague sitting close to Mrs. Manning told him that she had said: "Base and shameful England!"

Reporters who for weeks had been impressed by Marie's silence were now stunned by her violence. As she was led away from the dock, she was heard to "pour dreadful imprecations upon all around her." Turning down the refreshments that were offered her, she unleashed her fury against the jury, her legal advisors, and England. "Damnation seize you all," she cried again and again. When a handcuff was first placed on her wrist, she shook her clenched fists in the faces of the court officers. Manning, on the other hand, was observed to exhibit the same submission and dejection he had shown during the trial.

That same evening the Mannings were removed from Newgate Prison to Horsemonger Lane Gaol. At half past seven two cabs were driven up to the entrance of the prison opposite Fleet Lane, and the next moment Mrs. Manning emerged, accompanied by Mr. Wright, deputy governor of Newgate, to whose left wrist her right was handcuffed, and they took their places in the first vehicle. Manning silently walked to the second cab, securely handcuffed between two officers. By the time the first cab had reached Ludgate Hill, the second was rapidly following it through the dense crowd around the courthouse. The journey from one prison to the other did not take more than twenty minutes. While en route Marie's mood lightened; she seemed to lose all her previous desperation and talked to Wright in a "free, mild and gentle manner." She even joked coquettishly about the manacle that bound her to him and bid farewell to Old Newgate in a mock-heroic style.

Commenting on her speech in court, she said, "I showed them resolution, did I not?" She also spoke of Fred: "I had plenty of opportunity to speak to him in the jail and during the trial, but I would not. He did not speak to me thank God, the unmanly wretch"; and, since Fred's knees were not within reach, she kicked the opposite seat of the cab contemptuously. As the cab rolled along, an advertising van passed by, displaying enormous placards announcing a full report of the trial in a weekly journal. The van caught Marie's eyes and for a short time brought her passions back to a high pitch; she was outraged, she said, that her trial could be so shamelessly hawked.

On the arrival at Horsemonger Lane, a message was sent in to Mr. Keene, the governor, to announce the result of the trial. Under the guidance of a police matron, Mrs. Manning was conducted to one of the cells set apart for the condemned. As she entered the cell, she burst into tears and stamped the floor, "not in rage but in grief—her feelings no doubt being overcome as she reflected upon the great change that had taken place in her destinies." For the first time Marie seemed to move observers to pity: "The woman, though hardened, was not entirely deadened to feeling." During the early part of the night Marie could find only fitful rest, but toward morning she slept soundly and the next morning the Junoesque woman ate her usual hearty breakfast.

It was reported that Marie's outburst in the dock at the Old Bailey had induced the prison authorities to give directions that all means by which she could commit suicide should be kept out of her way. The precautions may have also been heightened because of another courtroom incident. Both the prisoners had been routinely searched on their arrival at Newgate Prison. However, according to a story in the *Daily News*, the Newgate officials decided on the second day of the trial to search Marie again and found in her pocket "a large piece of broken glass, a most dangerous missile, and one calculated to have inflicted

serious injury upon any person who might have been struck
with it." The glass fragment was taken from her and the *News*
wrote that, in light of the violence Marie had shown in the dock,
mischief had probably been prevented by the discovery. It was
conjectured that the glass had been given to Marie by some
person among the many strangers who had been admitted into
the dock during the latter part of the proceedings due to the
crowded condition of the courtroom. The discovery of the
broken glass was also reported by the *Morning Chronicle,* which,
however, cautioned against exaggerated accounts of the prisoner's violence: "The authorities of the Horsemonger Lane
Gaol exhibit great reserve in their communications respecting
the prisoners; but we believe there is no doubt that the reports
relating to the violent conduct of Mrs. Manning since her
removal have been very much exaggerated, and that she is at
present exhibiting a demeanour consonant with her awful
situation."

Manning appeared to react to his conviction more calmly
than Marie; on reaching his cell he immediately sat down and,
resting his head on his hands, appeared to be buried in thought.
He seemed "to delude himself with the idea that his life might
yet be spared."

The next morning at about eight the jail chaplain, Reverend
Rowe, called on each of the Mannings. He found Fred more
responsive, for Marie, according to the *Times,* refused at first to
see him, asserting that she had been unjustly convicted. The
Mannings were then led to the chapel, where they were given
seats in the section reserved for the condemned, together with a
man named Jordan, who had been sentenced to death for an
attempted murder in Dulwich Wood. Reverend Rowe delivered
an eloquent sermon, taking his text from Psalm 68: "Etheopia
shall soon stretch out her hands unto God."

Now that the press corps had escorted the Mannings safely to
death row, they were free to review the trial. It was agreed all
around that the trial was out of the common run. Indeed, to the
Observer it was "perhaps the most remarkable trial of the present
century." The newspaper detailed the grounds for this critical
judgment:

A husband and wife placed at the bar of justice, charged jointly
with the crime of murder under circumstances of peculiar
aggravation, was a fact calculated to arrest attention in no
ordinary degree. . . . It has undoubtedly happened in all times
and ages that certain examples have taken a stronger hold than
others of the public mind, have created more lively horror and
more continuous interest, and have been preserved in the
traditions of successive generations as illustrating the stage of
social progress at which they occurred. This is one of them.

The *Morning Post* ascribed the intense interest in the case to "the
enormity of [the Mannings'] guilt—the deep-laid and cold-
blooded scheme by which they entrapped their victim to his
destruction—the close relationship of the culprits, and their
utter and extraordinary faithlessness to each other when detection threatened to overtake them."

There was a strong consensus that the guilt of both the
Mannings had been plainly established. The *Times* referred to
the verdict as "the announcement of a foregone conclusion,"
and the *Daily News* commented: "Not a shadow of doubt can
remain that a cold-blooded, long-premeditated murder, with a
view to robbery, was committed on O'Connor, and that both of
the Mannings were active participators in the crime." The
Observer rated the case "among the clearest, perhaps, upon
record—always premising that class of analogous cases which is
supported by circumstantial evidence." About the only note of
doubt (and a muted one at that) was sounded by the *Morning
Chronicle*. Although the *Chronicle* regarded the guilt of the
Mannings as proved, it pointed to the "physical possibility" that
"the murder might have been committed by a third person
when the Mannings were absent from home." Therefore, to the
Chronicle, unlike the *Times*, the melodramatic attraction of the
trial had been enhanced by "the cloud of uncertainty which
enveloped the result."

Neither the trial nor the verdict had cast much light on the
relative degrees to which Fred and Marie Manning had participated in the crime. But the editorial writers were willing to fill
the gaps in the evidence on this point, and most of them fixed
the principal blame on Marie. To the *Morning Chronicle* she was

"an ex-Abigail, who lays her plot, and prepares the machinery for its execution, with an air of self-possessed villainy worthy of Lucretia Borgia or the Marquise de Brinvilliers." The *Times* expanded on this theme; though willing to consider the possibility that Fred Manning had first suggested the murder in a "maudlin fit," it had no doubt that Marie had become the dominant force in the commission of the crime and in the avoidance of its detection:

> For Manning himself there can be but the one feeling of loathing and disgust. If his was indeed the hand that struck the first blow, one thinks of the insensate brute but as of the butcher who slaughters the ox without a feeling of the bloody work in which he is engaged. We can picture to ourselves the fixed determination of the woman, and the shrinking repentance of the man, at the moment the deed was upon the point of accomplishment. It may well be that it was Manning who in his maudlin fits of wickedness first suggested the thought of the murder to his sterner partner, and even busied himself in the preparation for its actual commission; but we are much mistaken if it was not the wife who clenched his last scruples, and by her sarcasm and reproaches spirited him up to strike the fatal blow.
>
> Every incident of the evidence points to the female prisoner as the chief actor in the crime. She it was who, when they were balked of their purpose by the accidental presence of a stranger, on the night previous to the actual assassination, fondled and caressed the intended victim;—she it was who renewed the fatal invitation—who proceeded to his lodgings to extract his property—who received his friends after the murder, and feigned a hypocritical anxiety for his disappearance. In short, throughout the whole tale Mrs. Manning appears as the protagonist, and her brutal partner but as the minister and executor of her will.

To find a more even balance struck between the Mannings, it is necessary to put the London newspapers aside and turn to the editorial page of the *Manchester Guardian*. The *Guardian* acknowledged the "considerable possibility" that "judging from the determined and obdurate character of the female prisoner," the murder had been originally planned, and, to some extent, perpetrated by her. But the newspaper entered its

protest against attempts to excite public sympathy for Fred
Manning: "we feel no doubt, that although the murder may
have been originally suggested by the female prisoner, and
urged upon him with the influence which an energetic mind
and an indomitable will always possess over common and vulgar
natures, he was eventually as deeply concerned in the murder,
in the disposal of the body, and in the felonious abstraction of
the property, as his wife."

Despite the unanimity of the London newspapers in upholding the correctness of the conviction of both the Mannings, they
were also at one in roundly condemning the conduct of Serjeant
Wilkins. They smarted, of course, under his attack on the
quality of crime journalism but trained most of their fire on his
efforts to incriminate his client's wife by citing Manning's
statements against her and by addressing her directly in abusive
terms. The *Times* editorial was eloquent in its expression of
contempt for Wilkins:

> Fallen and degraded as were the wretched creatures at the bar, it
> was strange to find an English advocate rising in his place and
> permitting himself to be made the medium of conveying to the
> jury the dastardly lies and equivocations of such a ruffian as
> Manning. We will not, however, judge, but leave Mr. Serjeant
> Wilkins to the strictures of his brother advocate. . . . His mis-
> representation of the course pursued by what he is pleased to
> style "a degraded press" with regard to the murderers might call
> for admonition and rebuke; but, with the well-deserved sar-
> casms of Mr. Ballantine tingling in the ears, Mr. Serjeant Wilkins
> may safely be left to the public judgment on this and other
> matters connected with his defense of Manning.

Even the courtroom audience came in for its share of
criticism. On 29 October an observer of the second day's session
of the trial exercised the traditional English privilege of writing
an indignant letter to the *Times*: "Sir,—Could it be believed that
yesterday, while the awful sentence of death was being passed at
the Old Bailey on a female, others of her sex were, by the aid of
double opera-glasses, watching the misery of mind of the
wretched criminal at the bar? Yet such was the case: ladies on

the bench, having shaken off all the delicacy of the female, were actually doing so."

As in all ages, there was at least one writer who was ready to blame the crime on literature. In a letter to the editor of the *Illustrated London News*, published on 3 November, the murder method was attributed to the Mannings' reading of a tale by Alexandre Dumas entitled "The Thousand-and-One Phantoms, To Be Read Between Eleven O'Clock and Midnight." In that story a quarryman confesses to having murdered his wife in a cellar where he planned to bury her in a sack of lime. The writer of the letter did not regard it as "requisite to dwell on the pernicious influence exercised by publications in which the mode of committing every degree of crime so as to avoid the legal consequences is so distinctly pointed out."

CHAPTER FOURTEEN

Waiting for Mr. Calcraft

*Saturday night. He had only one night more to
live. And as he thought of this, the day broke—
Sunday.*

—Oliver Twist

uring the reign of Philip of Macedon, the king
was the law, and the sole hope after a judgment of conviction was that Philip might come
to his senses and reverse his own verdict. The
Roman historian Valerius Maximus put it aptly when he wrote
that the only appeal lay "from Philip drunk to Philip sober."

Marie Manning faced the same predicament after her conviction when she desired judicial review of the trial court's
denial of her application for a separate trial by a jury of mixed
nationality. It was not until 1907 that England established by
legislation a Court of Criminal Appeals with broad powers to
review criminal convictions. Marie, like all other criminal defendants prior to the 1907 act, had very limited postconviction
remedies. One method of review was to apply for a writ of error
under which certain portions of the record of the case could be
brought before the House of Lords. This procedure, if followed, would result in a substantial deferment of the execution
day, since the case could not be submitted to the House of Lords
until after the end of the session of Parliament. But this remedy
involved a formidable obstacle—the consent of the attorney
general must be obtained before the writ would issue. In an
article on 29 October 1849, the *Daily News* reported that Mrs.
Manning's counsel would apply for a writ of error but predicted
that Attorney General Jervis would refuse to agree to this
protracted procedure. A follow-up story on 5 November confirmed the correctness of this analysis. It reported that a

certificate had been signed by Mr. Parry to the effect that he considered the decision of the trial judges on the question of the mixed jury to be erroneous and that there were good grounds for appeal to the House of Lords. The certificate was forwarded to the attorney general, who, after consulting with his colleagues who conducted the case with him, wrote Mrs. Manning's solicitor, Solomon, refusing to give his consent. Jervis's decision was influenced by the fact that the three trial judges had been unanimous in their ruling on the point in issue.

This rejection of the writ of error left Marie with an alternative method of appeal that resembled the only one enjoyed by the subjects of Philip of Macedon: her counsel must argue again before some of the same judges who had already ruled against her. This appeal lay to the so-called Court of Crown Cases Reserved, which had been established by an 1848 statute in confirmation of ancient custom. The original practice was for a judge, if he had doubt about a legal issue, to defer a judgment of conviction or a sentence until he could discuss the matter informally with the other judges. This tradition had crystallized into a sort of appellate court, very strange to modern notions, in which one or more of the trial judges sat with other judges in the review of their own trial rulings. The hearing of Mrs. Manning's appeal by the Court of Crown Cases Reserved was set down for 7 November, and two of the six judges on that court would be Chief Baron Pollock and Justice Cresswell, who had presided at her trial.

One lone newspaper voice was raised in support of Mrs. Manning's position on the appeal. The *Observer* wrote: ". . . the point, in all likelihood, will be decided according to the ruling of the Chief Baron on the trial. That Mrs. Manning was guilty of the murder of O'Connor no one may doubt, therefore it would have been, perhaps, a wise and prudent course to have yielded to the application of her counsel for a mixed jury." The sustaining of the trial court's denial of Mrs. Manning's right to the mixed jury would lead to the paradoxical result that "she is in a worse position as an English wife than she would be as an English mistress."

While the appeal was pending, there was a startling new

development. Late on Saturday night, 3 November, Mr. Solomon received an anonymous letter which he thought was written in a female hand:

> I beg to state that I think Mrs. Manning had a right to be tried by a jury *de medietate linguae*, on account of her being a foreigner in the first place; secondly, if you will take the trouble to go to St. Marylebone Church and look at the books, you will find that George Frederick Manning now under sentence of death is the same person who was married in 1832 to Mary Roberts, and that his brother Richard Manning was witness to it; but if you should not find it so, you had better apply at No. 28, Camden cottages, where you may obtain further particulars.

If the information was true, then Marie's marriage to Manning was bigamous and would not have changed her status to that of a naturalized Englishwoman. On Sunday morning Solomon went to Marylebone Church to examine the marriage register. Although the records were not ordinarily made available on Sunday, he was given access to the register when he explained the urgency of his search. Reviewing the pages for 1832 he came upon the following entry on 2 March:

> George Frederick Manning, bachelor, and Mary Roberts, spinster, were married by banns.
>
> Sarah Lawrence }
Richard Manning } witnesses
Bryant Burgess, B.A., curate

Unfortunately for Marie, the name in the entry seemed to fit the case better than the date did. Fred Manning's brother Edmund burst the brief bubble of hope by a letter to the *Times* on 6 November:

> Sir,—Feeling your readiness at all times to correct any erroneous impressions calculated to prejudice the public mind, especially in the case to which I allude, as a brother of the unfortunate Frederick George Manning, I feel I should not be doing justice to myself, brothers, and the rest of the family, should I not contradict a statement set forth in your columns of yesterday with respect to a previous marriage having taken place between my brother and a certain Mary Roberts, in the year 1832, at

Marylebone Church, which statement would imply that he had been guilty of the crime of bigamy. I beg to state that he was born on the 20th of March, 1820, which will show the utter impossibility of such having taken place, as he could not have been, at the period of the marriage named by your correspondent, 13 years of age.

I am, Sir, your most obedient servant,

Edmund Manning

A charge of murder against his brother was bad enough, Edmund seemed to be saying, but bigamy was a disgrace the family could not bear.

So the path was cleared for the hearing of Marie Manning's appeal. The suspense and delay were becoming intolerable for those who looked forward to seeing the Mannings executed or, in the macabre Victorian phrase, "turned off." One of the expectant multitude was the critic John Forster, a friend and future biographer of Charles Dickens. On 7 November, the day of the appellate hearing, Jane Welsh Carlyle, the wife of the writer Thomas Carlyle, wrote to Forster to extend her sympathies on the slowness of the proceedings in the case: "What a bore that we cannot get done with the Mannings. I begin to fear you will not have the pleasure of seeing her turned off, after all." But Mrs. Carlyle had nothing to fear from the appellate proceeding. The court unanimously confirmed the ruling of the trial court that Mrs. Manning had become a full-fledged Englishwoman as a result of her marriage to Manning and had lost her right to be tried separately by a jury of mixed nationality. The date for the execution of the Mannings was set for the following Tuesday, 13 November.

Shortly after the news of the judges' ruling was brought to Horsemonger Lane Gaol, the prison authorities came to see Marie Manning in her cell and Chaplain Rowe informed her that her sentence would be carried out on the following Tuesday morning. Marie seemed extremely surprised at the announcement and repeated her complaint that she had been unjustly tried and convicted. She told the prison officials that her husband, if he were not unfeeling, could unravel all the circumstances relating to the murder and could exonerate her completely. She spoke in excited tones but soon put her hands to her face and cried bitterly. The chaplain exhorted her to use her last remaining days in prayer and repentance and to make a full confession of the crime, but she maintained her innocence and insisted that she had nothing to confess. The authorities, fearing she might attempt suicide, sent an additional woman to watch her; Mrs. Randall, a female searcher from the Southwark Police Station, arrived that night to assist two other women already on guard. Mrs. Randall had attended Mrs. Manning during the police court examinations, and Marie seemed quite as strongly attached to her as to the gallant Superintendent Moxey. As soon as Mrs. Randall came to her cell, Marie expressed her pleasure on seeing her and talked freely. She was innocent, she said, and would not be executed, for "some influential ladies would intercede for her in high quarters." When she was told that her legal advisors had already done all they could for her, she stamped her foot in a rage and exclaimed violently, "Done all they could! Why, they have done nothing; they and everybody else in the court decided upon hanging me before I was tried." Referring to her husband a few minutes afterward she added, "Ah, he is a vagabond. I never said anything about him. He knows who murdered poor O'Connor and can tell all." When her solicitor, Solomon, and her trial counsel were mentioned, she became very agitated and, shaking her fist, exclaimed, "Oh, if I only had them here I'd serve them out. They might have got me acquitted if they had done their duty." Against all offers of religious consolation she remained adamant; though she attended chapel services regularly, she paid little attention to Reverend Rowe and to a "charitable lady" who came to visit her.

Fred Manning, on the other hand, was an exemplary condemned murderer. He expressed several times his strong desire to see his wife. Although he continued in his habitual depressed state and ate much less than Marie, whose appetite never failed her, he occupied his time in reading improving religious works and writing.

Meantime, the police remained oddly busy. It is a striking feature of the Manning case that despite the expressed satisfaction of all observers with the crushing weight of the evidence against both prisoners, the police continued an active investigation of the details of the crime even after the conviction. Many of the clues being followed by the police were furnished by the cooperative Fred Manning. On Monday, 29 October, Manning, in an interview with his solicitor, Binns, and the deputy governor of the prison, stated that some securities that belonged to O'Connor had been destroyed by Mrs. Manning on the evening after the murder was committed. Marie had burned them, he said, in the back kitchen with several old papers and some rags. As his revelations continued to flow day by day, it became clear that, despite the contrary position taken at the trial, Fred had also taken possession of some of the dead man's property. He told his solicitor Binns that he brought some of O'Connor's railway shares with him to Jersey, where he destroyed them in a watercloset before his arrest. He produced a description of the securities for the benefit of O'Connor's family so that they might seek restoration of the securities from the railroads.

Fred acknowledged that the pistols used to commit the murder were indeed those found in the possession of Mr. Adams, the pawnbroker who had been unable to identify Manning as the pledgor of the guns. Fred also supplied a solution for the mystery of the missing clothes of O'Connor. The police had supposed that the clothes had been wrapped with the crowbar and thrown into the Thames, but Manning now told them that they had been disposed of in the fire in the back kitchen. When he was asked what had become of the missing crowbar, he told the authorities that it could be found at a certain railway station, which he named.

The Mannings also were beginning to turn their thoughts toward each other. Shortly after the trial it was reported that Manning had finally had his wish: he had written a letter to Marie, which was delivered by the prison authorities, and received a prompt response. On 10 November the text of the correspondence was published. The literacy and elevated tone of the letters suggest that though the hands may have been those of Fred and Marie, the voices belonged to Binns and Solomon. Fred's letter, dated 29 October, stated:

I address you as a fellow-sinner and a fellow-sufferer, and not as my wife, since the contract must be considered as cancelled, extending as it does only until death, and not beyond it, and both of us standing, as we do, on the brink of eternity. We may already consider ourselves as cut off from the world. The consciousness of this truth does not, however, prevent me from expressing my earnest solicitude for the happiness of your soul as well as my own. I do, therefore, beseech and implore of you to be truthful in all you utter, and that you may not be tempted to yield to any evil suggestions of the enemy of our souls' welfare to question for an instant the solemn truth that we shall shortly appear before our God in judgment—that His eye is upon us now. The time, though not, so far as I can learn, precisely fixed when we are to be launched into eternity, but we may be quite sure and certain that it is close at hand. And now, by all kindly feelings we have at any time entertained towards each other, I earnestly pray that you will look to God for the pardon you need, and of which I feel my own need also, believe me, through the merits of a crucified Redeemer, being satisfied that His all-sufficient atonement and intercession cannot benefit us unless we repent, and give proofs of that repentance. Believe me, I upbraid you not, but trust you will be assured that I forgive everyone, as I pray and hope to be forgiven by God; and now I close, as my feelings are too acute to write more. May the Lord be merciful, and may He be so consistent with His promises. Let us be truthful and sincere in all we say and do. This is the last letter you will ever receive from me. Now let me beg of you to grant me an interview this day, if possible. I have a great wish to have one before I depart this world.

F. G. Manning

Marie's response, which Fred received on the following day, echoed some of her husband's phrases and responded to his religious discourse, but the main burden of her letter was a plea to him to save her life by acknowledging her innocence of the crime:

I address you as my husband. I am far away from my happy native land on account of this contract and this land, which you have made to me a captivity. The peace and well-being of society, the laws of truth, which you have broken, have alike demanded my banishment from the country which gave me birth. But I am not going away from God; He is everywhere alike present, and at all times gracious to those that seek His mercy and His favour. What has brought me into this eternal consequence? If you live and die unforgiven by God, though those sins will be punished by the laws of man, they are still all registered by the only God. All that I have to say is this—I never made any statement of any kind to injure or condemn you in this matter—that you well know—from first to last. I am here condemned only by your statement. If it had proved beneficial to you, I should have been satisfied with all your doings, and the great expense of your learned counsellors, that did not benefit you, but plunged me unmercifully with you to this horrid fate.

Marie then proceeded to introduce into the case a new "third man"—a "young man from Guernsey" who she said fired the fatal shot:

All I have to beg of you now is to state facts, as you know that I was not in the house when O'Connor met with his death; but I was gone to see for him, and during that time he called in my absence, and was shot by that young man from Guernsey who was with you in the back parlour smoking; but that I did not know anything about it until the Saturday, and that it was all settled in the kitchen. I was in hopes you would have brought that young man forward on the trial, but that you did not do, but only blamed me, as you did, from the first day. But, my dear, as you now know that you cannot save yourself, I implore of you to state the facts which are true, and endeavour to save your wife. By so doing, it would be satisfaction to your own heart and soul to know that you are doing right and good towards me before you depart from this world. The Lord God will forgive you and comfort you. Believe me, I upbraid you not, but trust you will be assured that I forgive you, and everyone, as I pray and hope I may be forgiven by God. If you comply with this true statement, I shall be happy to see you until the last day. My hope and life is in your hands. You can, if you will, save me. Remember you cannot answer for our sins or transgressions, when all our secret sins shall be set in the light of His countenance, and when the wicked who carelessly lived and miserably died without the fear or favour of God, shall doubtless perish everlastingly. In that day a craven conscience shall proclaim a failing heart, and an angry Judge shall point to the wicked.

I humbly look to thee, Oh Lord. Thou hast set forth as a propitiation for the remission of sins that are past through Thy forebearance. I cannot write any longer, God bless you, and have mercy on us both.

M. Manning

Marie's letter did not move Manning to change his version of the crime. In interviews with his brother Edmund, Reverend Rowe, and prison authorities, he continued to maintain his innocence. When Edmund first visited him, he asked, "Surely, Frederick, you are not guilty of this horrible charge?" Fred immediately replied, "No, I am innocent. I have told Mr. Rowe everything. I have confessed all to him. Edmund, she murdered him. I was upstairs dressing myself at the time she shot him. I did not know she was going to do so. I had no hand in the murder. Mr. Rowe knows I am innocent."

After Edmund had reviewed the letters exchanged by the Mannings, he said, "Frederick, she exculpates herself from the charge, and accuses a third party; who does she mean?" He answered, "Her statement is altogether false; no one accompanied me to Jersey.* I know, Edmund, you will believe me when I assert that I am innocent, for you have always been my best friend, and I should never have married that woman if I had listened to your advice."

Both the Mannings retained hopes for a reprieve. It was reported that Manning intended to use the prison correspondence with his wife and also some disclosures with reference to the Great Western train robberies as a ground for an application he was filing with the Home Secretary for commutation of his sentence. The newspapers reported that many influential people had appealed to the throne in his behalf, including the philanthropic family of the Gurneys, bankers of Lombard Street, Mr. Sudlow of an eminent law firm, and Serjeant Wilkins; and there was a rumor that Benjamin Disraeli planned to lend his support. On Saturday afternoon, 10 November, Edmund, who had brought Fred's married sister to take her last

*Either the newspapers or the Mannings seem to have regarded the islands of Guernsey and Jersey as roughly interchangeable.

farewell a few days before, came to see him again. Fred asked his brother whether Mr. Binns had informed him that the application for a reprieve had been turned down by the Home Secretary. He also told Edmund that he had written another letter to Marie requesting an interview but he feared that she was as hardened as ever and would not see him. Returning again to the subject of the murder, he gave Edmund a pencil sketch he had made of the back kitchen, showing the position of O'Connor's body as he had first seen it. He took special care to explain the sketch to his brother and was very anxious to satisfy him that he had not participated in the actual murder. After they had conversed for a while, Fred asked Edmund to give his love and last blessing to his relatives and his respect to his former master, Mr. Reeves, a coach builder at Taunton, whom he wished to thank for all his kindness to him when he was a boy. As Edmund turned to leave, Manning asked Reverend Rowe to offer a prayer before they parted, and the chaplain complied with his wishes; the brothers kneeled and prayed together. Edmund asked Fred whether he should come to see him again. Fred told him that it would be of no use for him to do so and he would rather that he not return.

On Monday, 5 November, Marie Manning drew up a memorial to Queen Victoria, imploring her for a reprieve and reiterating her claim of innocence. She enclosed the memorial with a letter addressed to the Duchess of Sutherland in which she asked Her Grace to present it to the queen. The letter was mailed but was rejected on presentation at Stafford House, and on the following Saturday it was opened in due course at the dead letter office in St. Martin's-le-Grand. On Friday, impatient at having received no reply, Marie also wrote to the Home Secretary, Sir George Grey, requesting a reprieve. Donald Nicoll, a sheriff of London and Middlesex at the time, wrote long afterward that in fact "many persons of rank sought on behalf of Maria Manning the exercise of Royal clemency." There is a tradition that when Mrs. Manning was told that the queen would not intervene, she remarked bitterly: "Then she is no lady."

As the days went by the press published fragmented summaries of the new revelations Manning had been making in his prison interviews about the preparation and commission of the crime. It became more and more obvious that Fred was building Marie's role to even greater proportions. He now claimed that Marie had purchased the pistols at the shop of Mr. Blanch, a gunmaker in Gracechurch Street, who at her request instructed her how to load them; she directed Fred to purchase the crowbar to raise the stone and the lime to burn the body. The customary ambiguity remained about the role of the dust shovel she purchased the day before the murder. Fred was quoted as saying that it was used to dig the grave and again as maintaining inconsistently that the grave was dug as early as May and covered over with a kitchen shutter hidden by a carpet.

Fred even attributed his own passivity to Marie's calculation. He claimed that during the period of her preparation she purchased a dozen bottles of brandy and kept him generously supplied with his favorite liquor so that, to use his own words, "during the whole of this time I was not in my right senses." Even the bludgeoning of O'Connor Fred now asserted to be Marie's work. According to the newspaper summaries, he had said in his prison interviews that his wife came upstairs after shooting O'Connor in the basement and exclaimed, "I have done it—he is dead enough." Manning said he was dreadfully frightened and told her "she was a dead woman, and would be hung for the murder." She got into a passion with him and called him a "damned coward" and, pointing a pistol at him, said threateningly, "If you don't come down and see him, I will serve you the same." After some hesitation Manning did go down and was horrified to find O'Connor lying on his face, partially in a stooping posture, his head hanging into the grave and his hands up to the sides of the head. (It was reported that when Manning described this scene to his brother and sister, jail governor Keene, and Chaplain Rowe, he went down on his knees in the cell to illustrate the position of O'Connor.) About ten minutes or a quarter of an hour had expired since the shooting of O'Connor, but according to Fred's account, Mrs. Manning's anger was unappeased; she turned over the body and struck O'Connor's head three or four times with the crowbar screaming, "You damned old villain, you will never deceive me or anyone else again."

These preliminary reports of Manning's disclosures certainly were not designed to please everybody. The *Observer* dubbed his story a "quasi-confession" because of its many inconsistencies and Manning's patent objective of minimizing his own guilt at the expense of Marie. Its editorial of 11 November compared Manning to a Macbeth intent on the fruits of crime but spurred on by his wife's stronger will; but it was on his soul that the public opprobrium would lie far heavier: "She is a murderer of the worst class; he is the same; and he is also a conjugal traitor." Manning's attempt to trace the origin of Marie's hostility to O'Connor to her alleged anger over his refusal to rent a room at 3 Minver Place seemed strained, and even though Fred had buttressed this quarrel somewhat by the assertion that Marie also felt that O'Connor had cheated her in financial transactions, the newspapers still longed for a motive that would have a more passionate character. They supplied one themselves when they reported a rumor that O'Connor had made the mistake of informing Marie of his plans to marry another woman and that she murdered him so that her rival would not have a prior claim on his property. A reader of the *Observer* suggested that Marie's rage was fueled by grudges of love and money; that Patrick had probably shown Marie's love letters to other women as evidence of his prowess, and had also refused to return to Marie investments he had bought with her funds.

Ultimately the newspapers published what purported to be the full text of Manning's confession. In the final confession, as in the previews that the papers had already published, Manning ascribed O'Connor's fate to the hostility that Marie conceived by reason of his failure to rent a room at Minver Place. Marie told him that it was not the first time Patrick had cheated her so: he had been the sole cause of her taking the King John's Head on which they had lost one hundred pounds, and he had also induced her, with false promises of backing, to take a house in Mile End Road. It was Marie, Fred claimed, who initiated the lawsuit against O'Connor for the lost rent. The day previous to the time for their court appearance in the case, O'Connor paid thirty shillings to Manning in the presence of Marie and apologized for not taking the lodgings. Manning told him that it was a matter of indifference as it was of little account to him whether O'Connor lodged with them; however, Fred added, he had been informed that O'Connor had spoken disrespectfully of them and if he found this was true, he would bring an action against him for defamation. According to Fred, O'Connor almost shed tears as he solemnly declared he had always spoken of Manning in the highest terms, and held out his hand to him. O'Connor left the house on good terms with Fred, but when he was gone, Marie said, "That old villain has been the cause of my losing much money, and I am determined, as I am a living woman in this room, to have my revenge upon him." When he asked her what she meant, she replied, "I will shoot him if I am hanged for it, as he has deceived me so many times."

Marie immediately began to lay her plans, Fred told Chaplain Rowe. She said she would frequently ask him to dinner and would go to his house very often to find out the amount of money he had in his possession and the number of railway shares. One evening she found O'Connor in his room quite drunk; he had taken brandy at the docks as a preventive for cholera. He went into his bedroom and brought out all his scrip and bonds and showed them to her, telling her that he had made a will bequeathing thirteen hundred pounds to her that she would enjoy free of Manning's control. Fred said Marie told him that she believed "what the old villain said was a great lie; and that she was sure he would never leave her a shilling." "Now," he quoted her as saying, "I shall begin to get things ready to cook his goose."

Fred dated this conversation about 25 July. At that time he was planning to take a position as a town and country traveling salesman for a firm of stationers, but Marie told him that if he took the job she would follow him to every part of London he visited to keep him from "knocking about with whores," and that he had better let her carry out the plan as she was determined to have her revenge "upon that old vagabond." To prevent his going to visit his prospective employers, she locked up Fred's hat and coat and said, "Now I shall prepare his grave." Fred then regaled Chaplain Rowe with his account of Marie's preparation for the crime. She purchased a shovel at an ironmonger's shop in Tooley Street and began the next day to dig the grave, which was completed between two and three weeks previous to the murder. Fred added a touch of melodrama: O'Connor, he said, had been in the kitchen three or four times after the grave was finished and, in walking on a board laid over it, frequently questioned them as to what was being done. Marie told him that the landlord, Coleman, was having the drain altered, and O'Connor observed that it was taking a terribly long time.

On the twenty-sixth or twenty-seventh of July, Marie, according to Fred's account, got William Massey to write a letter to O'Connor to the following effect:

> Dear O'Connor,—I shall be happy to see you to dine with me and my sister, as she is coming from Derbyshire to remain a few weeks with me; she will be most happy to be introduced to you. Dinner will be ready at half-past five o'clock. If you are engaged, drop me a line. Trusting you are well,
>
> I am, dear O'Connor, yours truly,
> W. Massey

Fred said that the story about Massey's sister was untrue, but he did not explain to Reverend Rowe why the lodger lent himself to the deception. O'Connor came to their house on Thursday, 26 July, at the hour specified in the note. When he arrived, he asked for Miss Massey and her brother. Marie, Fred said, told O'Connor that they had just gone out but she expected them to return in time for dinner. Fred claimed that he was sitting in the parlor with O'Connor, telling him of his intention to bring an action against two men at Taunton for defamation (presumably in connection with the Great Western robberies). During that time Marie called him and asked why he did not leave the room for she wanted to get O'Connor into the kitchen to "cook his goose." Fred told her he would not have any such thing done, and while they quarreled O'Connor rose, put on his hat, and left the house. She ran after him and overtook him about three hundred yards from the house but could not persuade him to return. When she came back, she was disgusted with Fred: "You cur-hearted villain, you have prevented me carrying out my plan. I am now quite certain he will never come again." Fred told Reverend Rowe that he then asked her what would become of her soul if she committed a murder, to which she responded: "We have no souls; after we are dead we are like a lump of clay, and there is no more thought of us, and we shall never suffer hereafter for murdering the man."

According to Fred's confession, Marie was nothing if not persevering. The next morning she got Massey to write O'Connor another letter explaining that his sister and he had been called away to their uncle's and expressing the hope of being able to see him some day the following week. But the Massey connection was not pursued, and on Wednesday, 8 August, Marie sent O'Connor the letter of invitation that was introduced at the trial. This was the letter that arrived too late, and O'Connor escaped with his life Wednesday evening when he turned up in the company of his friend Walsh. Next morning, the day of the murder, Marie wrote again to O'Connor and took the note to the post office herself, telling Fred that this would make certain Patrick would receive it in time. Fred said that the note was as follows:

> Dear O'Connor,—I shall be happy to see you to dine with us this day at half-past five. I trust you are quite well. Yours truly,
>
> Maria Manning.

Fred said that O'Connor arrived at their house at ten minutes past five on Thursday. Previously Marie had laid the table for five persons. The dish covers and the table service were all in place, but the plates were empty, for Marie had prepared no food. When O'Connor entered the house, he asked where the Masseys were, and Marie said they were upstairs dressing. In fact, Massey was not in the house and his sister was not even in London; and, Fred said to Reverend Rowe, he was not even sure that Miss Massey had ever seen London at all. Marie asked O'Connor to go downstairs and wash his hands, which that less than fastidious gentleman declined to do. But she insisted, "Patrick, Miss Massey is a very particular young lady." After

O'Connor had been at the house for twenty minutes, Fred, who was in his bedroom washing, heard him go down the stairs. About a minute later he heard a pistol shot. His wife then came up to him and said: "Thank God, I have made him all right at last; it never will be found out, as we are on such exceedingly good terms. No one will ever have the least suspicion of my murdering him." Fred replied, "I am quite certain you will be hanged for this act," but she retorted, "It will not be you who will have to suffer; it will be me. I think no more of what I have done than if I had shot the cat that is on the wall."

It is at this point of his "confession" that Fred admitted his first involvement in the crime. He said Marie insisted on his going down to the back kitchen immediately, where he found O'Connor resting on the grave. His statement goes on: "He moaned, and I never liked him very well, and I battered in his skull with a ripping chisel."

According to Fred, Marie removed from the dead man's trousers pocket the key of his trunk and cash box; and within ten minutes after the murder, about twenty minutes to six, she proceeded to his lodgings to steal his property. As she was leaving home, Fred told her it would be impossible for him to stay in the house, and he went out into the garden and smoked a pipe on the garden wall. Marie returned from O'Connor's about twenty minutes to eight and, appearing greatly excited, told him she had brought the whole of O'Connor's shares and bonds with her. But when she looked through her haul, she found to her disappointment that the foreign bonds, which were worth between three and four thousand pounds, were not among the securities she had taken away, and she went back to O'Connor's place the next day to look for the missing securities.

Fred said that Thursday night, after Marie returned home from O'Connor's, she "went downstairs with a large pair of scissors and cut off the whole of his clothes and buried them, as well as the slippers that were upon the corpse; and then she got a strong piece of cord, and they both tied the legs back to the haunches; and having done so they put the body in the hole and covered it with lime, and then trod the earth in, which occupied a considerable time, and they did not retire till nearly midnight, and the next morning they again set to work at the grave, and concluded it about eleven o'clock, and then the wife said, 'Thank God we are safe; it is over; no one will think of looking there for him.'" Fred added that about a fortnight before they had purchased a pint and a half of vitriol, which was thrown over the body before the lime was applied.

Marie told him: "If anyone comes to inquire after O'Connor, let me answer, for I have the nerve of a horse." If ever the murder was found out, it would not be for her want of firmness. "If it is found out," she added, "you will stand in the same position as myself, because you assisted in the murder, but if anyone attempts to take me, I will first blow his brains out, and then my own." She was left with only one qualm: she regretted that she had not read prayers over the body.

On the following Saturday, Fred continued, Marie asked him to go to a sharebroker's to sell O'Connor's Eastern Counties Railway shares. He told her that it was impossible to sell the shares, as fifteen days' notice was required before sale, but she could not be put off; she told him that he could borrow money on the shares, and he went to the offices of Messrs. Killick & Co., where, impersonating Patrick O'Connor, he obtained 110 pounds for the shares from Mr. Bassett. Fred immediately went from there to the Bank of England, had the hundred-pound note changed, and returned home and gave the money to his wife.

Manning also told Chaplain Rowe about Marie's flight from London. He said that when the Bainbridges' servant whom he had sent for Marie could not find the house, he went home and found to his surprise that his wife had left in a cab with all her boxes. As a result of her desertion, he was "left penniless."

The final confession of Manning was a disappointment to those who had been hoping that he would show greater candor in the end and would fill the gaps left in the array of statements he had made in kaleidoscopic settings—in the Jersey cottage, on the Channel steamer and the train, and now in prison. But it was not to be. There was probably nobody who was more strongly aroused by what little new matter there was in the confession than William Massey, whom Manning seemed to be implicating as a witting or unwitting accomplice in baiting the murder trap. It was not true, he wrote to the *Times*, that he had written two letters to O'Connor on the subject of his visit to the Manning's house. He had written one letter at the request of Manning and his wife, but he could not detect one word in the two letters published in the confession that was in fact his.

Some of the newspapers, overcome by a love of symmetry, also published a so-called "confession" of Mrs. Manning. It was obviously apocryphal, since the source of the statement was vague and its narrative quite abbreviated. It was reported that "to those who entertain any doubts on the subject it may be desirable to know that the wretched woman herself made a confession of her guilt soon after her commitment for trial, and that the fact of such confession was well known to at least one of her legal advisers." Marie was said to have stated that, having made up her mind to shoot O'Connor on the evening of 9 August, she dressed herself so that she might start for his lodgings and arrive there as soon as possible after the murder. When O'Connor consented to go downstairs to wash his hands, the narrative proceeded, Marie followed him pretty closely, and as he put his foot on the last step, she fired the pistol at the back of his head and he instantly "tumbled onto his grave." She took the keys from the dying man's pocket, went upstairs, put on her bonnet and mantilla, and hailed a cab for Greenwood Street. She remained at O'Connor's lodgings for about an hour and used the keys to help herself to his securities and two watches. When she returned to Minver Place, she found her husband smoking his pipe in the garden. The statement quoted her as saying: "I then changed my dress, put on an old one, and assisted my husband to strip the body, tie up the legs, and bundle him into the hole which was the fit place for the wretch!" In doing so some blood got on her dress, and her subsequent efforts to remove it caused the stains that had been observed. Marie, it was asserted, had declared it to have been her intention to get as much of O'Connor's property as she could and, when once she left, never to return to see her husband; but the confession of her husband at the moment of her arrest had destroyed all her hopes and frustrated her attempts to prove an alibi.

The correspondence and confessions of the Mannings provided lively fare for their devoted readership in the weeks that followed the trial. But for the Mannings it was a period of waiting. They were waiting for Mr. Calcraft.

CHAPTER FIFTEEN

Oh Mrs. Manning! Don't You Cry for Me!

*All was brightness and promise, excepting in
the street below, . . . where, in the midst of so
much life, and hope, and renewal of existence,
stood the terrible instrument of death. It seemed
as if the very sun forebore to look upon it.*

—*Barnaby Rudge*

n his memoirs Marie Manning's counsel,
Ballantine, described one of Old Bailey's
greatest celebrities: "Rarely met with upon
festive occasions, he was, nevertheless, accustomed to present himself after dinner on the last day of the
sessions. He was a decently dressed, quiet-looking man. Upon
his appearance he was presented with a glass of wine. This he
drank to the health of his patrons, and expressed with becoming modesty his gratitude for past favours, and his hopes
for favours to come. He was Mr. Calcraft, the hangman." It was
William Calcraft, executioner for the City of London and
Middlesex, who was entrusted with the hanging of the
Mannings. Elected to his office in 1829, Calcraft served for
forty-five years, a record among England's executioners. His
tenure was not a happy period for the condemned, for Calcraft,
despite his dedication to his work, was a woeful incompetent.
Part of his problem traced from an old-fashioned or even
nostalgic strain in his personality, for he shunned the technical
innovations of modern hanging in favor of the antique "short
drop." His "clients" fell only a few feet after the trap opened
and often were "violently convulsed" for several minutes before
they died. Horace Bleackley has pointed out the irony that,
decade after decade while mid-Victorian England was priding
itself on its social progress, the Home Office allowed "an

ignorant and obstinate old hangman to choke his fellow creatures to death."

Yet Calcraft was a simple and kind man who did not seem destined by background or temperament for his chosen work. Prior to becoming an assistant executioner under his predecessor, Tom Cheshire, he had been a ladies' shoemaker and a private watchman at a brewery. He was a loving husband and father, and his pacific hobbies included the culture of flowers and bees, and the breeding of pigeons and prize rabbits. Noted for his shyness and his reluctance to talk about his work, Calcraft often left his home early in the morning or after dark to avoid recognition. His destination was often the Tiger public house at Hoxton, where he liked to talk and play skittles with his fellow rabbit fanciers. When he was at work he was a nervous performer and had "shown on more than one occasion, that his dread of facing the crowd was equal to his victim's dread of facing the gallows." In his latter days Calcraft was reported to have undergone a religious conversion, and he was seen with his wife in regular Sunday attendance at a church in Islington. It was apparent that he had seen the light, for he seemed to have lost his love for his work and had even stopped driving his profitable trade in the sale of his victims' clothes and of bits of the ropes that had hanged them.

Calcraft enjoyed a much better press than his famous predecessors, who were pictured in Victorian literature as criminals, brutes, and egoists. In 1838 Londoners were chuckling over the third edition of *The Autobiography of a Notorious Legal Functionary*, a satirical account of the early career of Jack Ketch, the infamous seventeenth-century hangman whose name became a term of opprobrium applied to all his successors. In this novel Ketch is the son of thieves and himself becomes a pickpocket, an unsuccessful burglar, and a conniver at a murder of revenge. He succeeds to the office of hangman after his uncle, who held the post, commits suicide; and on being examined as to his qualifications as an executioner, he is taught a useful credo: "Never hang the wrong man—never fail to hang the right one; and never hang yourself, as your poor simple uncle did."

In his early novel, *Barnaby Rudge* (1841), Charles Dickens presented the eighteenth-century hangman Edward ("Ned") Dennis as a nihilist and a sadist. Dennis, who in the novel as in real life was a participant in the destructive anti-Catholic riots by the followers of Lord George Gordon in 1780, shouts a very sweeping political slogan of his own: "Down with everybody, down with everything!" When he meets Hugh of Maypole, he cannot resist an immediate professional appraisal: "Did you ever see such a throat as his? Do but cast your eye upon it. That's a neck for stretching!" But joined to Dennis's cruelty and bent for destruction is an insistence on the "constitutional" status of his function and on his rights to profit from his executions. When he takes part in the storming of Newgate Prison by the rioters and the freeing of the prisoners, he tries unsuccessfully to prevent the liberation of four prisoners condemned to the gallows, and upbraids their rescuers: "Don't you know they're left for death on Thursday? Don't you respect the law—the constitootion—nothing? Let the four men be."

William Calcraft, unlike Ned Dennis, did not always permit self-interest to dictate his opinions about his professional responsibilities. After the conviction of the Mannings he went to see his superiors, the sheriffs of London and Middlesex, and told them he was reluctant to hang Mrs. Manning. A wife, he maintained, was under the control of her husband and, not being a free agent, should not suffer with him. His qualms were very disturbing to sheriff Donald Nicoll, who was mindful of the fact that, if substitutes could not be found, the sheriffs were personally responsible for carrying out the executions. But as in all ages, there was no shortage of volunteers for the task. Several applications were received; one came from a market gardener who boasted that he was "strong in the wrist" from his exercise in binding bunches of broccoli for the Covent Garden market. But the vegetarian was turned down, because Calcraft ultimately notified the sheriffs that he had quieted his scruples.

The usual scene of Mr. Calcraft's operations was Newgate Prison, but the Mannings were condemned to be hanged at Horsemonger Lane Gaol in Southwark. The jail was about a half mile to the southwest of Minver Place, and it was only a slight exaggeration when one commentator said that the Mannings were to be hanged within sight of the scene of their crime. Located on Horsemonger Lane (now Harper Road) close by the Surrey Sessions Courthouse, the jail was built at the end of the eighteenth century. Between 1813 and 1815 Leigh Hunt served part of his two-year sentence for libel at the Horsemonger Lane Gaol and was visited there by Lord Byron. The prison building was comparatively small, forming an irregular square of greater length than width. The roof was flat except where the surface was interrupted by projecting sky-lights. In the middle of the northerly side of the outer wall that surrounded the prison was built an entrance lodge whose roof rose thirty-five or forty feet. It was expected that the Mannings' gallows would be erected on the roof of the prison itself, but one eyewitness account maintains that it was, in fact, built on the western end of the roof of the entrance lodge. The prison was higher than the lodge and from the south shut out any view of executions on the lodge roof. Therefore, the faces of the Mannings would be turned northward toward London when they died.

In its fifty-odd years of history, Horsemonger Lane had witnessed executions for crimes great and small. One of the most notorious criminals executed at the prison was Colonel Despard, hanged in 1803 for plotting to assissinate King George III and seize the Tower of London and the Bank of England. Three years later, Horsemonger Lane Gaol was thronged to witness a triple feature, the executions of the murderer Richard Patch and the counterfeiters Benjamin Herring and his wife, Sarah. When the ropes had been placed around the necks of the Herrings, Benjamin kissed Sarah, "which had a most impressive effect." But the love scene above did not instill tender sentiments in all observers; the crowd was large and unruly, and two men and a child in its midst were trampled to death.

For several days before erection of the Mannings' gallows, feverish building activity was proceeding down below on the street to the north of the prison entrance. There was a large open area before the prison; the thoroughfare on the prison side of Horsemonger Lane was at least forty feet wide and extended beyond either end of the prison wall. Across the thoroughfare, opposite the prison wall, was a newly built row of houses, called Winter Terrace, whose gardens, planted with stunted poplars, were fenced from the street by low iron rails. The windows, roofs, and grounds of the Winter Terrace were being let to spectators at prices to fit every pocketbook. For a place at the windows of the houses directly in front of the prison entrance lodge the tariff was one pound, but for five shillings hundreds could be accommodated on temporary three-tier platforms being erected in the gardens in front of some of the Winter Terrace houses. These stands, which resembled "those one sees in front of the lesser booths on Epsom Race-course," were not erected by the house owners but by entrepreneurs who had rented the ground for the purpose, paying from seven pounds to twenty pounds depending on the surface area. The speculators were described as consisting chiefly of coster-mongers (peddlers who sold produce from carts) and "the lowest frequenters of the prize ring." Spaces were also being rented at two public houses at either end of Winter Terrace, the Masons' Arms on the west, where one could get a good view from a first-floor terrace at two pounds, and at the Albion on the east, where an amphitheater had been erected in the direction of the prison entrance with seats going for five shillings. From the tops of houses in surrounding streets a distant and presumably even more econmical view of the execution could be purchased.

In two of the Winter Terrace houses representatives of the press had obtained seats. This arrangement was necessary because an order of the Secretary of State, which had been enforced for several years, prohibited anyone except respon-sible officials from entering the jail on the morning of an execution. But other reservations of places had no professional justification. It was rumored that several members of the aristocracy had secured choice locations. At one house opposite the jail, it was reported, "the landlord makes no secret of the fact that his guests have required him to furnish a champagne breakfast at unlimited cost." Mention was made of "an old gentleman who, fearing to breast the crowd on the morning, had engaged a bed for the night thus ensuring the opportunity of gloating his eyes upon the drop at daybreak."

On Saturday, 10 November, the police took a number of countermeasures in the interest of safety. A number of men removed some loose flints that had been laid down on the road in front of the prison. This precaution was thought necessary "as much to avoid the possibility of mutual injury by the mob, as of popular vengeance on the convicts." To keep the crowd from congregating close to the entrance lodge, a portion of the area before the prison was barricaded and manned by a large police detachment, and many of the streets feeding into the area were also blocked off. Nevertheless, by Saturday Horsemonger Lane was already thronged; the neighborhood public houses were doing record business; and the erection of stands for viewing the execution proceeded apace.

During the day Reverend Rowe appeared before Police Magistrate Secker to request his intervention to stop the building boom at Horsemonger Lane. The chaplain told Secker that in front of nearly all of the houses in the locality the inhabitants had raised a number of slender scaffold poles tied with side pieces and surmounted by planks to serve as seats for people to witness the Tuesday execution. He was certain that, because of the negligent manner in which these platforms had been erected, some serious accident would occur unless the court ordered the stands pulled down. Magistrate Secker asked a good Victorian question: were the scaffolds erected on public property? When Reverend Rowe replied that they were built in the gardens of the Winter Terrace, the magistrate said that, if such was the case, he could not interfere. He was, however, sorry to hear that respectable people should act in such a disgusting manner. He hoped the public would have some regard for their morals and would have nothing to do with such people. Reverend Rowe then asked whether the property owners, in the event of accidents of a fatal nature, would be liable to be indicted for manslaughter. Secker said that he had no doubt they would be; he hoped, however, that the public would not endanger their lives for the sake of witnessing the execution of two fellow creatures.

But the harried magistrate had not heard the last of the entrepreneurs of Horsemonger Lane. Late on the same afternoon, another complaint about the mushrooming grandstands was submitted to him, this time by a tenant who charged that his landlord had erected a scaffolding to such a height that his room was cut off from the daylight and he could not do his work. Rights to the daylight were something with which the common law was accustomed to deal, and the magistrate directed one of his warrant officers to proceed to the spot and to ascertain whether the applicant's statement was true. The warrant officer returned with the landlord in tow and reported that a great portion of the scaffolding projected over the street and also shut out the light. The landlord denied the encroachment on the street; and as for the obstruction of light, he told Secker that his lodger had no basis to complain since he had been given a week's notice last Saturday to vacate the premises. The lodger was tenacious; he rejoined that the owner had wanted to get rid of him only to find an opportunty of letting the front window on the day of the execution, and he was determined not to leave. Secker said he wanted no part of their private quarrels but, convinced that the scaffolding did project over the public way, he ordered it removed.

The *Times* reported that the authorities could have taken stronger legal measures against the builders of the stands on Horsemonger Lane. It appeared that under the Gaol Act the erection of scaffolding of any kind within view of the prison could be prohibited, but the act required fourteen days' advance notice, which the authorities had failed to give. At Scotland Yard Superintendent Haynes huddled with his advisers to consider whether there was any other strategy that could be forged in the face of this administrative failure, but meanwhile the sale of places for viewing the execution turned into a real boom. In an allusion to the American Gold Rush then in progress, the *Times* reported that some of the best places in Horsemonger Lane were bringing "Californian prices." There was only one substantial risk in the local speculation; many of the would-be purchasers of seats were wondering whether the two convicts would be brought out for execution at the same time. Some persons connected with the prison had stated that an interval of about an hour would separate the executions of the two prisoners, and this led to great disappointment because the true aficionados of public hanging thought that the occasion would lose much of its special interest if both spouses were not "turned off" at the same time. But still the "to let" signs sprouted on the windows, and when a bargain for a seat was closed, a printed ticket was presented to the buyer in the following form:

> Admit the bearer
> to one front seat
> at Mr. _____ _____'s
> Number _____ Winter Terrace

Paid, £1 00s. 0d.

From an early hour on Sunday, large numbers of idlers were seen lounging about the prison, making running commentaries on the likely conduct of the criminals in their last days, "their remarks in some instances being of the most revolting description." It was not until shortly after noon that the curiosity of the crowd was gratified; the black timbers of the scaffold became visible atop the prison wall. The gallows was finally completed about four o'clock, and the noise of its erection was plainly audible in Marie's cell, which was situated almost opposite. The windows of her cell had been barricaded to spare her the sight of the men at work.

The battle against the grandstands resumed on Monday. As a result of an application to the Commissioners of Pavements, a number of officers went out in the morning to inspect the various scaffolds and temporary seats and ordered their removal in all cases where the slightest encroachment has been made on the public street. Both the Mason's Arms and the Albion Tavern were served with notices to remove the encroaching structures. At the same time Superintendent Haynes appeared before Magistrate A'Becket (who was sitting in place of

Secker) to play a new legal card. He argued that the New Building Act provided that before any building of a temporary kind could be erected for the purpose of an exhibition, a certificate must be obtained from the official referee. A'Becket accepted this position and recommended that the authorities serve immediate notice on the owners of the buildings that if the structures were not immediately pulled down they would be fined two hundred pounds. Haynes and his men left the court to carry out the court's order, and more of the jerry-built structures were pulled down.

Early Sunday morning the hardy spirit of Marie Manning finally broke; she attempted to kill herself. She had professed a strong attachment to the three female turnkeys who were watching her and often requested them to lie down and take a few hours rest, but they declined to do so, for they had noticed that she frequently pretended to be asleep when, in fact, she was watching their movements closely. At about three o'clock Sunday morning, however, two of them, tired out by their watch, fell asleep, and Marie attempted to strangle herself by grasping her throat and forcing her nails into her windpipe. The third guard saw her becoming convulsed and, waking the other attendants, was able with their aid to prevent Marie from succeeding in her attempt. When they had her under restraint, they examined her nails, which they found she had grown to great length and sharpened almost to a point.

Later in the morning Marie was sufficiently recovered to attend services with her husband at the prison chapel. The Mannings were so placed that neither could observe the other. On entering the chapel neither of them betrayed any extra-ordinary emotion, but as the service proceeded they both became distressed, and during portions of Chaplain Rowe's sermon they wept bitterly. The chaplain took as his text the second verse of Psalm 65: "O Thou that hearest prayer, unto Thee shall all flesh come." He began by remarking that if all his hearers knew how short a period existed between them and eternity they would each feel the necessity of so living their lives that they would be able to assist each other, and would thus merit assistance hereafter through the heavenly and divine grace of the blessed Redeemer. How much more forcibly did this apply, he said, to their unhappy brother and sister, whose days were numbered, and who had but a few hours to live. Calling on the Mannings to repent, he assured them that the mercy of God was all-sufficient to pardon the most guilty criminal, if truly penitent. He implored them to embrace the opportunity without delay of laying their hearts open before God and not to lose one moment of the short period allotted to them for existence in the world. He concluded: "God be merciful to you both, and to all of us sinners, and teach us to look to Jesus, the sinners' friend, as the only true source of absolution for our transgressions."

On the previous Friday evening Manning had written to Chaplain Rowe to seek his good offices in arranging the interview that Marie still denied him. "May I ask it of you," he wrote, "as an act of kindness, to learn from her whether an interview may not take place, as it is truly awful to contemplate the wickedness of any one who shall enter the presence, the awful presence, of God without being at peace with all men." Marie, however, had persistently refused to see Fred unless he first agreed to affirm her innocence, and despite her emotion at the Sunday chapel services, she still remained adamant. She met with Chaplain Rowe in the afternoon but declined his spiritual comfort and would not see her husband. On Sunday evening she went to bed early and did not rise until late on the following morning, although she had slept little. She expressed great indignation at the close guard kept over her bed and said she would not endure their watch again, for on the next and final night she would not go to bed at all.

The noise of the crowd around the jail could clearly be heard in her cell, and she was told that the scaffold had been erected. She said that the crowd would not see her since she would cover her face. All her words about her husband were bitter; she asked how he was and how he looked and, on being told that he was greatly emaciated, she remarked that she supposed his "fat old jowl" was thinner. She made frequent references to the railway robberies and declared that she had been the means of saving him from transportation as a participant in the crimes and regretted that she had done so, for if he had been sent out of the country, she would now be a happy woman, enjoying her liberty instead of facing execution. On Monday night Reverend Rowe visited Marie in her cell shortly after eight and remained with her for more than two hours. It was reported that during that period she made a "pretended confession" to him, "carefully excluding from that confession—if such rambling and evidently false statements which she made may be called—every appearance of an acknowledgment that she had any guilty participation in the murder of Patrick O'Connor." She pleaded entire ignorance of the crime, beyond the fact that it had been perpetrated by "the young man from Jersey," and would not respond to Rowe's questions as to how she obtained possession of O'Connor's keys.

According to the *Observer* Marie continued to give more careful thought to her dress than her soul. It reported that, as soon as she had been told that her appeal was decided against her, she asked to be supplied with some materials from among the things she had with her in the jail, "then very coolly set to work and made herself a new pair of drawers which she kept, and refused to wear until the morning of her execution, having made them expressly for the purpose of being hanged." When she arose on the morning of her execution, one of her watchers handed her a pair of cotton stockings which she at once gave her back again, saying, "No, not these, but silk ones." She directed that a pair of new white silk ones be given her, and she put them on with much care. The *Observer* tattled that "although naturally having a fine figure she had by art considerably improved herself by padding such portions of her dress as she thought would do so. Since her capture she had become very stout and as she increased in size she carefully removed the padding from her dress concealing it as much as possible from the view of those around her. On the night before her death she burned her bustles, not choosing to assign any reason for the act."

When Chaplain Rowe left Marie on Monday night, he went to see Fred and stayed with him until one o'clock in the morning. Fred seemed perfectly resigned to his fate but became very irritated when Rowe, respecting Marie's confidence, refused to

tell him what she had said about his part in the murder; both
the prisoners had failed in their frequent efforts to press Rowe
into the role of an informer. On the chaplain's leaving for the
night, Manning told him he hoped to see him the following
morning at five o'clock. During the night Manning remained
dressed and hardly slept, but read and reread the sixth and
seventh verses of Psalm 51:

> Behold, thou desirest truth in the inward parts: and in the
> hidden part thou shalt make me to know wisdom.
>
> Purge me with hyssop, and I shall be clean: wash me, and I shall
> be whiter than snow.

But when the morning came, he put aside his devotions and was
overcome with a sense of his own celebrity. As souvenirs he
wrote out notes for some of the turnkeys. One of them read:
"Frederick George Manning, age 28 years, died at Horsemonger Lane Gaol Tuesday, the 13th of November, 1849. I
have now only three hours to live in this world."

Between six and seven Chaplain Rowe was sent for, and on
entering Manning's cell he found him much calmer than on the
previous evening. Afterward, Rowe visited Marie and solemnly
enjoined her, as she was so soon to appear before her God, with
whom disguise was useless, that if she had anything to say or any
request to make, she should do so at once. Her reply was disappointing; she asked the chaplain to write to two ladies and to
express her heartfelt thanks for their kind efforts on her behalf,
even though they had not been of any avail. While the chaplain
still struggled to move Marie to repentance, Manning had
breakfast and was granted permission to walk in the prison
yard. He soon tired of the exercise and, entering the chapel, sat
down at one end of a bench placed directly in front of the
reading desk and pulpit. It was now about a quarter past eight.
After a while Manning told the turnkey who had accompanied
him that he wanted very much to see his wife. In a few minutes
Marie entered the chapel and sat on the same bench as her
husband, with two guards between them.

Fred leaned toward Marie and said, "I hope you are not
going to depart this life with animosity. Will you kiss me?"

The last meeting but one, from Huish's *The Progress of Crime*.

Marie said that she had no animosity towards him. She bent over to him and they kissed. Chaplain Rowe then administered the sacrament to them, and they kissed and embraced each other several times. Manning was heard to say to Marie, "I hope we shall meet in heaven." At this moment the prison governor, Keene, came in and told them that it was time to make ready. Mr. Calcraft also appeared, and the Mannings were led to different parts of the chapel for the pinioning of their arms. Fred Manning submitted to the procedure patiently. While being pinioned he asked Calcraft whether he would suffer much pain. Calcraft replied that if he kept himself still he would suffer no pain at all, and Manning seemed considerably relieved. He addressed some polite words to the chaplain: "I was petulant last night, and I hope you will forgive me, making allowances for my situation."

Marie's pinioning was more difficult. When Calcraft entered the room where she was waiting for him, Marie nearly fainted, and it was necessary to administer some brandy to her. On recovering, she took out of her pocket a small black silk handkerchief, which she requested be placed over her eyes before she left the room. The prison surgeon, Harris, took the handkerchief and bound it carefully over her eyes, after which, at her request, he threw over her head a black lace veil, which she tied tightly under her chin. Calcraft then approached and pinioned her arms. The hangman suggested that she wear a cloak over her shoulders in order to hide the ropes, but she objected strongly to this and the cloak was put aside. At this point one of the female turnkeys burst into tears, but Marie said to her calmly, "Do not cry, but pray for me." She was then led out into the chapel yard, where her husband waited for her. The procession moved toward the scaffold headed by Mr. Keene. Chaplain Rowe walked immediately in advance of Manning, who was flanked by two of the turnkeys, and about two paces behind came the female convict supported by the surgeon, Mr. Harris, and by Mr. Wheatley, an officer of the jail. She walked with some hesitation from being blindfolded and more than once requested Harris to be careful she did not come into contact with anything. She complained that the cords hurt her wrists.

Reporters wrote that in their progress through the chapel corridor the Mannings passed over their own graves, in which was placed a coating of lime, "an instance of retributive justice for the crime of which they had been so righteously convicted."

The crowd below had swollen to about thirty thousand, packing the stands that had survived the police campaign and thronging streets, windows, gardens, and rooftops. On Monday evening a stream of spectators had begun to pour into Horse-monger Lane before the watchful eyes of five hundred police-men positioned outside the prison. The *Times* reporter de-scribed the crowd as "the dregs and offscourings of the popula-tion of London, the different elements that composed the disorderly rabble crew being mingled together in wild and unsightly disorder, the 'navvy' and Irish labourer smoking clay pipes and muzzy with beer, pickpockets plying their light-fingered art, little ragged boys climbing up posts, and standing on some dangerous elevation, or tumbling down again, and disappearing among the sea of heads." But on the outskirts of the crowd, grouped in smaller numbers, the reporter spotted "a very different class of people—men and women too,—who had paid their two or three guineas to gratify a morbid curiosity, and who, from the fashionable clubs at the west end, and from their luxurious homes, came to fill the windows, the gardens and the housetops of a few miserable little houses, in order to enjoy the excitement of seeing two fellow-creatures die by an ignominious death upon the scaffold."

The crowd had come to brave the cold winter night with their vigil, and the roar of their collective voice never stopped. To keep their spirits high and their blood circulating they broke up into dancing parties and performed quadrilles, polkas, or jigs. Above the general clamor the voices of amateur vocalists could be heard. One anonymous wit achieved instant popularity with a parody of Stephen Foster's latest hit, "Oh! Susanna," which was taken up by the crowd: "Oh Mrs. Manning! Don't you cry for me!" In counterpoint to the song, the proprietors of the grandstands, accosting every respectably dressed person they saw, chanted praises of the strength, security, and cheapness of their structures and of the "splendid view." The public houses in the neighborhood were filled, every house was lighted, shops of all kinds were open, and "hundreds of itinerant basketmen were crying Manning's biscuits and Maria Manning's peppermints for sale." Squibs and firecrackers flew through the air punctuating the merrymaking.

Shortly after seven Calcraft and several assistants appeared on the gallows and tested its working order. They received no notice from the crowd, which was hilariously absorbed in the efforts of several spectators to escape the pressure of the mob by scrambling over the closely packed heads that surrounded them. The crowd thought the execution would take place at eight o'clock, but the hour came and went with nothing to be seen but two men loitering lazily near the gallows. At about half past eight a fire broke out at the back of the jail, and for five minutes the gallows was shrouded in smoke. When the smoke was blown away, the "sun broke out with great splendour." Then it was nine, and shortly afterward the jail procession, to the tolling of the prison bell, emerged from a small door in the inner side of a piece of brickwork at the east end of the roof. Thousands of spectators strained their eyes watching for the first appearance of the Mannings. Fred came first, supported by the two jailers and accompanied by Chaplain Rowe, who read the usual church service. Fred was wearing a black suit, and his shirt collar had been loosened for the convenience of Mr. Calcraft. His legs seemed to fail him, and he was scarcely able to move. He first turned to the east, apparently reluctant to face the crowd beneath him. "A gleam of sunshine fell upon his features while in this position, and showed that the pallor of his countenance still continued." Marie, dressed in a handsome black satin gown, followed him with firm strides and did not exhibit any signs of agitation. When she approached the scaffold, Fred gradually turned in the direction of the crowd while Calcraft proceeded to draw a white nightcap over his head and to adjust the rope. In the meantime, Marie had mounted the scaffold, and when she took her place under the gallows beam, she did not tremble but stood "as fixed as a marble statue." Perhaps her firmness communicated itself at last to Fred, for he leaned over in Marie's direction as far as the rope would permit

The last scene, from Huish's *The Progress of Crime*.

and, whispering something, held out his pinioned hand to her. One of the turnkeys brought Fred's hands into contact with those of his wife, and the couple took their final leave of each other. For the parting kiss of Benjamin and Sarah Herring that had moved the ancestors of the Horsemonger Lane crowd forty years before, the Mannings had been able to substitute only a crippled handshake.

Calcraft put a nightcap over Marie's head and then the noose; the scaffold was cleared of all occupants but the Mannings, the chaplain, and the executioner. Reverend Rowe, making one last attempt to bring Marie Manning to repentance, asked if she had anything to say to him, and she replied, "Nothing, but to thank you much for all your kindness." As he left, the Mannings again approached each other, extending their hands, after which they resumed their positions. An instant later Calcraft withdrew the bolt and the drop of the scaffold fell. According to some accounts it appeared that the hangman for once had done his work well and that the Mannings died almost without a struggle; "at least," said the *Daily News*, "there was far less muscular action than is usual." But to make sure that the reality of death matched the appearance, their bodies were left hanging for about an hour.

At the conclusion of the hanging the crowd began to separate, and it became apparent that, as at the Herrings' execution, death was not only on the prison roof but in the street below. As the ground became cleared, "hats, bonnets, shawls, shoes and other articles of dress were thickly strewed on the ground which had the appearance of having been the field of some frightful struggle." A man who had placed a leg between some iron railings to resist the pressure of the crowd fractured his thigh when the crowd swayed. After having been dragged out, he was conveyed to a hospital on a stretcher. While the crowd was pushing between two of the barricades near Newington Causeway at the western end of Horsemonger Lane, several people made an attempt to get out. Among them was a young woman named Catherine Reed, who fell down in a faint and was trodden by the mob. She was taken to Guy's Hospital with terrible injuries and died the next day. Near the place where

Miss Reed fell, a young man named Thomas Overall was also forced down in the midst of the crowd and was so seriously injured that he was also rushed to Guy's Hospital, where he was reported to be in a very dangerous condition.

The crowd had already dispersed when Calcraft lowered the Mannings' bodies and removed the ropes from their necks. They were then carried to an upper room in the lobby on the roof where, it was reported, they were both dissected by the medical authorities; the purpose of this procedure, if performed, was unclear, since the regular practice of dissecting bodies of executed criminals had been abolished by statute in 1832. The report of the *Observer* did not bear out the impression of the crowd that both Mannings had died peacefully. Fred's features "did not indicate that his sufferings had been at all intense, for beyond a slight swelling of the face and a muscular contortion of the lips, he bore all the appearance of a calm sleep." But Marie's features "were fearfully distorted, and plainly showed that before life had ceased her sufferings must have been very acute." After completion of the medical examination, the Mannings' bodies were covered except their heads, which were shorn of their hair to permit casts to be made. The press was not told whether the casts were being made for phrenological purposes or for public exhibition. The early Victorians had a passion for the science of phrenology, which purported to find badges of criminality in the bumps on the heads of hanged men. The *Observer* tended to doubt that the casts could have been made for exhibition, because Manning had strongly expressed the wish that his head not be put on show after his death. During the day, however, several county magistrates were granted their wish to view the Mannings' bodies, but Governor Keene sternly barred all others, although applications had been received from "high and influential offices." The public read that Keene was not successful in defending Marie's hair; in its story on the execution, the *Observer* claimed that "several members of the police force having obtained admission to the room managed to possess themselves of some of the long and beautiful tresses of the female, which they afterwards disposed of at high prices to those whose filthy and depraved taste renders them ambitious to obtain such revolting relics of notorious criminals." This statement stung the authorities of the prison and Scotland Yard, who ordered an investigation. Superintendent Haynes, in a memorandum preserved in the Yard's dossier, reported to Comissioner Mayne that there was no truth in the *Observer* article. Haynes enclosed a copy of a letter from prison surgeon Harris stating: ". . . fore-seeing some improper use might be made of it, I with my own hands cut off all her hair both in front and behind, as close as I well could with scissors, and the same is now in my possession." He added indelicately that "she had very little hair, most of it being false."

But Harris's disclaimer does not go far to reduce the impression that the indignities meted out to the Mannings' bodies at Horsemonger Lane on November 13 rivaled the grim burial at Minver Place. Finally, when the doctors, modelers, magistrates, and barber had gone, the Mannings' bodies were placed on separate shelves and at a late hour at night were buried side by side in the passage fronting the entrance of the prison chapel.

The day's excitement was too much for the sensitive hangman. After the Mannings had been executed, Calcraft went down from the roof of the lodge to one of the rooms underneath. He looked extremely pale and trembled strongly. On being asked by one of the prison authorities what was the matter with him, he replied in a faint voice "that he was very nervous that morning, and that he should like to have a mouthful of air." One of the turnkeys took hold of his arm and escorted him into the prison yard, where they walked back and forth for nearly half an hour. Only then had Calcraft sufficiently recovered to aid his associates in taking down the Mannings' bodies. When he left the jail he exclaimed that "he did not much like hanging a man and his wife."

CHAPTER SIXTEEN

The Moral Lesson at Horsemonger Lane

But, after all, what is it? A tumble and a kick!
And, anyhow, 'tis seemingly all over precious
quick,
And shows that some, no matter for what
they've done, dies game!
Ho, ho! if ever my time comes, I hope to do the
same!

—"The Lesson of the Scaffold,"
from *Punch*

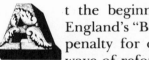t the beginning of the nineteenth century, England's "Bloody Code" prescribed the death penalty for over two hundred crimes, but a wave of reform reduced this number to eight by 1838. As Victoria took the throne, demands were being increasingly heard for the abolition of capital punishment even for murder. As early as 1830 this position had been put forward by the social philosopher Jeremy Bentham, and in 1840 William Ewart introduced a parliamentary motion for the "entire Abolition of the Punishment of Death." The motion was defeated by nearly two to one, but more than ninety votes were cast in favor of its passage. Subsequently, alternative proposals were made to retain the death penalty for murder but to reduce the number of other capital crimes.

These legislative efforts were paralleled by a literary campaign against capital punishment. In the year of Victoria's accession, 1837, R. H. Barham, author of *The Ingoldsby Legends,* published a poem inspired by the hanging of Greenacre, "The Execution: A Sporting Anecdote." Lord Tomnoddy, who finds the opera season at low ebb, asks his coachman what a nobleman may find to do and is taken to a hanging. He soon drinks himself into a stupor on gin toddy and misses the tragedy of the condemned man's despair:

> God! 'tis a fearsome thing to see
> That pale wan man's mute agony,—
> The glare of that wild, despairing eye,
> Now bent on the crowd, now turn'd to the sky.

The poet's vision of the man on the brink of the gallows anticipated the experience that Oscar Wilde at the end of the century recorded in *The Ballad of Reading Gaol:*

> I never saw sad men who looked
>   With such a wistful eye
> Upon that little tent of blue
>   We prisoners called the sky.

But Lord Tomnoddy saw none of this and in fact slept through the execution:

> Why, Captain!—my Lord!—Here's the devil to pay!
> The fellow's been cut down and taken away!—
>   What's to be done?
>   We've miss'd all the fun!

The nobleman philosophically went home to bed, for it "was perfectly plain that they could not well hang the man over again."

Punch, on page one of its very first issue in 1841, announced its intention to attack and ridicule capital punishment. Taking its cue from its namesake, the puppet Punch who hangs the executioner Jack Ketch at the end of the traditional Punch and Judy show, the magazine proclaimed its enmity to the hangman in its manifesto "The Moral of Punch": "We now come to the last great lesson of our motley teacher—the gallows! that accursed tree which has its *root* in injuries. How clearly PUNCH exposes the fallacy of that dreadful law which authorises the destruction of life! PUNCH sometimes destroys the hangman: and why not? Where is the divine injunction against the shedder of man's blood to rest? None *can* answer! To us there is but ONE disposer of life." *Punch's* crusade against the hangman was led by one of its greatest satirists, Douglas Jerrold. Writing under his pen-name, "Q," Jerrold, in a column in 1842, trained his savage wit on a newspaper account of a hanging that had attracted a huge crowd, which came and went in a holiday mood; the last religious service for the condemned man at Newgate chapel had been observed by the Lady Mayoress and her invited friends from the prison governor's pew. But Jerrold's emotions were engaged beyond the reaches of satire; he believed deeply that the use of death as a punishment was a sacrilegious distortion of the process through which God ordained that all must pass, regardless of the quality of their lives. In Jerrold's story, "The Lesson of Life," a hangman expresses the view that no death on the gallows can arouse as much horror as the sight of a good man dying in his bed. To Jerrold capital punishment was not only a crime against life; it was a sin against death.

None of the Victorian writers has left a richer or more complex legacy of writings on capital punishment than Charles Dickens. In "A Visit to Newgate" (1836), an article that the twenty-three-year-old Dickens wrote for inclusion in *Sketches by Boz*, his tour of the prison ends in the condemned cell, where he reconstructs in imagination the convict's thoughts in the night before the last dawn—the hope of reprieve, memories of his wife "before misery and ill-treatment had altered her looks, and vice had changed his nature," recollections of the trial, wild dreams of escape, a long tract of unconsciousness, and then the all too real form of the turnkey in the "dull grey light of morning." This theme is reproduced and its treatment deepened in the chapter "Fagin's Last Night Alive," in *Oliver Twist* (1837–39). Execution is one of the principal subjects of Dickens's early novel *Barnaby Rudge* (1841), whose preface invokes the memory of Mary Jones, a nineteen-year-old mother of two who was hanged in the eighteenth century for attempted shoplifting after the impressing of her husband into military service and seizure of his goods for debt had reduced her to begging in the streets. *Barnaby Rudge* provides another wrenching description of the hours of waiting for execution, though Dickens passes over the hanging in merciful silence. Earlier in the novel, in the scene of the storming of Newgate prison by the

Gordon rioters, the youthful Dickens presented the pleas of the condemned prisoners for liberation in terms that marked out plainly his opposition to the death penalty: "The terrible energy with which they spoke, would have moved any person, no matter how good or just (if any good or just person could have strayed into that sad place that night), to have them set at liberty: and, while he would have left any other punishment to its free course, to have saved them from this last dreadful and repulsive penalty; which never turned a man inclined to evil, and has hardened thousands who were half inclined to good."

In 1840 Dickens attended the execution of Courvoisier. He and William Makepeace Thackeray saw each other in the crowd but neither could catch the other's eye. Thackeray felt, to his surprise, such a strong personal empathy with Courvoisier that he could not bring himself to watch the hanging. He expressed his feelings in his article "On Going to See a Man Hanged" (1840), in which he wrote that he was left with "an extraordinary feeling of terror and shame," springing from his partaking with forty thousand others in "this hideous debauchery, which is more exciting than sleep, or than wine, or the last new ballet."

Dickens did not react to the sight with the emotional immediacy of Thackeray. Indeed, public executions continued to exert on him what he called the "attraction of repulsion." Philip Collins, in his admirable work *Dickens and Crime,* has defended Dickens against the charge of being a "masculine Madame Defarge," but the fact is that he attended three or possibly four executions. Thackeray, so far as we know, gave up death as a spectator sport after the Courvoisier execution, and once turned down an invitation to a foreign beheading, commenting, "*j'y ai été* [I've been there already], as the Frenchman said of hunting."

Despite the ambivalence of the emotions that were stirred in him by the observation of executions, the Courvoisier hanging undoubtedly had a great impact on Dickens's conscience. He recalled the scene vividly six years later in the first of a series of four long articles to the *Daily News* in which he advocated the total abolition of capital punishment. He wrote of the effect of the execution on the crowd in attendance: "No sorrow, no salutary terror, no abhorrence, no seriousness; nothing but ribaldry, debauchery, levity, drunkenness, and flaunting vice in fifty other shapes. I should have deemed it impossible that I could have ever felt any large assemblage of my fellow-creatures to be so odious." In his arguments against capital punishment, Dickens emphasized as had Thackeray its tendency to barbarize and desensitize the community. He also quoted several examples of hangings in error (including a Report of a New York Select Committee) and cited statistics that abolition of the death penalty in certain foreign countries had not led to increases in their murder rates. As an additional blow to the deterrence theory, he cited a favorite statistic of abolitionists: that according to a prison chaplain in Bristol, only 3 of the 167 prisoners he had attended under sentence of death had not been spectators at public executions.

The uniqueness of Dickens's letters, however, lies not in his assembling of these arguments but in the application of his novelist's imagination to the potentially harmful role of the gallows in shaping the evil resolves of the would-be murderer. He noted that for the murderer with exhibitionistic instincts the death penalty and its attendant notoriety, far from acting as a deterrent, in fact provide an incentive. The "ill-regulated mind" of the murderer actuated by revenge, Dickens argued further, might impel him to kill on the basis of the mechanistic calculation that capital punishment, by demanding life as the price of a life, had removed the "base and cowardly character of murder" and that society, by hanging him, would receive its just bargain. Pursuing this line of thought, Dickens feared that the prospect of hanging might also incite the wife-murderer who could feel that his crime was not the cowardly slaughter of a woman but a heroic challenge to the shadow of the gallows and a response to its dark fascination: "Present this black idea of violence to a bad mind contemplating violence; hold up before a man remotely compassing the death of another person, the spectacle of his own ghastly and untimely death by man's hands; and out of the depths of his own nature you shall assuredly raise up that which lures and tempts him on."

Feeling once again "attraction of repulsion," Dickens was tempted to attend the hanging of the Mannings, but he had difficulty making up his mind to go. On 7 November, a week before the date set for the execution, he wrote his friend John Leech, who was a cartoonist on the *Punch* staff: "I give in, about the Mannings. The doleful weather, the beastly nature of the scene, the having no excuse for going (after seeing Courvoisier) and the constantly recurring desire to avoid another such horrible and odious impression, decide me to cry off." But by the following Monday, Dickens had reversed his decision and engaged a rooftop opposite the jail. He sent a letter to Leech by messenger inviting him to join him, John Forster, and two other friends: "We have taken the whole of the roof (and the back kitchen) for the extremely moderate sum of Ten Guineas, or two guineas each. The passage would clearly have been a dismal failure, and I am not sure but that even this arrangement may turn out a [ditto]." Dickens suggested that the group begin the night's festivities by meeting for supper at the Piazza Coffee House in Covent Garden *"at 11 exactly."* Acording to the recollections of Henry Manistre, Dickens did not pass the night resting on his rooftop but conceived the idea of taking a walk through working-class neighborhoods for the purpose of gathering the residents' impressions of the coming execution. Manistre recalled their nocturnal wandering: "We started from Horsemonger Jail—Mr. D., Mr. William Twelle, a wealthy coppersmith; Mr. Cinton, proprietor of a glass factory establishment; John Grant, the London representative of a great Manchester house, myself, and one other. We crossed London Bridge, then through Cheapside, Fleet Street, Strand, clear out to Sterge Lane. We dropped into gin palaces—among filth and vile vapour—a long weary tramp to daybreak, and so back to Horsemonger Jail again."

Dickens went to the execution with the avowed intention of "observing the crowd gathered to behold it." As he looked on with his friends from their rented observation post, he was horrified by the crowd's callous and riotous behavior, and the disgust it aroused in him appeared to obliterate any response he may have felt to the hangings or to the last moments of the criminals on the scaffold. He immediately composed a letter to the *Times,* in which he set aside "the abstract question of capital punishment" and argued instead that hangings so long as they continued should be conducted privately within prison walls. He reported the terrible scene he had witnessed:

I believe that a sight so inconceivably awful as the wickedness and levity of the immense crowd collected at that execution this morning could be imagined by no man, and could be presented in no heathen land under the sun. The horrors of the gibbet and of the crime which brought the wretched murderers to it faded in my mind before the atrocious bearing, looks, and language of the assembled spectators. When I came upon the scene at midnight, the *shrillness* of the cries and howls that were raised from time to time, denoting that they came from a concourse of boys and girls already assembled in the best places, made my blood run cold. As the night went on, screeching, and laughing, and yelling in strong chorus of parodies on negro melodies, with substitutions of "Mrs. Manning" for "Susannah," and the like, were added to these. When the day dawned, thieves, low prostitutes, ruffians and vagabonds of every kind, flocked on to the ground, with every variety of offensive and foul behaviour. Fightings, faintings, whistlings, imitations of Punch, brutal jokes, tumultuous demonstrations of indecent delight when swooning women were dragged out of the crowd by the police, with their dresses disordered, gave a new zest to the general entertainment. When the sun rose brightly—as it did—it gilded thousands upon thousands of upturned faces, so inexpressibly odious in their brutal mirth or callousness, that a man had cause to feel ashamed of the shape he wore, and to shrink from himself, as fashioned in the image of the Devil. When the two miserable creasures who attracted all this ghastly sight about them were turned quivering into the air, there was no more emotion, no more pity, no more thought that two immortal souls had gone to judgment, no more restraint in any of the previous obscenities, than if the name of Christ had never been heard in this world, and there were no beliefs among men but that they perished like the beasts.

In conclusion, Dickens wrote that he did not believe that "any community can prosper where such a scene of horror and demoralisation as was enacted this morning outside Horsemonger Lane Gaol is presented at the very doors of good citizens, and is passed by unknown or forgotten."

Dickens's companion John Leech had not come to Horsemonger Lane as an idle spectator; sharing his friend's condemnation of public hanging, he planned to sketch the scene for *Punch*. Leech had already done an execution scene in one of his illustrations for Albert Smith's 1846 novel based on the career of the seventeenth-century poisoner, the Marquise de Brinvilliers, to whom Marie Manning had been compared. The print shows the marquise being carted to the stake through a crowded square; surrounded by the black-garbed coachman and priest, the ghostly white figure of the marquise cowers and gazes timorously at the jeering mob. Leech's illustration of the execution of the Mannings appeared in *Punch*'s issue for the following week above the mocking caption, "The Great Moral Lesson at Horsemonger Lane Gaol, Nov. 13." The Mannings do not appear, for the subject of Leech's satirical vision was the merrymaking of the crowd. In the background two children dance at the foot of the prison wall; another hoists himself on a playmate's shoulders to grasp the knocker of the prison entrance while others peep beneath the gate. In the middle ground stern-faced policemen guard a barrier restraining a grinning, brutish crowd, and on the near side of the barrier other spectators smoke and drink at a public house as they await the hour of the hanging.

Under Leech's drawing *Punch* published a poem for the occasion, "The Lesson of the Scaffold; or, The Ruffian's Holiday." Written in the vernacular of the mob, the poem points out the only "moral lesson" that was apparently drawn from the hanging:

> . . . that some, no matter for what they've done, dies game!
> Ho, ho! if ever my time comes, I hope to do the same!

But the impressionable thirty-seven-year-old bachelor John Forster, who viewed the execution with Dickens and Leech, only had eyes for Marie Manning. In a gushing letter to the novelist Sir Edward Bulwer Lytton written shortly afterward, he

The Great Moral Lesson at Horsemonger Lane Gaol, Nov. 13.

John Leech's "The Great Moral Lesson at Horsemonger Lane Gaol."

wrote of her in terms that, he admitted, expressed nothing short of "heroine-worship":

> You should have seen this woman ascend the drop, blindfold, and with a black lace veil over her face—with a step as firm as if she had been walking to a feast. She was *beautifully dressed*, every part of her noble figure finely and fully expressed by close fitting black satin, spotless white collar round her neck loose enough to allow the rope without its removal, and gloves on her manicured hands. She stood while the rope was adjusted as steadily as the scaffold itself, and when flung off, seemed to die at once. But there was nothing hideous in her as she flung to and fro afterwards. The wretch beside her was as a filthy shapeless scarecrow—she had lost nothing of her graceful aspect. This is heroine-worship, I think!

Bulwer Lytton may have been puzzled as to how Forster's vision could have been so penetrating that he could see Marie's "manicured hands" within her gloves, but a second letter from Forster a month later made it obvious that Marie's last admirer had obtained from prison officials the most intimate details about his heroine:

> After I wrote to you about that executed criminal—the woman Manning, I heard what fell from her as she stood on the drop. "Mind you do your work well!" she said to the hangman as he adjusted the rope. . . . Then—when the [parson] had retired— she called to the surgeon, who had led her (blindfold) up the scaffold, and said these words, the last she spoke on this earth. "I am poorly, at present; I trust to you that it shall not be made known." It was true—and she had obtained a clean napkin not ten minutes before she ascended the drop. A sensitive clean- liness of body seems to have been her passion—and the doctor who examined the bodies after death, and who said he had never seen so beautiful a figure, compared her feet to those of a marble statue.

Bulwer Lytton must have smiled at the effusions of his susceptible friend, and readers of *Punch* no doubt nodded with approval at Leech's sketch of Horsemonger Lane, but it was Dickens's letter to the *Times* that was destined to become the most lasting memorial of the Mannings' hanging. The letter drew a large number of responses from readers of the newspaper, both supporting and opposing his position. One reader supplemented Dicken's condemnation of the crowd by reporting on the equally contemptible behavior of the upper classes; he was afraid that Dickens was not so placed that he could look into the rooms of the Winter Terrace, "where the outfall of the moral sewerage of what is called *respectable society* found its vent—where respectable (?) persons used opera-glasses to assist their sight in watching the agonies of a man and wife strangled a few yards from them—where champagne and cigars helped to while away the hours. The letter concluded that "there may be a moral to such people in a woman hung in satin for a crime to which she was led by profligacy and the coveting of scrip." But others disagreed. One reader, while referring to Dicken's letter as striking and of much interest, submitted that he carried his deductions too far and did not sufficiently explain himself. Dickens, according to the correspondent who signed his name "Milo," seemed to imply that public executions were a leading cause of the depravity he described, but in fact the real causes were far too constant and deep-seated to be affected by such rare occurrences as public hangings. Milo suggested that the Home Secretary and Mr. Dickens "investigate the causes and suggest the means of eradicating the many real sources of the evil." Another reader rejected what he called the two principal deductions to be drawn from Dickens's letter and from the subsequent reader's letter criticizing the behavior of the upper classes, namely, that it was a disgraceful action to go to see a murderer hanged and that it was doubly disgraceful to look at the process of hanging through an opera glass. The writer asserted on the contrary that "in going to see the murderer hung we go to see the earth cleansed from the foul stain of his being, and, more than this, to assure ourselves that it is really done." He added in conclusion that he wrote disinterestedly, since he had not seen the Mannings or any other criminals hanged.

On 14 November the *Times* itself entered the fray with its own editorial. In contrast with Dickens and most of its other readers who wrote on the execution, the *Times* remained obsessed with

Mrs. Manning. She was a "Lady Macbeth on the Bermondsey stage . . . Jezebel the daring foreigner, the profane unbeliever . . . the ready arguer, the greedy aggrandizer, the forger, the intriguer, the resolute, the painted and attired even unto death." Turning to Dickens's letter, the *Times* praised his "knowledge of the human heart and its workings under the infinite varieties and accidents of modern life" but was not prepared to follow him to his conclusion. It appeared to the *Times* that "so tremendous an act as a national homicide should be publicly as well as solemnly done. Popular jealousy demands it. Were it otherwise, the mass of the people would never be sure that great offenders were really executed, or that the humbler class of criminals were not executed in greater numbers than the State chose to confess. The mystery of the prison walls would be "intolerable." The *Times* thought it "altogether fair" to attribute the mirth of the crowd to the night's exposure, a long suspended expectation, and the common human tendency to "hide the deepest feeling with the wildest excesses of manner and of language." The *Manchester Guardian*, however, took issue with the *Times* and sided with Dickens in urging private executions. Its editorial maintained that the sight of executions, instead of acting as a deterrent, might engender a feeling of familiarity that robbed the punishment of half its terrors; private execution, on the other hand, would produce the positive benefit of ending the hero worship of condemned criminals. The *Guardian* could not believe that the mass of the people would trust only their own eyes for assurance that great offenders had actually been put to death.

Meanwhile, Dickens was becoming overwhelmed by personal letters relating to the position he had taken in his letter to the *Times;* in fact, as he wrote in a letter to Reverend Edward Tagart, he was soon "in the midst of such a roaring sea of correspondence . . . that I seem to have no hope of land." On 15 November Dickens responded to a letter from Henry Christy, a rich philanthropist who proposed to reproduce Dickens's letter as a pamphlet and enclose it in some widely circulated publication. Dickens said that the only publication in which his influence could assist Christy in carrying out his plan was *David Copperfield,* which was then being serialized, but that in such case "considerably more than double the number you propose to print would be required." In the evening Dickens replied to a letter from another quarter. Charles Gilpin, founder of the Society for Promoting the Abolition of Capital Punishment, had invited Dickens to attend a meeting sponsored by the society on the following Monday. In his response Dickens declined the invitation, explaining that in his view "the general mind is not in that state in which the total abolition of capital punishment can be advantageously advocated by Public meetings." Dickens believed that "the enormous crimes which have been committed within the last year or two, and are fresh, unhappily, in the public memory, have indisposed many good people to share in the responsibility of abandoning the last punishment of the Law." But he thought that "there are many such who would lend their utmost aid to an effort for the suppression of *public* executions for evermore, though they cannot conscientiously abrogate capital punishment in extreme cases." He had therefore "resolved to limit my endeavours to the bringing about of that improvement as one greatly to be desired, certain to be supported by a very general concurrence, and irresistible (as I think) if temperately urged, by any Government."

Gilpin's letter had quoted a recent letter from Douglas Jerrold in which that staunch opponent of capital punishment had ridiculed the "Mystery" of private hanging. On 17 November Dickens wrote to Jerrold, arguing that there was no punishment, except death, to which mystery did not attach; the prison vans were mysterious vehicles, he wrote, and was there no mystery about transportation of criminals to penal colonies and the anonymous lives of convicts in prison? At the same time, Dickens composed a second letter to the *Times* making the same points and setting forth detailed arguments in support of his proposal of private hanging. He suggested a number of procedures for assuring that private hangings would be carried out faithfully: required attendance by the prison governor, other officers, and a "witness jury" of twenty-four citizens; official certification of the hanging and burial; and "during the hour of the body's hanging I would have the bells of all the churches in that town or city tolled, and all the shops shut up, that all might be reminded of what was being done." At the end of his letter, Dickens showed that the inflexibility of Gilpin, Jerrold, and their fellow abolitionists was getting under his skin; he wrote that of those who desired total abolition of capital punishment he would "say nothing, considering them, however good and pure in intention, unreasonable, and not to be argued with." Dickens's estrangement from the abolitionists was deepened by a reply he received from Douglas Jerrold branding Dickens's advocacy of private executions as a mischievous compromise tending to "continue the hangman among us."

When abolitionists wrote to him in more measured terms, Dickens still was willing to assure them that his heart was with them. In response to a letter from a woman named Miss Joll inquiring how he now stood on the question of capital punishment, he wrote: "He is, on principle, opposed to capital punishment, but believing that many earnest and sincere people who are favourable to its retention in extreme cases would unite in any temperate effort to abolish the evils of public executions, and that the consequences of public executions are disgraceful and horrible, he has taken the course with which Miss Joll is acquainted as most hopeful, and as one undoubtedly calculated to benefit society at large." But to his friend W. F. de Cerjat he wrote in unflattering terms about the total abolitionists. He first recalled the horror of the experience that had led him to mount his campaign for private hanging: "You have no idea what that hanging of the Mannings really was. The conduct of the people was so indescribably frightful, that I felt for some time afterwards almost as if I were living in a city of devils. I feel, at this hour, as if I never could go near the place again." His letters had made a "great to-do" and had "led to a great agitation of the subject," but he had no confidence that any change would be made, mainly because "the total abolitionists are utterly reckless and dishonest (generally speaking), and would play the deuce with any such proposition in Parliament."

But although Dickens's letters had made a "great to-do," not everyone was impressed. Many years later J. Ashby-Sterry was chatting with an ex-policeman who had been on duty at Horsemonger Lane on the day of the Mannings' execution and the whole night before and gave a "very graphic and thrilling account of the whole proceedings." Ashby-Sterry observed that the policeman doubtless remembered Mr. Dickens's celebrated letter on the subject that appeared in the *Times* the next morning and was thunderstruck by the response: "Mr. who, sir? Can't say as I ever heerd on the gent!'"

On Monday evening, 19 November 1849, the public meeting in favor of total abolition of the death penalty, which Dickens had declined to attend, was held at the Bridge House Hotel in Southwark with about three hundred people in the audience. The meeting was chaired by Charles Gilpin, and among the dignitaries on the platform was William Ewart, who had introduced the parliamentary motion for abolition in 1840. In his introductory address, Gilpin attacked the behavior of the spectators at Horsemonger Lane, not only the multitudes but West End people, and highborn ladies who behaved in such a manner that for his own part "he confessed there was too much of the Maria Manning in such conduct for him to make him feel very comfortable in such company." He also castigated the press for reporting the particulars of the Mannings' last hours—that Manning ate an indifferent breakfast and his wife a little better; he thought that such things were calculated to stimulate in criminals a morbid desire for public approval or even for public execution.

Gilpin asserted to cheers that the late execution and the "horrible abominations attendant upon it" had "shaken the gibbet to the foundation." Referring then to Dickens's letter to the *Times*, Gilpin spoke of the great writer with respect and, though differing with his position, told the meeting he felt sure that Dickens still shared their principles but considered secret executions a step in the right direction. However, he said that they had not come to the meeting, and indeed were not at liberty, "to substitute one kind of strangling for another—the strangling in prison, for that of a public execution on the scaffold." Gilpin exhibited a letter from Douglas Jerrold (whom he called a man not second to Charles Dickens for his hold on

the public mind) that expressed the opinion that "the genius
of English society will never permit private hanging" and that
"the brutality of the mob even is preferable to the darkness
of secrecy." But the chairman then proceeded to read other
communications that responded to Dickens's compromise with
more asperity: Richard Cobden was quoted as warning, "Take
heed of the new dodge—private executions," and a letter was
read from John Bright that suggested that the proposal for
private hanging "seems to be dictated by the mere liking to put
somebody to death."

Mr. Ewart then proposed the principal resolution to be laid
before the meeting, to the effect that the punishment of death is
opposed to the spirit of Christianity; that it does not repress
crime but has grossly demoralizing effects; that it sometimes
causes the destruction of the innocent by judicial process and at
other times favors the escape of the guilty; and that it ought
to be immediately and totally abolished. Ewart spoke of his
continued dedication to total abolition of the death penalty and
declared his utter repugnance to private executions as an
evasion of the main question. He told the meeting that by
inflicting capital punishment, the government shifted public
attention from the crime to the punishment and "invested the
scaffold with a false dignity, and raised the convict to a martyr."
The audience laughed when he recalled having seen newspapers refer to Manning's wife as a Clytemnestra or Lady
Macbeth. He thought all that exaltation of a criminal would be
lost if the death penalty was abolished.

So far the meeting appeared to have been conducted with
dignity, but a minister named Henry Christmas, of Zion
College, seemed to feel it was his role to provide comic relief.
He certainly had not been put on the program as a stand-up
comedian, for Reverend Christmas had acquired some reputation in abolitionist circles for his writings arguing the absence of
biblical authority for capital punishment and had been quoted
with approval by Dickens in one of his letters to the *Daily News* in
1846. But tonight Christmas was in a facetious mood. He began
by telling the audience that those who would retain capital
punishment argued that it was commanded by the Holy Scrip-

tures. But how could this be so? Cain was a murderer, yet Reverend Christmas had never heard of Cain being hanged. Moses killed an Egyptian and hid him in the sands, looking cautiously about him the while, for fear the policeman might be watching him, but he never heard of Moses being hanged.

Ewart's principal motion was put to the meeting and carried unanimously, and then Reverend H. Richard moved that a petition based on the resolution be presented to Parliament by the representatives of the Borough of Southwark. Whoever saw the spectacle lately exhibited in Southwark, he said, must have felt that it was a disgrace to civilized and Christian England. We were accustomed, he told the audience, to look down on the games of ancient Rome in which gladiators were butchered to make a Roman holiday, but what should be said of "the bringing forward of two helpless wretches, pinioned and blindfolded, to make an English holiday?" One of the few dissenting voices was then heard from the audience protesting that that was a misrepresentation of the intention. But Richard maintained that it did not misrepresent the effect.

John Robertson, in seconding the motion of Reverend Richard, argued that the gallows, far from deterring crime, "taught murder, and this was the evil of it." He reminded the audience that at the very time that Mrs. Manning and her husband were first entertaining the notion of murdering O'Connor, Rush had just been executed; and that the evidence of Massey had been that considerations respecting the execution of Rush were mixed up with conversations with Manning as to the most vulnerable part of the human head. Mr. Scoble, in supporting the same resolution, commented on the failure of the Mannings to be brought to repentance by the prospect of hanging. Up to a short time before the execution they had some hopes of a reprieve, and the speaker thought they were right to have been optimistic since the Home Secretary had "just respited a man who had been guilty of as cruel and as cowardly an act as even that for which the Mannings suffered, only that the intended victim recovered." He submitted that the vacillation on the part of the government took away from the supposed influence that capital punishments were thought to have on criminals. To the end Mrs. Manning seemed to him to be oblivious of the rope: "What influence had the gallows on the wretched woman Maria Manning, when it would appear that her only desire at the last moment was, that she should appear respectable on the scaffold? This was shown by her needlework, by her attiring herself in a silk dress, and by her having on silk instead of cotton stockings."

The second resolution was then put by Chairman Gilpin and agreed to, and the meeting adjourned. Despite the moments of humor, the meeting had been unaccountably tense. The audience "evidently heard with considerable uneasiness a tinkling noise which was audible at intervals towards the doors of the room." The chairman had quieted their nerves by assuring them that the noise was one quite common at public gatherings—it was "caused by the collection of a subscription to defray the expenses of the meeting."

The *Times,* in an editorial of 21 November, rebuked the levity of the speakers and audience at the abolitionist meeting; this gathering "showed quite as little disposition to view [capital punishment] in its own proper light as the less pretentious rabble" at Horsemonger Lane. The chairman and Bright were scolded for implying that Dickens's advocacy of private hanging was dishonest or bloodthirsty. However, the editorial reserved most of its criticism for the biblical quips of Reverend Christmas. The *Morning Post* seconded the attack on Christmas, quoting a joke of the "reverend, but not very reverent gentleman—a joke which told with such amazing effect on the risible faculties of the audience that we have no doubt the worthy parson, encouraged by this essay, is even now agonizingly labouring at a Comic Pentateuch, to be published in due course at the *Punch* office." Now the journalists had touched off a fight within their own ranks for *Punch,* unsmiling for the moment, claimed angrily that it had been charged falsely with "impiety." As for Dickens, who was beginning to tire of the controversy, he was able to throw off the abolitionists' attacks on him by a brief humorous reference in an address on 21 November to an appropriate audience, the Newsvendors' Benovolent Institution: ". . . yesterday an afflicted wife and family heard from [the newsvendor] that a husband and father was roaming about the world with an unsatiated thirst for human blood."

The dispute of Dickens with the advocates of outright abolition of capital punishment was like an internal family quarrel, in which emotions run high but are soon calmed by the claims of kinship. But England also heard other voices about capital punishment, voices that were harsher and not easily stilled. One such outcry was heard from Thomas Carlyle in his bitterly polemical essay, "Model Prisons," which appeared on 1 March 1850 as one of his *Latter-Day Pamphlets.* The main force of Carlyle's attack was directed against reformers who seemed to him to show more interest in improving prison conditions than in bettering the lot of the vastly larger number of law-abiding citizens. But scattering his shot in all directions, Carlyle angrily rejected the notion that punishment could only be justified on the basis of its deterrent effect. His asserted the existence of a religious right and obligation to take revenge on murderers as enemies of God: "The soul of every god-created man flames wholly into one divine blaze of sacred wrath at sight of such a Devil's-messenger; authentic first-hand monition from the Eternal Maker himself as to what is next to be done. Do it, or be thyself an ally of Devil's-messengers; a sheep for two-legged human wolves, well deserving to be eaten, as thou soon wilt be!" Many reviewers were shocked by Carlyle's lack of moderation, both in thought and language. *Punch* referred to the essay as "barking and froth" and wondered whether Carlyle was developing rabid symptoms. Anticipating that readers would have difficulty making sense of the turgid writing of the *Latter-Day Pamphlets, Punch* also published a bilingual edition of a characteristic Carlylean passage, one column in the author's original version, and the other in English.

A point of view similar to Carlyle's was espoused, though in more restrained language, by an editorial of the *Times* on 20 November rejecting the arguments advanced by Dickens in his second letter of 17 November and upholding both capital punishment and public attendance at hangings. The *Times* did not admit that "a man is . . . hanged in the sight of day in order simply that those who witness his death may be deterred from imitating his crime"; instead, the editorial held that "such death was the due wages of his sin. . . . He is hanged publicly because the visible self-investiture of a community with this awful power is, in its nature, one of the most solemn public acts which that community could perform."

The English loved Dickens but they listened to Carlyle. Public hanging was not abolished until 1868, Parliament being stirred to that action by the disgraceful behavior of the crowd at the execution of Franz Müller four years before. Capital punishment was abolished in England about a century after Dickens's death.

CHAPTER SEVENTEEN

Homicide Fair Revisited

. . . it has been, from first to last, a pernicious instance and encouragement of the demoralising practice of trading in Death.

—Charles Dickens, from *Household Words,* 27 November 1852

The first volume of Henry Mayhew's *London Labour and the London Poor,* which originally appeared in 1851, provides firsthand evidence that the Manning case was big business for the thriving street trade in tales, ballads, and souvenirs of crime. Mayhew's book gives a lively description of the techniques of the street sellers of "literature" who vied with the costermongers for the ears of the passerby. The sales were pushed by a class of fast-talking street orators appropriately known as "patterers." The "running" or "flying" patterer roved the streets of London with his stock of crime papers, crying "murder," "horrible," or "barbarous" but keeping the details to himself. If his paper related to a well-known case such as that of the Mannings, he would also shout the names of the criminals quite distinctly. His literary wares included the broadside (or broadsheet), a single sheet describing a crime, trial, execution, "last dying speech," or (if the seller was really lucky) the "full confession" of the culprit. Sometimes his offering would include a "book," a pamphlet whose length was strictly limited to eight pages.

The running patterer who specialized in crime also sported the title of "crime hunter" or "death hunter" and was a severe critic of the commercial possibilities of the current cases. One of these specialists confided to Mayhew that the Bermondsey case had its shortcomings. First of all, he thought that the numerous court hearings had defused the crime's sensational appeal: "We might have done very well, indeed, out of the Mannings, but there was too many examinations for it to be any great account to us." He had unfortunately spent much of his recent time in the country, where trade in the Mannings was less brisk than in the metropolis. "I've been away with the Mannings in the country ever since. I've been through Hertfordshire, Cambridgeshire, and Suffolk, along with George Frederick Manning and his wife—travelled from 800 to 1,000 miles with 'em, but I could have done much better if I had stopped in London." What had put the biggest dent in the patterer's profit, however, was Mrs. Manning's inconsiderate refusal to confess: "Every day I was anxiously looking for a confession from Mrs. Manning. All I wanted was for her to clear her conscience before she left this here whale of tears (that's what I always calls it in the patter), and when I read in the papers . . . her last words on the brink of heternity . . . , I guv her up entirely—had completely done with her. In course the public looks to us for the last words of all monsters in human form, and as for Mrs. Manning's, they were not worth the printing." However, the enterprising death hunter was not without remedy if the season's crop of crime was disappointing. He simply sold stories of concocted murders and fictitious robberies, which the trade called "cocks."

Other street salesmen remained in one place (at least until hustled along by the police). These "standing patterers" attempted to call attention to their papers (or more often pamphlets) by means of a board with colored pictures on it, illustrating the contents of what they had for sale, or by gathering a crowd around them through horrible descriptions of their merchandise. The street artists chose striking colors—scarlet, light blue, and orange (not yellow which "ain't a good candlelight colour")—and left nothing to the imagination. The paintings were in watercolor rubbed with gum resin to guard against the rain. Mayhew writes that the board used to advertise literature on the Mannings was among the most elaborate, consisting of many compartments showing the circumstances of the murder, the discovery of the body, the trial, and other scenes. A standing patterer told Mayhew that the public (particularly out of town) greatly admired the picture of Mrs. Manning, beautifully "dressed for dinner" in black satin with "a low front," firing a pistol at O'Connor, while Manning, in shirt sleeves, looked on in evident alarm. The patterer commented:

> The people said, "O look at him a-washing hisself; he's a doing it so nattral and ain't a-thinking he's a-going to be murdered. But was he really so ugly as that? Lor! such a beautiful woman to have to do with him." You see, sir, O'Connor weren't flattered, and perhaps Mrs. Manning was. I have heard the same sort of remarks both in town and country. I patters hard on the woman such times, as I points them out on my board in murders or any crimes. I says: "When there's mischief a woman's always the first. Look at Mrs. Manning there on that werry board—the work of one of the first artists in London—it's a faithful likeness, taken from life at one of her examinations, look at *her*. She fires the pistol, as you can see, and her husband was her tool."

Popular street artists were commissioned to paint a board for a fee ranging from three shillings to three shillings sixpence, depending on the extent of the pictured details. Sometimes, in the case of a surefire case like the Mannings', the artist would work on speculation. There was no great risk for any entrepreneurs in the Mannings' case, since we are told by Mayhew that broadsheets on the case sold two and a half million copies. One broadsheet shows the Mannings hanging like marionettes above the crowd at Horsemonger Lane and exhorts the reader in crude verses: "They pity all who see us suffer, man and wife on the fatal tree: for years to come will be remembered the Mannings' deeds in Bermondsey." Another broadsheet published in Carlisle briefly described the execution and appended a poem contrasting Marie's wickedness with her husband's "contrition for his guilty deeds." Woodcuts of the Mannings and their victim also moved briskly, and so headlong was the scramble for the marketplace that one "likeness" of O'Connor, as Mayhew detected from the presence of a fur collar and an order with its insignia round the neck, was in fact a doctored portrait "of the sovereign in whose service O'Connor was once an excise-officer—King William IV." The balladeers also seized upon the Mannings as a popular theme for their lyrics. One example, "Life of the Mannings,' appears in John Ashton's *Modern Street Ballads* (London 1888). There is quite a bit of poetic license in the piece, and sometimes plain inaccuracy; Marie becomes a Swede, and O'Connor is forced into the traditional role of the sincere lover. Despite these carping comments, the following poem was a best-seller of 1849:

LIFE OF THE MANNINGS.

EXECUTED AT HORSEMONGER LANE GAOL ON
TUESDAY, 13 NOV., 1849.

SEE the scaffold it is mounted,
And the doomed ones do appear,
Seemingly borne wan with sorrow,
Grief and anguish, pain and care.
They cried, the moment is approaching,
When we, together, must leave this life,
And no one has the least compassion
On Frederick Manning and his wife.

Maria Manning came from Sweden,
Brought up respectably, we hear,
And Frederick Manning came from Taunton,
In the county of Somersetshire.
Maria lived with noble ladies,
In ease and splendour and delight,
But on one sad and fatal morning,
She was made Frederick Manning's wife.

She first was courted by O'Connor,
Who was a lover most sincere,
He was possessed with wealth and riches,
And loved Maria Roux most dear.
But she preferred her present husband.
As it appeared, and with delight,
Slighted sore Patrick O'Connor,
And was made Frederick Manning's wife.

And when O'Connor knew the story,
Down his cheeks rolled floods of tears,
He beat his breast and wept in sorrow,
Wrung his hands and tore his hair;
Maria, dear, how could you leave me?

Wretched you have made my life,
Tell me why you did deceive me,
For to be Fred Manning's wife?

At length they all were reconciled,
And met together night and day,
Maria, by O'Connor's riches,
Dressed in splendour fine and gay.
Though married, yet she corresponded.
With O'Connor, all was right,
And oft he went to see Maria,
Frederick Manning's lawful wife.

At length they plann'd their friend to murder,
And for his company did crave,
The dreadful weapons they prepared,
And in the kitchen dug his grave.
And, as they fondly did caress him,
They slew him—what a dreadful sight,
First they mangled, after robbed him,
Frederick Manning and his wife.

They absconded but were apprehended,
And for the cruel deed were tried,
When placed at the Bar of Newgate,
They both the crime strongly denied.
At length the Jury them convicted,
And doomed them for to leave this life,
The Judge pronounced the awful sentence,
On Frederick Manning, and his wife.

Return, he said, to whence they brought you,
From thence unto the fatal tree,
And there together be suspended,
Where multitudes your fate may see.
Your hours, recollect, are numbered,
You betrayed a friend, and took his life,
For such there's not one spark of pity,
For Frederick Manning and his wife.

See what numbers are approaching,
To Horse Monger's fatal tree,
Full of blooming health and vigour,
What a dreadful sight to see.

Old and young, pray take a warning,
Females, lead a virtuous life,
Think upon that fatal morning,
Frederick Manning and his wife.

A wide audience was also assured for stenographic accounts
of the trial garnished with portraits and memoirs of the
murderers and their victim. In the issue of the *Illustrated
London News* that appeared on 20 October 1849, a week before
the trial, W. M. Clark advertised that in the next few days he
would publish at a price of sixpence *The Trial of Manning and his
Wife.* He "begged to say" that he had "engaged Eminent
Short-hand Writers, from whom he will receive every particular
of the above Trial." The product rolled off the presses on
schedule and was offered for sale on 29 October. When a
competitive report of the trial published by George Vickers was
released, it bore on its back cover a notice that Robert Huish's
Memoirs of Marie Manning was now appearing in three penny
installments. The crime merchants had moved with breath-
taking speed.

The case also became the theme of a religious tract by
Reverend Erskine Neale entitled *The Track of The Murderer
Marked Out By an Invisible Hand: Reflections Suggested By the Case
of The Mannings.* Reverend Neale found the hand of providence
at work in the apprehension of the Mannings through apparent
trifles: the failure of the Edinburgh brokers to destroy the note
of Marie's local address, and Fred's excessive brandy purchases
in Jersey.

The Manning case does not seem to have been adapted for
the stage with the same sensational success won by some of the
earlier nineteenth-century murders such as the Red Barn
Murder or the case of Thurtell and Hunt. The Thurtell play,
called *The Gamblers; or, The Murderers at the Desolate Cottage,*
opened six weeks before the trial, and a carriage billed as the
"identical chaise" used in the murder rolled nightly across the
stage until Thurtell's lawyer obtained an injunction against
further performances. None of such promotional ingenuity
marks the theatrical history of the Mannings, but at least the
memory of the case could be drawn on at the box office a

decade later. On 5 March 1860 the Britannia Theatre or Saloon, in High Street Hoxton, offered *Marie de Roux; or, The Progress of Crime,* an anonymously written drama that was presumably based on Robert Huish's novel.

The Mannings also were sold on the street as toys, a rude imitation of an ingenious device known as the Thaumascope ("wonderscope"). On a broadsheet were printed black marks that at first glance did not appear to define any object, but on closer examination the outlines of a face, and sometimes a figure, could be made out. When the white or black portion of the paper was cut away, what remained, when a light source was properly brought to bear, threw a huge shadow on the wall that could be increased or diminished by moving the light. During the same winter shadow figures of the Mannings were offered for sale with those of Queen Victoria, Prince Albert, the Princess Royal, and the Prince of Wales. Even the potters of the Sutherlands' Staffordshire did not neglect the case. For the mantelpieces of Victorian homes they produced a nine-inch figurine of Mrs. Manning as a "baby-faced" murderess, and a companion image of her jowly husband. Perhaps *Punch* was not indulging in excessive satire when it suggested that the ultimate product of Homicide Fair would be "murder-dolls," little images of the popular criminals of the day. "It is to be expected," *Punch* wrote, "that the smaller fry will take delight in having, as puppets to amuse their play hours, the miniature representations of those atrocious monsters in whom their parents take an interest."

Punch's real target was the life-sized "murder dolls" that the adults adored, the "waxen horrors" of Madame Tussaud's museum. In 1849 and 1850 *Punch* conducted an unrelenting campaign against Madame Tussaud's Chamber of Horrors as one of the most contaminating sources of "murder mania" in London. Fred Manning shared *Punch*'s view; at the conclusion of his last meeting with his brother and sister he said to prison Governor Keene when they were leaving: "Mr. Keene, I have to ask you one great favour—that you will not, for the sake of my family, allow any one to take a cast of my head, to be exhibited at Madame Tussaud's." But no powers on earth could keep

Photograph of Marie Manning. Courtesy Madame Tussaud's Archive, London.

Photograph of Fred Manning. By permission of the Dickens House.

Staffordshire figure of Mr. Manning. By permission of the Dickens House.

Staffordshire figure of Mrs. Manning. By permission of the Dickens House.

models of the Mannings out of the Chamber of Horrors. Their waxen figures "taken from life at the trials" were displayed to the public at Madame Tussaud's on 13 November, the day of the execution, and they were joined by a plaster cast of O'Connor, and a plan of the back kitchen of Minver Place. Other figures sprouted elsewhere; on 24 November a Manchester waxwork museum respectfully announced that it had added to its collection "correct likenesses" of the Mannings.

But Fred's worry had focused on the display of a cast of his head. Were his wishes going to be honored? The *Observer* had hoped so and had speculated that the casts that were taken after the hangings were intended for phrenological study. Another newspaper confirmed this speculation, reporting that "the phrenological development of the heads is said to agree in a very remarkable manner with the character of the convicts as at present known," and that a synopsis of the study would be published. But Marie's head, at least, did not escape the fate her husband had feared for himself. Her death mask was prepared by Joseph Tussaud, Madame Tussaud's son, and was exhibited at the Chamber of Horrors between 1891 and 1894.

Punch sent its representative to view the Manning wax figures when they were added to Madame Tussaud's collection. The exhibit was described in a bitterly worded article, "The Mannings at Home." Madame Tussaud, who was still alive and well and taking tickets at the door, is described as the "artistic continuation of Mr. Calcraft," the "wax witch" who takes up the hangman's work when he is done and beautifies it. *Punch* reported that it had "witnessed the crowd that—prompt to Madame Tussaud's card of invitation, that, like a blotch of blood, stands filthily out from the columns of the papers—gathered in Baker Street, to see Maria Manning and George Manning, in wax at home." Sardonic praise was lavished on Marie's wax image: "Maria Manning, as done in wax, is really a *chef d'oeuvre*. Dear thing! she would be a treasure as a lady's-maid at a hundred a-year, with all the cast dresses. Never did assassination look so amiable—so like a quality to be introduced to the bosom of families. . . . She only wanted a lamb to be quite a duck. . . . if the rue be wanting, the black satin gown is unexceptionable. There she stands in silk attire, a beauteous thing, to be daily rained upon by a shower of sixpences." And *Punch* also found Fred to be greatly improved in appearance, having "the look of a very clean undertaker, a little above his business."

All this exploitation of the Manning case was bound to furnish a tempting subject for satire, and *Punch* had shown the way. Before the year 1849 was over, the Manning madness was wildly caricatured by the author and dramatist R. H. Horne in his pamphlet *Murder-Heroes and The Diseased Drama of Their Crime, Trial, Sentence, & Execution*. The cover contained an illustration of a gallows over the caption "One of our Oldest Institutions" and promised the following revelations:

> All they said and did
> How they were dressed,
> What they ate and drank,
> How polite and grateful they were,
> And with what sort of step they
> ASCENDED THE SCAFFOLD

Horne's spoof tells the imaginary narrative of the murder hero Gottlieb Einhalter, a little old man who shoots people all over Europe through a pistol barrel concealed in his wooden leg. When arrested he confesses that he "had devoted all his energies to rectify the evils of over population so clearly displayed in the Divine book . . . of the great English Malthus!" Petted and lionized, Einhalter achieves his greatest sensation on the verge of his execution; attempting to shoot his sweetheart through his pistol-leg, he blows himself up and deprives the French Academy of his "finely-developed cranium." *Bentley's Miscellany* referred to Horne's work as "a timely satire upon the recent epidemic communicated to the people by the trial and execution of the Mannings."

CHAPTER EIGHTEEN

The "Demise" of Black Satin

We felt a fatal presentiment that the shop was doomed—and so it was.

—Sketches by Boz

The black satin that Marie wore at her trial and execution had caught the eye of the public. Yet it was characteristic and respectable dress for a woman who had been a lady's maid to the nobility and looked back upon her service at Stafford House as permanently fixing her genteel station in life. The English fashion historian C. Willett Cunnington observes that "all through the Victorian era the 'black silk dress' was regarded as an invaluable standby, denoting respectability without undue pride, and was much used, therefore, on ceremonious occasions, in the presence of 'our betters', or death, or similar superior forces." Marie had worn her black satin in the presence of the Duchess of Sutherland (in fact, Donald Nicoll was told that the dress was given her by a member of the Sutherland family); and it suited her well when she faced the superior forces of the law, and when she confronted death as it came to her in the person of Mr. Calcraft on the roof of Horsemonger Lane Gaol.

In light of contemporary fashions it would seem, then, that Marie's dress was entirely appropriate, but we are nonetheless told that the public, in revulsion from the Bermondsey Horror, immediately stopped wearing black satin dresses after the execution. The late nineteenth century crime writers who have briefly described the Manning case usually pass along that intriguing fashion note. Donald Nicoll, who, it will be remembered, was sheriff of London and Middlesex at the time of the trial, may be the only one of these authors who had firsthand knowledge of the case. He recalled: "After this it was useless for linendrapers to advertise black satins to be sold at even half their cost, as the material remained upon their shelves till Mrs. Manning was forgotten." An article in a series entitled "Celebrated Crimes and Criminals" first published in the *Sporting Times* and later (in 1890) as a book made the following comment on Marie's hanging: "Mrs. Manning, who was most scruuplosuly attired, wore a black satin dress on this eventful occasion, a fact which brought this costly material into an unpopularity which lasted for many years afterwards." Major Arthur Griffiths, in his *Mysteries of Police and Crime* (1898), recites the tradition as hearsay: "Mrs. Manning wore a black satin gown on the scaffold—a circumstance that caused a strong prejudice to be held against that material, which is said to have remained out of fashion in consequence till quite recent years." In *Studies in Black and Red* (1896), Joseph Forster, who hated Mrs. Manning with a passion, remarked sarcastically that he hoped the black satin dress she wore at her hanging "was some slight comfort to her," and added that "in consequence black satin went out of fashion for a considerable period, the trade in that fabric being correspondingly injured." By the time we reach the twentieth century, Mrs. Manning's effect on the satin trade is blown up into an economic disaster of the first magnitude. Charles Kingston writes that "this last appearance of Maria Manning had disastrous consequences for the trade in that material. For many years afterwards no woman would think of wearing black satin, which had become such a startling reminder of a most horrible crime, and consequently thousands of persons were thrown out of work, and numerous small traders went bankrupt." Bernard O'Donnell wrote in 1951 that black satin went out of fashion for nearly thirty years after the Manning execution.

If it were only the crime writers who had handed down this obituary of black satin, we might be inclined to reject it outright as part of the romance that clings to an interesting murderess. But caution must be taken against undue skepticism because the essential truth of the tradition is accepted by the fashion historians. Wilfred Mark Webb, writing in *The Heritage of Dress*, not only asserts as fact that black satin went out of fashion after Mrs. Manning's hanging but gives other examples of fashion changes induced by executions. He informs us that the wearing of nightgowns in the street was stopped by a woman being executed in her bedgown, and that "the use of yellow starch had its death-blow when the hangman appeared in orange collar and cuffs." Having little faith in the independence of the judiciary at least in matters of fashion, Webb also claims that a judge has been known to plot the destruction of a style people wanted suppressed "by ordering the hangman who officiated to deck himself in the objectionable garment." He concludes by passing judgment on the unfortunate black satin: "Now, however, as there are no public executions, there is not this opportunity of getting rid of obnoxious styles, and society ought to look about for another means to repress them." C. Willett Cunnington, in the introduction to his important survey *English Women's Clothing in the Nineteenth Century* (1937), comments with more restraint: "All through the century black with a lustre surface (such as satin) was fashionable for visiting or evening toilette, except for a few years after the execution of the murderess Mrs. Manning, who was hanged in black satin."

None of these writers cites contemporary evidence for the rejection of black satin after 1849, and it is therefore appropriate to take a look now at available Victorian sources of fashion information. After all, black satin was not only a staple in the everyday wardrobe but one of the principal fabrics for mourning dress, and it would seem harder to kill off than the eccentric habit of promenading in nightgowns.

A prime reference source is the fashion magazines of the period. A review of the monthly columns on "London Fashions" in *The Ladies' Cabinet of Fashion Music and Romance* for the period from January 1850 through March 1852 indicates nothing to support the tradition of the immediate baleful effect of Mrs. Manning's famous dress. In December 1849 Queen Dowager Adelaide, the widow of William IV, died and Queen Victoria ordered a period of national mourning. In its London Fashions column for January 1850, *Ladies' Cabinet* stated that the death of the Queen Dowager had "cast a temporary gloom over the fashionable world," which was now in half mourning. For promenade dress velvets and satins were reported to be most in vogue, and "robes of black velvet or of black satin are the most fashionable." In February the same column reported that "black satin, or dark colours, are much worn for half dress." No black satin fashions are noted in most of the following winter, but in April 1851, as spring approached, "we also see many redingotes of black satin, the corsage with basques, trimmed with ribbon, or with narrow lace frilled." In March 1852 it is announced that "redingotes of black satin are much in favour, ornamented with passementerie in jet."

Another London fashion magazine of the same period, *The London and Paris Ladies' Magazine of Fashion Polite Literature, Etc.*, also continued to comment on black satins. In January 1850, during the period of half mourning for the Queen Dowager, the *Ladies' Magazine* pictured as a walking dress a "redingote of black satin; the corsage is open, with revers of sable fur." In March, as one of its dinner dresses, a robe of black satin was shown, with a low body and chemisette of cambric and a casaweck (short quilted outdoor mantle) of pink taffeta. Black satin was also featured in the following winter of 1850–51. The November issue shows a walking dress that is a "robe of black satin with a mantelet of velvet," and in December the large plate of fashion engravings shows a style that Mrs. Manning herself might have worn: "Robe of black satin, with five flounces of black lace headed by ruches; the body is quite plain; pardessus of the same, trimmed round the bottom with three rows of lace, and finished round the neck and front by several rows of narrow lace." Marie might even have fancied the pink silk capote (bonnet) that the mannequin wears, because she often liked to relieve her basic black with colorful accessories. Another carriage dress of black satin was shown in the January 1851 issue, where the blackness of the dress fabric is again reinforced by black ornamentation, this time in lace and velvet. Other black satin dresses appeared in October and November 1851.

Ladies' Magazine, like the other English fashion periodicals, reported current trends from Paris, and it is likely that modish

Englishwomen, in planning fabric purchases, looked more often at Paris styles than at the local gallows. The report of the "French correspondent" of the *Ladies' Magazine* indicates a possible reason for the decline in black satin purchases (if it did occur) that is more prosaic and plausible than Mrs. Manning's hanging—it was coming to be replaced to some extent by velvet, which "now forms, according to present ideas, a toilette for useful simple wear, as formerly levantine and satin were used." Certainly the magazine found no flagging of the popular favor in which the color black was held. On the contrary, the "French correspondent" reported in October 1851 that "black has become an indispensable part of a lady's toilette; it is not as formerly reserved for mourning."

Neither of these fashion journals made any mention of Mrs. Manning's dress. It should not be supposed that this silence can be attributed to squeamishness or to the feeling that acknowledgment of an acquaintance with a lurid murder case would be unladylike. The interest in the Mannings and other murders and executions was by no means limited to the Victorian male. Indeed, the December 1849 issue of *Ladies' Magazine* ran the following advertisement announcing the addition of the Mannings to the Chamber of Horrors at Madame Tussaud's.

Maria Manning, George Manning,
and
Bloomfield Rush,
Taken from Life at the Trials; a Cast in Plaster of
Mr. O'Connor,
with plan of the kitchen where he was murdered:
Models of Stanfield Hall,
The Seat of the late T. Jermy, Esq., and Potash Farm, the Residence
of the Assassin, are now added to the Chamber of Horrors, at
Madame Tussaud & Sons' Exhibition,
Bazaar, Baker Street, Portman Square.
Open from 11 in the Morning till 10 at Night.
Admittance, Large Room, 1s.—Small Room, 6d.
"This is one of the best Exhibitions in the metropolis."—*The Times.*

The advertisement was still running in January and March 1851. *Ladies' Cabinet* ignored the Mannings but had other crime tidbits for its readers, including articles on the beheading of Charles I and executions in Canton.

An analysis of the advertisements of the silk mercers in the *Illustrated London News,* a weekly, from late 1849 to the end of 1851, does not show any radical shift in offerings or pricing of black satins. The three principal shops that advertised were King and Co. of Regent Street, its former partner, W. W. Sheath, and Beech & Berrall of Edgeware Road, a more economy-minded operation that sold a large amount of merchandise acquired in special purchases. Since black satins, apart from their use for mourning dress, were worn primarily in the winter, the advertisements for the material appear most heavily in the fall and winter months with closeout sales in the spring. In October and November 1849, the months of the Mannings' trial and executions, black satins were advertised by all three firms. Then on December 8, following the death of Queen Dowager Adelaide, both King and Sheath placed a number of advertisements for black fabrics, including black satins ranging from thirty-six shillings the full dress to three guineas for the richest quality. On 15 December John George, a competitor who was in the course of a going-out-of-business sale, announced a further reduction in the price of his colored silks because the royal mourning period required black.

In the course of 1850 Beech & Berrall placed at least twenty-five advertisements for black satins, with clearance sales on winter fabrics including black satins continuing well into the summer. King placed eleven weekly ads for Mrs. Manning's favorite fabric and only rarely offered a price reduction to its more affluent trade. Sheath, whose advertisements were less frequent and without great detail, listed black satin twice in early 1850.

Fabric advertisements are less common in 1851, but in the first six months King advertised black satin seven times and Beech & Berrall five times. Only one advertisement might lend some credence to the possibility that there was distress trading in the material. In a notice of a twenty-day sale of special-purchase merchandise in February and March, Beech & Berrall announced that the stock included five thousand yards of the richest black satins and added that this was "a most important portion of the stock inasmuch as good Black Satin is not influenced by fashion, but like current coin, always treasured with a feeling of security." The advertising copywriter may either have been trying to ward off the curse of Mrs. Manning or merely explaining a badly balanced sale inventory. In any event, King at the same time was offering black satin at its 1850 price range, twenty-one shillings, sixpence to three guineas the full dress.

The Great Crystal Palace Exhibition was held in 1851, less than two years after the Manning execution. The list of prize medals awarded at the exhibition for silk and velvet shows that seven manufacturers won awards for black satins, among them one British firm and others from Europe (which dominated the satin trade), including exhibitors from France, Switzerland, and Austria. The ghost of Mrs. Manning had not frightened these manufacturers from the hall or blurred the vision of the award committee.

In light of this evidence, admittedly scattered, that black satin had not vanished completely from the London fashion scene, what can we make of the traditions attching to Mrs. Manning's dress and its powerful influence? When the "murder mania" of early and mid-Victorian England is considered, it seems at least as likely that the dress of a famous murderess would inspire a fashion as destroy it. Certainly *Punch* thought so and counted on Mrs. Manning to be a trendsetter. In a satirical letter entitled "Old Bailey Ladies" published immediately after the trial, a young woman writes a friend her enthusiastic fashion notes from the courtroom: "MRS. MANNING was very nicely dressed, indeed. When I looked at her, I thought the jury must find such a black satin gown not guilty—but they didn't. Besides the black satin, she had a plaid shawl of the Stuart pattern. Wore a very beautiful cap, that I have no doubt will be fashionable." There is at least one authenticated example of a new style being set by a Victorian murder. Franz Müller robbed and murdered an elderly man named Briggs on a train and inadvertently exchanged hats with his victim. The clinching evidence against Müller was the identification of the victim's hat, whose crown the murderer had cut down an inch and a half so as to remove the portion on which the hatter had written Briggs's name; the oddly proportioned hat gave rise to a new style in men's headgear—a hat shaped like a topper but reduced to half the ordinary height—the so-called "Muller-cut-down."

There seems at least one safe conclusion about the role of Mrs. Manning in fashion history—that, to borrow a phrase from Mark Twain, the reports of the death of black satin have been greatly exaggerated.

CHAPTER NINETEEN

Marie and Mademoiselle Hortense

Through all the good taste of her dress and little adornments . . . she seems to go about like a very neat She-Wolf imperfectly tamed.

—Bleak House

 s 1849 waned the newspapers continued to publish reports of the aftermath of the Manning case, and reverberations of the events and personalities that give their case its special character were still heard.

A controversy was created in the columns of the *Times* by the report that in the last hours of the Mannings the Sacrament had been administered to them by Chaplain Rowe. A reader identifying himself as a "Northumberland Rector" wrote that he would not have been so "painfully struck" by this occurrence had the criminals been professing members of the Church of Rome and the rites been administered by the "Romish priest," who "gives absolution in such cases as a matter of course." But in the Protestant church, he asserted, the rite was administered "as a means of grace to those only who draw near to it in a spirit of Christian repentance, faith and charity," and the "Rector" was tempted to ask Rowe how Mrs. Manning in particular could meet this prerequisite, having attempted suicide shortly before her execution and persisting in her denial of guilt. Chaplain Rowe responded, writing that, far from having suggested the propriety of their receiving Holy Communion, he had discouraged the desire the prisoners had expressed to receive it and did not comply with it until he had emphasized every exhortation in the Communion service, particularly the warning of the danger of receiving Communion unworthily. As for Mrs. Manning, he added, she had never admitted the atheistic sentiments ascribed to her by her husband but "was always anxious to receive spiritual instruction." The religious dispute was rounded out by a letter from a Catholic priest who stated that in the Catholic church as well, Holy Communion was never given except after previous confession and absolution, and that absolution was not given without sufficient evidence of penitential sorrow. He maintained that any Catholic priest would have regarded the administration of Holy Communion to persons in the state in which the Mannings were described to have been as "an act of the most fearful sacrilege."

In an editorial of 17 November 1849, the *Illustrated London News* took note of the queen's proclamation naming the previous Thursday as a day of thanksgiving for the recession of the cholera epidemic, but urged Parliament to remedy the growing evils of large towns and cities, and notably London, which "buries its dead in its bosom—pollutes its tidal river, till it is unfit to drink—deprives the larger portion of its population of air, light, and water—and suffers accumulations of nameless filth to poison the atmosphere for miles around." In March 1850 *Punch* hailed the issuance of a report that recommended the end of London burials and the establishment of a vast cemetery in the countryside.

Marie Manning did not receive the same support from her aristocratic employers as the Swiss valet Courvoisier had been rendered by his; Lady Julia Lockwood and Mr. Fector, M.P., whom Courvoisier had served, appeared as character witnesses at his trial. In December 1849 readers learned of an event that might help explain why the Duchess of Sutherland had not responded to Marie's pleas for assistance. She and the duke were busy making preparations for the celebration at Trentham of the coming of age of their eldest son, the Marquis of Stafford, on 19 December; the festivities were pictured in the *Illustrated London News* in the following month. But the Sutherland family may not only have been distracted by this great celebration; they had no recent experience with dealing with a murder within the household circle. The family's last successful application for a reprieve had been made in behalf of a

Sutherland ancestor who was implicated in the assassination of Piers Gaveston in 1312.

In late December 1849 it was reported that the Secretary of State had, upon the recommendation of the Commissioners of Police, granted rewards to the members of the police who had been active in the detection and conviction of the Mannings, ranging from fifteen pounds for Inspector Field to five pounds each for Constables Barnes and Burton. In the following year Inspector Field received further celebrity as Inspector "Wield" and then under his own name in Charles Dickens's series on London detectives in *Household Words,* and his looks and mannerisms were immortalized: "Inspector Wield is a middle-aged man of a portly presence, with a large, moist, knowing eye, a husky voice, and a habit of emphasizing his conversation by the aid of a corpulent fore-finger, which is constantly in juxta-position with his eyes or nose."

The news item about the police rewards made on Commissioner Mayne's recommendation did not give the public more than a slight hint that Mayne's administrative involvement in the Manning case was far from being ended by the execution of the criminals. An examination of the Scotland Yard dossier leaves one with admiration for Mayne's patience and care as an administrator and also with wonder that, trapped as he was in a bureaucratic maze, he was ever able to get about with his police work. The police rewards themselves came under attack in February 1850 when the Home Secretary complained about their "duplication" by later rewards made by the Solicitor of the Treasury for work and expenses of the police in connection with the court proceedings against the Mannings; the Home Secretary ultimately relented with a warning to Mayne that in the future all recommendations to the government for police rewards were to be made at the same time. Commissioner Mayne was also required to process and substantiate numerous claims of private parties for a share in the government's posted rewards for information leading to the Mannings' arrest. A particularly ticklish situation was presented by the Heulin brothers of Jersey; both filed a claim but George, who had located Manning at Prospect Cottage, thought that the full reward should come to him. Mayne was also bogged down in reviewing the expense reports of Superintendent Moxey and his fellow officers of the Edinburgh police force. Moxey found to his chagrin that English thrift was more than a match for the more famous Scottish variety, and his requested per diem of three guineas became the subject of voluminous correspondence among Scotland Yard, the Treasury and the Home Office. In addition, Mayne had to referee claims of compensation for damage allegedly caused by the police investigation; he authorized a payment of six pounds, ten shillings to Mr. Coleman for the repair of 3 Minver Place and rejected the claim of the furniture dealer Bainbridge based on the assertion that, due to emotional distress caused by police questioning, his wife had given premature birth to a baby boy who had subsequently died.

But the principal housekeeping headache of Scotland Yard was the disposition of the Mannings' property and the application of the proceeds to the unpaid balance of the costs of their defense. Marie's French securities brought a little over fifty-one pounds, and the only other assets were clothing, jewelry, and household goods. In a report of 4 February 1850 to the Commissioners of the Treasury, the Solicitor, George Maule, recommended the sale of this property by the police at the best possible price but in a way that would "prevent the doing this by means which might be used in order to enhance the price at the sale beyond its real value at the expense of the public morals." Mr. Maule's proposal, which was approved by the Treasury and passed on to Mayne, meant simply that the Mannings' property was to be sold under strict anonymity so as to avoid souvenir fever. The police accepted their task with their customary diligence. All names were cut from the clothing. When Superintendent Haynes stored the Manning property at a warehouse pending delivery to the auctioneer, he followed the example of his former quarry, Marie Manning, by making the deposit under an assumed name, "Mr. Wilson, London." The auctioneers, Messrs. Debenham & Storr's, King Street, Covent Garden, were cautioned, at Mayne's orders, that "the names of the persons [the property] belonged to should not transpire, which they have promised shall not be made known."

The sale, which was carried out on Friday, 8 March 1850, was advertised in the auction catalogue merely as

Fifth Day's Sale
or
Valuable Forfeited Property
and Other Effects.

The auction netted about fifty-one pounds. One of the biggest prices was five pounds, two shillings, sixpence which brought the happy bidder a gold Geneva hunting watch, a gold chain, two split rings, seal, and key. For eight shillings someone acquired Marie Manning's library, which consisted of the Biblical Keepsake; Cook's Letter Writer (which must have been useful to Marie, busy correspondent that she was); Nugent's French Dictionary; Souvenirs Historiques; the Psalms of David; and Sacred Poetry. For some reason the auctioneer, while observing its promise of secrecy, printed one item of clothing in italics: "A rich black satin dress." It went for one pound, eight shillings to a purchaser who had not yet learned of the reputed demise of black satin.

The Mannings' hangman was back in the news in March 1850. *Punch* gleefully reported that he had been summoned to court for refusing to assist in the support of his mother. Calcraft pleaded proverty. He testified that his regular Newgate salary was only one guinea, but *Punch* pointed out that he had not mentioned his income from country hangings and was also moonlighting as a shoemaker. The account of Calcraft's hearing stated that "the court was inconveniently crowded by persons, amongst whom were a number of well-dressed women, anxious to obtain a sight of the defendant." This tidbit caused *Punch* to call Marie Manning to mind: "By the way, a certain late patient of Mr. Calcraft's was remarkable for dressing well. Perhaps the well-dressed women gloating on him at Worship Street reminded him of her. Possibly it is not in externals alone that the ladies who could revel in such contemplation resembled Maria Manning."

The fame of the Mannings was by no means limited to the street peddlers of Homicide Fair, for in 1849 and the years that followed they seemed to be on every tongue in the literary world as well. Jane Carlyle, who had extended her sympathy to John Forster because of the postponement of the execution, could not rid herself of her obsession with the case. Writing to Helen Welsh in November 1849, Jane revealed the full extent to which she had become a fan: "Have you taken much interest in these 'interesting but ferocious' beings the Mannings—the General Public has talked of little else here—and even now that they are got well hanged out of the road 'additional particulars' are turning up daily." Jane added that she would send along pictures of the Mannings and noted that "*Maria* has a strange likeness (never tell it)—Lady Ashburton!" Undoubtedly she had discussed the case with her acerbic husband, Thomas Carlyle, and even he could not fail to share her fascination with Marie Manning, in whom he saw (or perhaps ironically professed to see) the unrealized potentiality of heroism: "A Mrs. Manning 'dying game,' alas, is not that the foiled potentiality of a kind of heroine too? Not a heroic Judith, not a mother of the Gracchi now, but a hideous murderess, fit to be the mother of hyenas! To such extent can potentialities be foiled."

From afar in Venice the young Effie Ruskin, wife of the art critic John Ruskin, revealed in her correspondence that the Mannings had become a passion of the entire family. In a letter of 27 November she thanked her mother for telling her about the Mannings. "We were all much interested," she wrote, "and had not heard of them since we read in the last Papers." John's father had previously sent them the Mannings' prison correspondence. Effie's letter to her father on 18 December showed that the case was still very much on her mind. She thought that the news about the administration of the Sacrament to Mrs. Manning was "horrible," but showing the traditional snobbery of a tourist, she still managed to prefer Marie to the local residents: ". . . she is only one woman in a century and the Italians here appear to me to be too degraded & ignorant to be so clever or so knowing as she."

The case had even become a household word in the circle of

Queen Victoria and her advisors. On 8 October 1850 Lord Palmerston wrote to the queen to comment on an instance of uncharacteristically rude treatment of a visiting foreign dignitary—the attack on Hungarian General Haynau by draymen during his visit to an English brewery. Haynau had earned a bad reputation in the recent Hungarian war for ordering the flogging of women, and Palmerston compared the public hatred of the general to the revulsion evoked by the Mannings: "But General Haynau was looked upon as a great moral criminal; and the feeling in regard to him was of the same nature as that which was manifested towards Tawell and the Mannings, with this only difference, that General Haynau's bad deeds were committed upon a far larger scale, and upon a far larger number of victims."

The name of the Mannings left a faint trace in the second novel of Wilkie Collins, *Basil*, begun in 1850. When the son of a forger in that novel decides to assume an alias to conceal his relationship with the criminal, Collins has him take the name "Mannion," a distorted version of the Manning name. It was certain that Charles Dickens had not forgotten the name. At the end of 1850, remembering all the quarrels that had arisen as a result of his letters to the *Times,* he wrote that he had come to think of Manning as "a most unpromising name." And yet both the Mannings remained in Dickens's thoughts. Neither of them had aroused any of his sympathy, and he had no doubt of their guilt. He did not give the slightest credence to their protestations of innocence or their reported expressions of confidence that they would be acquitted or reprieved. Indeed, several years after the Manning execution, in his essay "The Demeanour of Murderers," Dickens propounded the theory that the same self-possession, coolness, and equanimity that make it possible for the murderer to kill also enabled him to proclaim his innocence and safety to the very end. It was for that reason, Dickens commented, that he was little impressed by Mr. Manning's observation that "when all the nonsense was over, and the thing wound up, he had an idea of establishing himself in the West Indies." But as with all his contemporaries, Dickens seemed to remember Marie as the principal villain. Her image was clearly fixed in his imagination when he turned to his masterpiece *Bleak House,* which began to appear in 1852. At Chesney Wold, Lincolnshire, the home of Sir Leicester Dedlock, Dickens introduced with ominous emphasis Mademoiselle Hortense, Lady Dedlock's French maid:

> My Lady's maid is a Frenchwoman of two-and-thirty, from somewhere in the southern country about Avignon and Marseilles—a large-eyed brown woman with black hair; who would be handsome, but for a certain feline mouth, and general uncomfortable tightness of face, rendering the jaws too eager, and the skull too prominent. There is something indefinably keen and wan about her anatomy; and she has a watchful way of looking out of the corners of her eyes without turning her head, which could be pleasantly dispensed with—especially when she is in an ill humour and near knives.

Hortense's fine clothes conceal only thinly her wolfish instincts: "Through all the good taste of her dress and little adornments, these objections so express themselves, that she seems to go about like a very neat She-Wolf imperfectly tamed."

One peculiarly disagreeable trait soon detaches itself from this portrait of Hortense: she is forever watching, and her eyes are everywhere. When Lady Dedlock is having her hair undressed and looks in the mirror she sees "a pair of black eyes curiously observing her." And when the community of Chesney Wold gathers for services in the litle church in the estate park, Hortense's relentless eyes sweep over the congregation: "One face, and not an agreeable one, though it was handsome, seemed maliciously watchful . . . of every one and everything there. It was a Frenchwoman's." Hortense's persistent spying begins to appear more dangerous when Dickens shows her also to be proud, imperious, and violent. When Lady Dedlock demonstrates a preference for her pretty young maid Rose, Hortense cools her passionate resentment by walking off barefoot through the rain-soaked grass. At least the park keeper thought, as he saw her depart, she hoped to cool herself down, but his wife had another explanation of the attraction of the wet grass: "Or unless she fancies it's blood. . . . She'd as soon walk through that as anything else, I think, when her own's up!"

The keeper's wife had the sharper vision, for Hortense was setting out on a trail of blood. Discharged from Lady Dedlock's service, Hortense nurses a grudge against her former employer. Dickens drops a clever hint that the scorned maid may turn to violence, when the proprietor of a shabby London shooting gallery, Mr. George, in discussing his mixed clientele, confides: "I have had French women come, before now, and show themselves dabs at pistol-shooting." Soon Hortense finds a human target, in fact two. Her criminal plot has its roots and its camouflage in Lady Dedlock's scandalous past. For though she is now the haughty reigning beauty of high society, Lady Dedlock had a dreadful Victorian secret: before she was married to Sir Leicester she carried on a love affair with a young army officer, Captain Hawdon, and gave birth to a daughter. Sir Leicester's solicitor, Tulkinghorn, gets wind of the secret, and on one fatal occasion enlists Hortense's help in his investigations. It was very dangerous to employ Hortense, as both Tulkinghorn and Lady Dedlock were to learn. Rebuffed by Tulkinghorn in her demands to be paid more money for her brief part in his dark inquiries and for her silence, and still enraged over her dismissal by Lady Dedlock, Hortense shoots the lawyer through the heart, throws the murder weapon into the Thames, and sends letters to Sir Leicester charging his wife with the crime.

Dickens's contemporaries had no difficulty recognizing Marie Manning as the inspiration for the murderous Mademoiselle Hortense. Sheriff Donald Nicoll, who recalled that Dickens had attended the Mannings' trial, quoted Percy Fitzgerald, an early biographer of Dickens, as stating that "Maria Manning's broken English, her impatient gestures, and her volubility are . . . imitated in the novel 'Bleak House' with marvellous exactness." If Fitzgerald is right, then in the characteristic speech patterns of Hortense, her use of French words only slightly Anglicized and her literal adaptations of French phrases, her trouble with word endings, her rolled r's, and her energetic sentences delivered with fists clenched, Dickens may have given us the best record we have of Marie's voice and gestures: "'Discharge, too!' cries Mademoiselle, furiously, 'by her Ladyship! Eh, my faith, a pretty Ladyship! Why, I r-r-r-ruin my character by remaining with a Ladyship so infame!'"

Pitted against Hortense is a Scotland Yard detective, Inspector Bucket. The lavishly detailed description of Bucket, "fat forefinger" and all, proclaimed his original to be Inspector Field, one of the real-life pursuers of Marie Manning. Bucket's appealing personal traits are an eloquent memorial of Dickens's admiration and affection for Field. The fictional detective is genial, friendly, charismatic, talkative, even confidential, but he is all those things only to the extent that he wants to be and he never forgets his mission. More often than not Bucket puts his irresistible charm to the service of a deadly purpose. When he drops in at the musical instruments shop of the Bagnets, he orders a cello for a friend and stays on to celebrate Mrs. Bagnet's birthday, drinking to her health, praising the Bagnets' children, and keeping time to their eldest's performance on the fife; but when he leaves the jolly party, the inspector arrests the Bagnets' birthday guest. It would be an understatement to acknowledge that Bucket is not a man strongly moved by a love of justice. In fact, it is often hard to be certain whether he is serving the public or Sir Leicester Dedlock, and he is capable of the use of bribery and threats to bar the gates of the community to a poor sick boy who knows too much of Lady Dedlock's secret. Still, there are some occasions when he shows a genuine sympathy for victims of poverty, humiliation, or grief. Above all, Dickens emphasizes the professionalism of Bucket that typified the methodical competence of Field and the newly organized Scotland Yard. Self-controlled, unobtrusive, and a master of disguise, Bucket observes quietly and comes and goes as if invisible. He recognizes every criminal and policeman he meets on the street, and he makes himself known to them by the slightest of gestures. But beyond sheer competence there is one essential power in Inspector Bucket that makes it impossible for his prey to elude him: he is dogged and unrelenting to a degree that sets him apart from other men. Dickens wrote of him: "Time and place cannot bind Mr. Bucket. Like man in the abstract, he is here to-day and gone to-morrow—but very unlike man indeed, he is here again the next day."

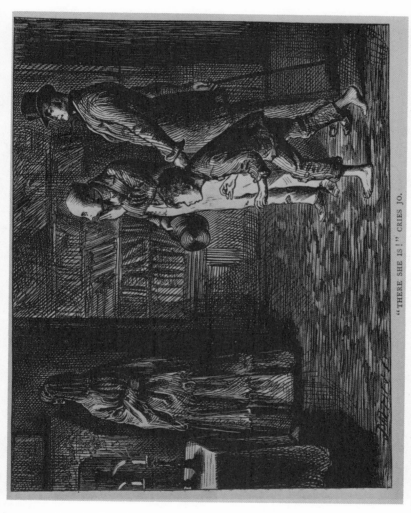

"THERE SHE IS !" CRIES JO.

Mlle Hortense Impersonating Lady Dedlock; illustration to *Bleak House* by Frederick Barnard.

MR. BUCKET IN LADY DEDLOCK'S BOUDOIR.

Inspector Bucket investigating; illustration to *Bleak House* by Frederick Barnard.

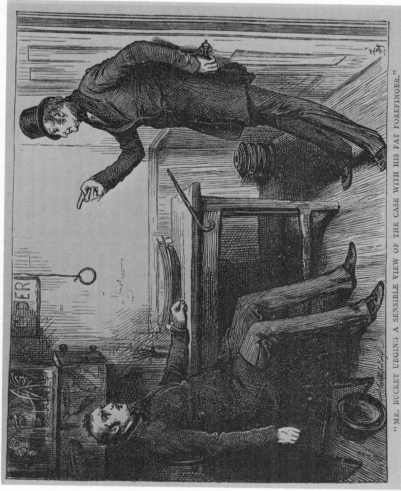

"MR. BUCKET URGING A SENSIBLE VIEW OF THE CASE WITH HIS FAT FOREFINGER."

Inspector Bucket's "Fat Forefinger"; illustration to *Bleak House* by Frederick Barnard.

Many of the plot devices, scenes, and themes of *Bleak House* raise echoes of the Manning case and its setting. By choosing the pistol as Hortense's weapon, Dickens may have reflected his acceptance of Fred Manning's final version of his wife's murder role, and the watery burial of the weapon recalls Scotland Yard's frustrating search for the Manning gun. The clothing of Mademoiselle Hortense, like the genteel attire of Marie Manning, plays a central role: Lady Dedlock disguises herself in Hortense's dress when she goes on a nocturnal expedition to learn about her dead lover, Captain Hawdon. (There is no mention of the fabric favored by Hortense, though, and the only black satin referred to by Dickens is in the waistcoat of her victim, Tulkinghorn.) The inquest on Hawdon's death is conducted in a public house that is just as undignified a setting as the tavern at the Leather Market. "The Coroner frequents more public-houses than any man alive," Dickens wrote of the inquest in *Bleak House*. "The smell of sawdust, beer, tobacco-smoke, and spirits is inseparable in his vocation from death in its most awful shapes." And the penny-a-liners who left a record of sensational criminal cases such as the murder of O'Connor are in attendance at the *Bleak House* inquest, "two gentlemen not very neat about the cuffs and buttons . . . the public chroniclers of such inquiries, by the line." But the inquest scene would remind Dickens's readers of many deaths as well as O'Connor's; what unmistakably evokes the Bermondsey case is the fact that the inquest and all the court proceedings of *Bleak House* are overshadowed by contagion and wholesale death due to poverty and social neglect. Although in the novel smallpox is on the rampage rather than cholera, Tom-all-Alone's, the fever-stricken slum described by Dickens, resembles Bermondsey in 1849: "for months and months, the people 'have been down by dozens,' and have been carried out, dead and dying 'like sheep with the rot.' . . . It is a fine steaming night to turn the slaughter-houses, the unwholesome trades, the sewerage, bad water, and burial grounds to account, and give the Registrar of Deaths some extra business."

Bleak House was not greeted as an instant classic and received at best mixed reviews. *Bentley's Miscellany,* for example, complained of the novel's "almost entire absence of humour" and the domination of "the grotesque and the contemptible." The *Athenaeum* had quite a different criticism; it seemed to feel a sense of deprivation in Dickens's failure to include scenes of the trial and execution of the murderess: "we can dispense with the excitement of the trial of Mademoiselle Hortense, the murderess, and the horrors of her execution,—but such events there must have been;—and to have overlooked them so completely as Mr. Dickens has done in winding up his story, is an arbitrary exercise of his art." These omissions, however, cannot have been mere accidents. Perhaps Dickens felt that no trial scenes even his pen could create would outdo the drama of Marie Manning's speech from the dock. As for his overlooking "the horrors of [Hortense's] execution," the *Athenaeum* should have remembered that Dickens had consistently treated descriptions of execution with great restraint in his earlier novels. He now had a stronger reason for silence; affected as powerfully as he had been by the mob of Horsemonger Lane, he had recorded his reactions for all time in the columns of the *London Times* and on this theme he simply had no more to say.*

*It is possible that the Manning case is also reflected in the quicklime burial in Dickens's final work, *Edwin Drood.*

CHAPTER TWENTY

The Second Murder Plot

"Now, what I want is, Facts."

—*Hard Times*

In her fictional role as Mademoiselle Hortense, Marie Manning lives on, but other monuments of her case have proved more fragile. Horsemonger Lane Gaol itself was torn down in 1880, leaving only the facade of the entrance lodge standing when J. Ashby-Sterry surveyed Dickensian locales in Southwark eight years later. Today all traces of the prison are gone, and where it once stood schoolchildren can be seen playing soccer in a recreational park; Minver Place and its memories have yielded to a glum-looking highrise apartment project. In 1930 archaeology brought the Mannings briefly to light again; on a cupboard shelf in a weights and measures building on Harper Road (formerly Horsemonger Lane), workmen discovered two tablets that proved to be the gravestones of the Mannings, which had been removed from the wall of the old prison's courtyard and preserved unknown for generations. The stones now repose in the collection of the Cuming Museum in Southwark. But in another museum, Madame Tussaud's, the Mannings have lost their place: the wax models of the once famous couple have been exiled to the repository of Tussaud's older figures at Wookey Hole in Somerset.

With the passage of time Marie Manning's reputation has worsened, and posterity has firmly identified her as the instigator and principal perpetrator of the Bermondsey Horror. Her own trial lawyer, Serjeant Ballantine, contributed to this judgment, for as he reflected in his memoirs on his unsuccessful defense, he wrote of his suspicion that "she was the power that really originated the deed of blood." As we have seen, Marie is

The gravestone of Fred Manning. Reproduced by permission of the London Borough of Southwark: Cuming Museum.

The gravestone of Marie Manning. Reproduced by permission of the London Borough of Southwark: Cuming Museum.

one of the very few English criminals who have been given an
entry in the *Dictionary of National Biography,* which relegates her
husband to the fine print. A final blow to Marie's already evil
name was struck by F. Tennyson Jesse, the usually judicious
high priestess of twentieth-century crime writing, who somehow was impelled to find a strain of sexual perversity in the
crime. With no support in the record of the case or in the least
responsible of the journalistic accounts, Miss Jesse wrote that
Marie, whom she described as "that chubby and redoubtable
Swiss with her broad, bland face and deeply dimpled mouth,"
had incited her husband to the killing of O'Connor "to whom
she made love over the grave that was already dug." One only
hopes that Miss Jesse did not literally mean that the meticulous
Marie could be so overcome by passion that she would subject
her elegant attire to the rigors of lovemaking on the floor of the
back kitchen.

If the evidence introduced at the trial is consulted, it is not
easy to see why the Victorians or their successors have chosen
Marie as the dominant actor in the crime. Certainly, the proof
against Fred appeared to be strong. The prosecution, building
their case on the careful work of Scotland Yard, showed that:
(1) Fred purchased the quicklime in which O'Connor's body
was encased; (2) he purchased a crowbar that could have been
used to inflict O'Connor's head injuries; and (3) he confessed to
the police that he was present at the scene of the crime, though
he equivocated as to his role in the murder and the disposition
of the body.

To this solid judicial evidence public opinion could have added
plausible theories as to Manning's motivation and his predis-
position for the crime. Theft was at least on the surface the most
immediate motive, and it seemed that Fred had, in his dealings
with Poole and Nightingale, been no stranger to robberies.
And, though Fred had evidently borne with patience or indifference Marie's longstanding affair with O'Connor, his
temper seemed to flare from time to time, as in the ridiculous
lawsuit against Patrick over the thirty shillings of lost rent. In
any event, the desire to eliminate a sexual rival, even if not an
automatic response in every husband's breast, was surely an

instinct that the public can readily recognize. But tradition has refused to regard marital jealousy as the key to the Manning case and blames the crime on Marie.

Why did this happen? Surely the prosecution's case against Marie was much weaker than the damning proof against Fred. The evidence against Marie, and the failures of such evidence, may be summarized as follows:

1. Marie lived at 3 Minver Place as Fred's wife during the time that the crime was prepared and must have known about the preparations.

2. She received the crowbar at the house.

3. She may have tipped Richard Welsh, who had previously delivered the lime, although Welsh's story changed from hearing to hearing and ultimately he could not affirmatively identify her.

4. She purchased a shovel that was not physically suitable for digging O'Connor's grave. Moreover, the purchase was made only the day before the murder, whereas the prosecution's theory was that the murder had been premeditated and the grave dug long before the murder.

5. Marie never confessed any role in the murder. She never admitted that she was at Minver Place at the time of the murder, and the prosecution had no proof that she was there. If the testimony of James Coleman was correct, O'Connor had not yet arrived at the Mannings' house at 5:10, and the Armes sisters, who were not favorable to Marie, consistently placed her around 5:45 at O'Connor's lodgings. Police experiments had shown the distance between the two residences to be forty-two minutes on foot and thirty-five minutes by omnibus (assuming no wait at the bus stop). A cab could have made the trip in twenty-five minutes, but the police had not located any cabdriver who could testify to having carried Mrs. Manning on the evening of 9 August. Faced with this evidence, the attorney general was himself skeptical of his ability to convince the jury that Marie arrived at O'Connor's place *after* the murder with his keys in hand; he therefore

theorized, in his opening statement, that it was only on the *following evening* that she stole his property.

6. Marie stole property of O'Connor's after his death using keys probably taken from his pocket; her willingness to take the property was essential to the criminal plot since she, but not Fred Manning, had free access to O'Connor's rooms.

The last point has power and lends considerable support to the jury's conviction of Marie, but still one wonders whether, in the absence of additional factors, the jury would have found it sufficient proof against her. The accepted social wisdom was that wives generally did what their husbands told them to, and a murderer might instruct his wife to steal without converting her into a murderess. The delicacy with which the legal significance of Marie's theft was regarded was suggested by the *Observer* article cited earlier: what convinced that newspaper that Marie was a murderess, rather than a dutiful accessory of her husband, was not that she stole O'Connor's property but that *she did not share the proceeds of the theft with her husband.* But Marie's decision to take off for Scotland with the loot might have been reached *after* the murder, and in fact the Lord Chief Baron had instructed the jury to disregard the Mannings' subsequent quarrels.

Whether or not it was right about how to assess the evidence of the theft, the *Observer* had put its finger on another key element that both the jury and posterity found crucial to the case against Marie: her strength of will and her repeated show of independence from her husband. In the courtroom and on the roof of Horsemonger Lane Gaol her fortitude shamed her husband's nervousness. She had been able to face the inquiries of the police at Minver Place while Fred hid. Not only had she run off with O'Connor's property, but she had had the unwifely audacity, according to the testimony of the stockbroker Stephens, to contemplate the making of stock transactions without her husband's knowledge. Moreover, Marie was a foreign wife, who, it was feared, had not learned the submissiveness of her English sisters.

But more than anything else it was Fred Manning's incriminating statements that damned Marie in court and ever afterward. Despite the legal fiction that Chief Baron Pollock, by his instruction to the jury, could induce them to disregard Manning's allegations as evidence against Marie, it is not sensible to suppose that the jury could obey him, particularly since the statements, nailed home cruelly and unfairly by Serjeant Wilkins in his closing arguments, had so much more to say of Marie's role in the crime than of Fred's. In fact, Horace Wyndham, in his article on the case in his collection *Feminine Frailty*, wrote that it was doubtful that Marie could have been convicted if she had won her application for a separate trial and Fred's statements had accordingly become inadmissible.

To a significant extent, posterity's view of Marie as the dominant party in the crime was strengthened by the release after the trial of Manning's prison "confession" to Chaplain Rowe. It is a fact that, when the confession first appeared in print, newspapers expressed doubts as to the candor of Manning's statements. But in the confession, which Rowe read at a press conference held at noon on 13 November, shortly after the execution, there seemed to be at last a chronologically detailed narrative of the crime; Manning persisted in assigning Marie responsibility for the instigation of the plot and the firing of the pistol but now confessed that when he came down to the cellar he found O'Connor still alive and moaning and hit him with the ripping chisel because he had never liked him very well. As the years went by, the contemporary reservations about Manning's confession faded, together with memories of the trial, and the short accounts of the case written since the late nineteenth century seem to take the confession as gospel.

A copy of the original twenty-five page handwritten text of the confession still survives in the collection of Madame Tussaud's but has apparently been ignored by previous commentators on the case. Dated 9 November 1849, the text was written by Reverend Rowe based on Fred Manning's disclosures to him; it is signed by Frederick George Manning, under the following affidavit also in his handwriting: "I do hereby solemnly declare that the aforegoing account is [sic] written by the Rev'd W S Rowe the Chaplian [*sic*] at my dictation is correct and true."

On close examination, two variations appear between the original and published versions that cast further doubt about the reliability of the document in fixing Marie's role in the crime. The first difference is the location of Fred's confession that he had wielded the crowbar. In the newspaper version this crucial admission appears in its proper chronological place in the narrative—after Marie came upstairs and told Fred that she had shot O'Connor. But in the manuscript, Fred's acceptance of responsibility for the blows of the crowbar is tacked on at the very end of the statement immediately before the signatures. This concluding passage reads: "I have one thing further to add.—On the fatal day after my wife had shot O'Connor, I went downstairs and found him lying as I have described in a pencil sketch, he was moaning. I never liked him much, and I beat in his skull with the ripping chisel. I have no more to say." It therefore seems clear that far from spilling out an orderly account of the full history of the crime in a spirit of contrition, Manning withheld until the last possible moment the admission of any active role on his own part, thereby rendering more suspect his charges against his wife that occupy most of the document.

This rearrangement of the order of the confession, which appears in all the newspapers I have consulted, is puzzling. It seems that this alteration must be attributed to Reverend Rowe himself, since he is reported to have "read" the confession to the press and since minor variations among the various newspaper versions indicate that they do not all derive from the notes of a single shorthand reporter who might otherwise be suspected of editorial tinkering with the sequence of the confession. Why would Chaplain Rowe have made this revision? Perhaps he was so moved by his final success in obtaining Manning's admission of guilt that he could not resist the temptation to change its location so as to lend added credibility to the document. It might be more charitable to assume that the placement of Manning's admission in its proper time frame was intended to make the statement more coherent to the press and its readers,

Fred Manning's sketch of O'Connor's body in the kitchen. The sketch accompanies the manuscript of his "confession" to Reverend Rowe. Note the words "Shoot at his spot." Courtesy Madame Tussaud's Archive, London.

but this explanation is less than satisfactory since another passage about Manning's participation in the burial is, even in the newspaper versions, left dangling in the latter part of the statement after the description of Manning's flight to Jersey.

The second variation between the manuscript of the confession and its published version is equally puzzling and much more troublesome. As we have seen, a major weakness in the theory attributing the pistol shot to Marie was the real uncertainty that Marie was at 3 Minver Place when O'Connor arrived. In the published version of Manning's confession, three critical points in the chronology of 9 August are purportedly fixed: (1) O'Connor is said to have arrived at 3 Minver Place at "ten minutes past five"; (2) at the time Marie persuaded him to go downstairs, O'Connor "had been in the house twenty minutes"; and (3) Marie left home "within ten minutes after the murder viz. 20 minutes to six." Even on its own terms this chronology is flatly inconsistent with the testimony of the Armes sisters, for Marie could not have left Minver Place at 5:40 and arrived at O'Connor's lodgings five minutes later, at 5:45, when the sisters claimed to have seen her at their door. But when the manuscript is consulted, matters become worse, for there Chaplain Rowe recorded Manning as having stated that the time of O'Connor's arrival at Minver Place was "1/2 past 5." If this later arrival time is correct, then Marie, in order to leave at 5:40, "ten minutes after the murder," would have been required, in a single instant, to greet O'Connor at the door, inveigle him downstairs, and shoot him. Moreover, if Marie's departure time is right, this supersonic activity would have been contradicted by the statement elsewhere in the confession that O'Connor had been in the house for twenty minutes before he went downstairs. If, on the other hand, O'Connor arrived at 5:30 and was in fact shot twenty minutes later, and Marie left home ten minutes after the murder, then the confession had erred on her time of departure, which could not have been earlier than 6:00, *fifteen minutes after the Armes sisters had seen her at Patrick's lodgings.*

The change in O'Connor's arrival time cannot be attributed to inaccurate shorthand reporting of Rowe's interview, since all the newspapers I have reviewed made the same change to ten minutes past five. It is unlikely that, even if we allow for the possible excitement of the moment, Reverend Rowe could have accidentally misread the manuscript to the press, for the words "1/2 past 5" are plainly written. The most plausible explanation is that Rowe made the editorial decision to move the arrival time twenty minutes back in order to harmonize it with the other statements in the confession that Marie left home at 5:40 and that a total of thirty minutes had elapsed between O'Connor's arrival and her departure. In any event, the newspapers' version, by placing O'Connor's arrival earlier, lent greater credibility to Fred's charge that Marie fired the gun.

It is only fitting that the altered version of Fred's prison confession permanently established Marie's reputation as the criminal mainly responsible for O'Connor's death, since his earlier statements to the police had sealed her fate in the courtroom. His allegations against her began at the moment of his arrest, but as certain enigmatic features of the case are reflected upon, the possibility emerges that the charges made by Fred against Marie were not the spontaneous responses of a trapped fugitive or a hostile reaction to Marie's having fled with the fruits of the crime. Instead, it appears that Fred had planned from the outset that, if the murder was discovered, the sole blame would fall on his wife. While the plot against Patrick O'Connor went forward, Fred was revolving in his unintelligent mind a second murder plot, a strategy to use Marie as a shield between himself and Mr. Calcraft.

A clue to Fred's plot against Marie turned up on the day of the hanging, when newspapers reported that the missing crowbar had finally been found. It was stated that, through information supplied by Manning to Reverend Rowe, the implement had been discovered, carefully wrapped up in a brown paper parcel, at the railroad station at Lewes, a town in the south of England near Brighton. According to the *Daily News*, human hair and spots of blood were plainly discernible on the crowbar and there was "very little doubt, from the appearance, that it was the instrument by which O'Connor's death was finally effected." The *Times* was certain that Manning had left the weapon in one of the railway carriages while on his way to escape to Jersey from Southampton.

Mr. Weatherhead, a clerk on the Brighton Railway, was reported to have brought the crowbar up to "the London authorities" on the day before the execution. Obviously, none of the "authorities" thought that the new evidence had any bearing on the appeal of Marie Manning for clemency. Yet the *Times* and other sources reported a most curious detail about the parcel in which the crowbar was wrapped: it bore the address "*Mrs.* Smith, passenger from Brighton to Lewes."

It does not seem possible that the crowbar found at Lewes station had been planted there by a third party as a prank, since there is documentary confirmation of the fact that the police were led to it as a result of Manning's revelations to Chaplain Rowe. The manuscript of Manning's confession (in a portion not included in the newspaper versions) states: "The Ripping Chisel I left at the Brighton Station *at Brighton* tied in Brown paper on the 10th August (Friday) together with an old *Brown* umbrella with the top of the handle off. These things were left as two parcels in the name of _____ of Lewes to be left till called for." This statement asserts that Manning disposed of the crowbar, not on his way to Jersey as the *Times* had supposed, but on the day after the murder. It will be noted that Rowe left blank the name in which the parcel was left. If the newspaper accounts are correct, the missing name was "Mrs. Smith." Why had Manning chosen that name? Although the murder had not been discovered on 10 August when Manning claimed to have deposited the crowbar and Mrs. Manning was not arrested as "Mrs. Smith" until after his flight to Jersey, the couple may have prearranged the use of the Smith name while they were still together at Minver Place. Therefore, assuming that the press report of the label is accurate, there is reason to believe that Manning had attempted, in the deposit of the "ripping chisel," to implicate Marie in its possession. When he wrote a woman's name on the parcel, he was still unaccused and hoped to heap the full blame for the murder on his wife. Perhaps the blank left in Rowe's manuscript of the confession reflects Manning's reluctance to admit his cowardice in putting Marie's brand on the blunt instrument.

Manning's use of the name "Mrs. Smith" on the wrapping of the crowbar suggests that at least by the day after the murder he had formed an intention to blame the murder on Marie. But if one looks back from this vantage point at certain of the evidence at the trial that is otherwise inexplicable, it seems likely that the intention to betray Marie had crystallized at the very beginning of Fred's murder plans. It must be granted that there is a danger of overrationalizing Manning's thinking, for a man who conceived that changing his address to 7 Weston Street in a note endorsement was an effective disguise was not a clever planner. But perhaps it was Manning's very stupidity that led him to take the following steps to maximize Marie's apparent participation in the murder:

1. He arranged that Marie, and not he, would receive the delivery of lime.

2. He directed the delivery man, Danby, to carry the crowbar to his home, where Marie met the man at the door, and thereby enabled him to identify her from the witness stand. Fred did this even though he had intercepted Danby in the open street, ordered the tool to be wrapped, and could have carried it home himself.

3. He caused Marie to send O'Connor an unnecessary flurry of letters of invitation in order to build up documentary evidence against her. Ballantine had actually suggested this theory to the jury in his closing argument, but it obviously made no great impression on them or on courtroom observers. Yet, there is much to be said for it. The letter of 8 August ultimately served no purpose other than evidence, since it was posted so late that it never arrived until the day after the dinner to which O'Connor was invited. The letter of 9 August was also pointless. Since O'Connor called at Minver Place late in the evening of 8 August, the Mannings could have asked him then to return for dinner the next evening. It was suggested in the

press that they had not done so for fear that Mr. Walsh, who accompanied him, would hear the invitation and would suspect the Mannings when O'Connor disappeared. But the fact is that, after O'Connor's murder, Marie Manning never denied the dinner invitation of 9 August and in fact claimed as an alibi that she went searching for O'Connor when he did not arrive at the appointed hour. Another possible explanation for the Mannings' failure to extend their final invitation orally might be that O'Connor appeared intoxicated or ill, but he was well enough to find his way home alone.

If Fred's confessions and his apparent plotting against Marie are put aside, as they should be, we are left with the central, unyielding mystery of the case: to what degree did Marie participate in the crime and what was the motivation of her conduct in relation to the crime and in her flight from her husband? It seems a fair speculation that at some point before the crime was committed Marie (1) became aware of the murder plan; (2) decided at the very least not to warn O'Connor; and (3) may also have resolved to steal his securities. The development of the murder plot against O'Connor shows signs of hesitation and uncertainty on the part of the Mannings, and it seems most likely that Fred conceived the idea and had some difficulty winning Marie's acquiescence, either because of her conflicting feelings about O'Connor or her doubts as to the ability of her incompetent husband to translate his ideas into effective action. Despite the contemporary rumors or guesses, we simply do not know why she fell out with O'Connor. Crook that he was, it is tempting to think that he had played fast and loose with her investments, but the Armes sisters had apparently never heard any quarrel as the lovers gazed at O'Connor's railway securities. The report that he was planning to desert her for another woman was romantic, but their liaison did not seem passionate; and O'Connor was not so old that Marie could have thought that his marriage would cheat her of an expectancy of inheritance in the near future. It may be that, seemingly trapped without exit in a degrading relation with two unsavory men, Marie finally saw that in the enmity of Fred to Patrick there was a hope of escape from them both. She had fled from her husband before, and perhaps as soon as she acquiesced in his plan to murder O'Connor, she silently made up her mind to leave him for the last time. If that was so, then three plots may have moved forward simultaneously: the murder plot against Patrick, Fred's clumsy plot to place sole blame on Marie that hanged her but did not save him, and Marie's plot to cheat her husband of the proceeds of the crime and to flee to a new independence. Under no analysis of the case does Marie, the betrayer of an old friend and lover, appear as a sympathetic character except in the loneliness of her defense against the double forces arrayed by the prosecution and Serjeant Wilkins; and if Dickens may overdraw her villainy in *Bleak House*, it is easier to accept his exaggeration of her vice than John Forster's gallows romance.

But still her trial, because of the abuse of her husband's incriminating statements against her, was unfair, and her hanging was an anomaly under legal concepts prevailing at the time. In an article that appeared shortly after the execution, the *Illustrated London News* reported that it had been able to discover only one earlier English case in which a woman had been hanged for assisting her husband in a murder:

> Probably the only instance on record in the English calendar of a man and his wife being executed together for murder, is that of Michael Van Berghen, a foreigner, and Katherine his wife, who were both hanged, with their servant, in East Smithfield, in 1700, for an affair of a similar character to that of the Mannings, and committed not far from the same locality. Van Berghen and his wife kept a public-house on the Thames side, opposite Rotherhithe; their victim was a gentleman named Oliver Norris, who was entrapped into their house, and there robbed and murdered by them. . . . the horrid affair . . . created great sensation at the period it occurred.

In both the Greenacre and Good cases, two of the recent murder sensations of Homicide Fair, mistresses of the murderer had been treated more leniently than Marie Manning. It will be recalled that Sarah Gale, Greenacre's mistress, was charged only as an accessory after the fact and transported for life, though she had apparently cleaned the murder house to conceal the crime, had shared the spoils, and had made statements to friends indicating that she encouraged Greenacre to commit the murder. And in the case of Molly "Good," even the charges against her for assisting her lover's flight were eventually dropped. But the Crown faced a dilemma in the case of Marie Manning. She was clearly guilty of concealing the murder and forwarding its purpose by stealing O'Connor's property, but, since she was the murderer's wife, the common law did not permit her prosecution as an accessory after the fact. She could obviously have been charged with theft, but the Crown, its hand greatly strengthened by Manning's statements, decided on the unusual step of charging her with actual participation in her husband's crime.

In discussing the denial of Marie's application for a trial by a mixed jury, the *Observer* had been alone in noting the paradox that had Marie lived with Fred Manning as his mistress she would have benefited by the right to a separate trial that was denied her as a wife. An even more dramatic paradox arose from the distinction the common law made between mistress and wife in the matter of criminal responsibility. If Marie had never exchanged her fatal wedding vows with Fred at St. James's Church in Piccadilly, she would very likely have been prosecuted, like Sarah Gale, as an accessory after the fact and would then have escaped the gallows.

For the *Observer* was right. In a murder case in 1849, it was better to be an English mistress than an English wife.

Acknowledgments

Although it was a sensation in its day and is regarded as a classic Victorian crime, the Manning case has never before been the subject of a full-length study. My effort to piece together the facts and social setting of the case turned into a project in criminous archaeology in which I could not have succeeded without the assistance and guidance of a large number of libraries and institutions and their staffs. I acknowledge my particular indebtedness and gratitude to the Bodleian Library; the British Library; the Cleveland Public Library; the Cuming Museum (Southwark); Dickens House Museum; Freiberger Library of Case Western Reserve Library; the Guildhall Library; Madame Tussaud's Limited; the Metropolitan Police (New Scotland Yard); the New York Public Library; and the Public Record Office, London.

For information relating to fashion history, I am indebted to Brighton Polytechnic; Courtaulds, Limited; Fashion Institute of Technology; Gallery of English Costume (Manchester); the Metropolitan Museum of Art; the Museum of London; Shirley Institute (Manchester); the Victoria and Albert Museum; and the Western Reserve Historical Society.

In most cases, the help I received was the result of courtesy and professionalism; but in at least one instance it was due to the British passion for murder cases (see chapter 6). One gray day in London my wife and I hailed a taxi and set off across the river for Bermondsey to photograph the scenes where the Manning melodrama played itself out. Our driver was reasonably polite but we detected a trace of grumpiness that perhaps reflected the unsmiling weather. We stopped at Weston Street and my wife (who is better than I at photography and many other things) began to take pictures of the housing project that has replaced the murder house. Curiosity finally got the better of our driver and he could not help asking what we were doing. When we told him that a famous murder had been committed there a century and a quarter ago, his eyes were suddenly agleam; he leapt from the cab, suggested camera angles to my wife, and proposed that we return at night to quiz the customers at the neighborhood pub. He was sure that their families had lived near Weston Street since time immemorial and that they would know all about the murder. Although we never got back to the pub, my final expression of thanks is to that taxi driver.

Selective Bibliography

CONTEMPORARY REPORTS AND DOCUMENTS OF THE MANNING CASE

Account of the Last Days, Confessions, and Execution of the Mannings, for the Murder of Patrick O'Connor at Bermondsey, An. Leith, 1849.

Annual Register 1849. Pp. 429–47.

Authentic Report of the Trial of the Mannings for the Murder of Patrick O'Connor. London, 1849.

Bermondsey Murder, The: A Full Report of the Trial of Frederick George Manning and Maria Manning for the Murder of Patrick O'Connor. London, 1849.

Central Criminal Court (Old Bailey) Session Papers, Twelfth Session. 1848–49. Pp. 654–79.

Huish, Robert. *The Progress of Crime; or, The Authentic Memoirs of Maria Manning.* London, 1849.

"Last Days of the Mannings, The: Their Confessions and Execution." *New Wonderful Magazine.* 2 vols. London, n.d. Vol. 2, pp. 341–51.

Manuscript confession of Frederick Manning. Madame Tussaud's Archive, London.

Reg. v. Maria Manning. Reports of State Trials (New Series). Vol. 7, p. 1029. 1849. Report of the decision on Marie Manning's appeal.

Scotland Yard dossier of the Manning case. Public Record Office, London.

"Trial of Frederick Geo. Manning, and Maria His Wife, For the Murder and Robbery of Patrick O'Connor, the Customs Gauger." *New Wonderful Magazine.* 2 vols. London, n.d. Vol. 2, pp. 265–96.

Verbatim Report of the Trial of George and Maria Manning, for the Murder of Patrick O'Connor. London, 1849.

CONTEMPORARY NEWSPAPERS AND PERIODICALS

For contemporary reports of the investigation of the crime and the trial and execution of the Mannings, I have relied heavily on the following London newspapers: the *Daily News,* the *Morning Advertiser,* the *Morning Chronicle,* the *Morning Post,* the *Observer,* and the *Times;* I also consulted the *Manchester*

Guardian. I have reviewed, in addition, a number of British periodicals of the period from 1848 to 1851. My principal sources were *Punch*, the *Illustrated London News*, and *Household Words*, and I have also drawn on material from *Ainsworth's Magazine*, the *Athenaeum*, *Bentley's Miscellany*, *Chambers' Edinburgh Journal*, *Eliza Cook's Journal*, *Fraser's Magazine*, the *Gentleman's Magazine*, and the *Quarterly Review*.

For information on the fate of black satin in 1850 and 1851, I have consulted *The Ladies Cabinet of Fashion Music & Romance* and *The London and Paris Ladies Magazine of Fashion Polite Literature, Etc.*

ADDITIONAL CONTEMPORARY SOURCES RELATING TO THE MANNING CASE AND OTHER TRIALS

Apprehension and Examination of Daniel Good The Murderer! London, 1842. Bound with newspaper accounts of the Good trial; in the collection of the author.

Ballantine, Mr. Serjeant. *Some Experiences of a Barrister's Life.* 5th ed. London, 1882. Pp. 184–86. Unflattering comments on Ballantine's long-lost client Marie Manning.

Execution of Fred. Geo. Manning and Maria, His Wife, The. Broadside and ballad published by Stewart, Printer, of Botchergate, Carlisle, and reproduced in Charles Hindley, *Curiosities of Street Literature* (London, 1871), p. 197.

Geo. F. and Mrs. Manning. Broadside. London, 1849.

Horne, R. H. *Murder-Heroes and the Diseased Drama of Their Crime, Trial, Sentence & Execution.* London, 1849.

"Life of the Mannings." Street ballad. In John Ashton, *Modern Street Ballads* (London, 1888), p. 368.

Mayhew, Henry. *London Labour and the London Poor.* London, 1861–62. Reprint. 4 vols. New York, 1968. Vol. 1, pp. 223–304.

Neale, Rev. Erskine. *The Track of the Murderer Marked Out by an Invisible Hand: Reflections Suggested by the Case of the Mannings.* London, 1849.

Pelham, Camden. *The Chronicles of Crime; or, The New Newgate Calendar.* 2 vols. London, 1886, Vol. 2, pp. 428–53. Account of Greenacre case.

Trial of Franz Muller, The. Notable British Trials. Edited by H. B. Irving. Edinburgh, 1911.

Trial of J. Blomfield Rush, The. Notable British Trials. Edited by W. Teignmouth Shore. Edinburgh, 1928.

Weekly Chronicle, Sunday, 9 April 1837. The trial of Greenacre.

LATER ACCOUNTS OF THE MANNING CASE

Adam, H. L. *Woman and Crime.* London, 1912. Pp. 134–39.

Dodds, John W. *The Age of Paradox: A Biography of England, 1841–1851.* New York, 1952. Pp. 387–91.

Forster, Joseph. *Studies in Black and Red.* London, 1896. Pp. 101–12.

Griffiths, Major Arthur. *Mysteries of Police and Crime.* 2 vols. London, 1899. Vol. 2, pp. 37–41.

Irving, H. B. *A Book of Remarkable Criminals.* London, 1918. Pp. 17–18.

Kingston, Charles. *Famous Judges and Famous Trials.* New York, n.d. Pp. 196–202.

Lambton, Arthur. *"Thou Shalt Do No Murder."* London, n.d. Pp. 220–25.

Logan, Guy B. H. *Verdict and Sentence.* London, 1935. Pp. 17–60.

[Maycock, Sir Willoughby.] *Celebrated Crimes and Criminals.* London, 1890. Pp. 51–72.

O'Donnell, Bernard. *Should Women Hang?* London, 1956. Pp. 83–87.

Whitelaw, David. *Corpus Delicti: An Enquiry into the Various Methods by which Famous Murderers Have Disposed of the Bodies of Their Victims.* London, 1936. Pp. 115–17.

Wilson, Patrick. *Murderess: A Study of the Women Executed in Britain Since 1843.* London, 1971.

Wyndham, Horace. *Feminine Frailty.* London, 1929. Pp. 161–87.

DICKENS

Works

If one is to comprehend fully Dickens's rich and often conflictive thinking and writing on crime, it is necessary to begin with *Sketches by Boz* and to end (in suspense) with the fragment of *Edwin Drood.* In *The Woman Who Murdered Black Satin* I refer principally to the following books, articles and letters of Dickens:

"A Visit to Newgate," in *Sketches by Boz* (1836)

Oliver Twist (1837–39)

Barnaby Rudge (1841)

Bleak House (1852–53)

Letters to the *Daily News* of 28 February, and 9, 13, and 16 March 1846 (four letters on capital punishment)

Letters to the *Times* of 14 and 19 November 1849 (letters against public hanging inspired by Dickens's attendance at the Manning hangings)

"Lying Awake," *Household Words* 30 October 1852 (Dickens's nightmarish recollection of the Manning hanging)

"A Detective Police Party" (includes comical account of the sea chase of the Mannings) and "On Duty with Inspector Field," in *Reprinted Pieces* (1858)

For private correspondence of Dickens relating to the 1849 controversy over public hanging and capital punishment, I have consulted the Nonesuch Edition. Unfortunately the definitive Pilgrim Edition has only reached 1846. Life is short, and the Pilgrim Edition is long.

For a speech of Dickens quoted in chapter 16, I have drawn on K. J. Fielding, ed., *The Speeches of Charles Dickens* (Oxford, 1960).

Biographies and Studies

Ashby-Sterry, J. "Charles Dickens in Southwark." *English Illustrated Magazine*, November 1888, pp. 105–15.

Collins, Philip. *Dickens and Crime*. London, 1962.

Cruikshank, R. J. *Charles Dickens and Early Victorian England*. New York, 1949.

Fitzgerald, Percy. *The Life of Charles Dickens as Revealed in His Writings*. 2 vols. London, 1905. Vol. 2, pp. 133–34.

Forster, John. *The Life of Charles Dickens* (1872–74). 2 vols. London, 1927.

Holdsworth, William S. *Charles Dickens as a Legal Historian*. New Haven, 1928.

Johnson, Edgar. *Charles Dickens: His Tragedy and Triumph*. 2 vols. New York, 1952.

Leavis, F. R., and Leavis, Q. D. *Dickens the Novelist*. New York, 1970.

Marcus, Steven. *Dickens: From Pickwick to Dombey*. New York, 1965.

Pugh, Edwin. *The Dickens Originals*. London, 1912. Pp. 253–59.

Valentine, R. B. "The Original of Hortense and the Trial of Marcia *[sic]* Manning for Murder." *The Dickensian* 19 (January 1923): 21–22.

Wright, Thomas. *The Life of Charles Dickens*. New York, 1936. Pp. 200–201. Henry Manistre's recollection of the night before the Manning execution.

BACKGROUND SOURCES

Crime, Courts, Police, and Prisons

Altick, Richard D. *Victorian Studies in Scarlet: Murders and Manners in the Age of Victoria*. New York, 1970. I owe a special debt to this important study of the impact of crime on the lives and work of nineteenth-century English writers.

Autobiography of a Notorious Legal Functionary, The. 3d ed. London, 1838. Novel based on the life of the hangman Jack Ketch.

Babington, Anthony. *The English Bastille: A History of Newgate Gaol and Prison Conditions in Britain, 1188–1902*. London, 1971.

Bleackley, Horace. *The Hangmen of England*. London, 1929. Pp. 207–27. Biography of Calcraft.

Borowitz, Albert. *Innocence and Arsenic: Studies in Crime and Literature*. New York, 1977. See especially "Why Thackeray Went to See a Man Hanged."

————. "Under Sentence of Death." *American Bar Association Journal* 64 (August 1978): 1259–65.

Bridges, Yseult. *Two Studies in Crime*. London, 1959. Pp. 7–128. Study of the Courvoisier case.

Browne, Douglas G. *The Rise of Scotland Yard*. London, 1956.

Chesney, Kellow. *The Anti-Society: An Account of the Victorian Underworld*. Boston, 1970.

Cobb, Belton. *The First Detectives: And the Early Career of Richard Mayne, Commissioner of Police.* London, n.d.

Crew, Albert. *The Old Bailey.* London, 1933.

Derriman, James. *Pageantry of the Law.* London, 1955.

Griffiths, Arthur. *The Chronicles of Newgate.* London, 1896.

Hall, Sir John. *The Bravo Mystery and Other Cases.* London, 1923. Pp. 105–39. Account of the Northumberland Street case.

Hartman, Mary S. *Victorian Murderesses.* New York, 1976.

Hibbert, Christopher. *The Roots of Evil: A Social History of Crime and Punishment.* London, 1963.

Holdsworth, W. S. *A History of English Law.* 3d ed. 7 vols. London, 1922. Vol. 1: *The Judicial System.*

Jesse, F. Tennyson. *Murder and Its Motives.* New ed. London, 1952. In this otherwise scrupulously accurate survey of classic crimes, the author invents (at p. 24) the repellent scene of Marie Manning making love to O'Connor "over the grave that was already dug."

Laurence, John. *A History of Capital Punishment.* New York, 1960.

Lee, Captain W. L. Melville. *A History of Police in England.* London, 1901.

Nicoll, Donald. *"Man's Revenge."* London, n.d.

O'Donnell, Bernard. *The Old Bailey and Its Trials.* New York, 1951.

Pearsall, Ronald. *Night's Black Angels: The Many Faces of Victorian Cruelty.* New York, 1975.

Radzinowicz, Leon. *A History of English Criminal Law and Its Administration from 1750.* 4 vols. London, 1948–68.

Rumbelow, Donald. *I Spy Blue: The Police and Crime in the City of London from Elizabeth I to Victoria.* London, 1971.

Tobias, J. J. *Nineteenth-Century Crime: Prevention and Punishment.* Newton Abbot, 1972.

———. *Urban Crime in Victorian England.* New York, 1972.

Letters, Memoirs, and Biographies

Bartlett, David W. *What I Saw in London; or, Men and Things in the Great Metropolis.* Auburn, 1852.

Carlyle, Jane Welsh. *Jane Welsh Carlyle: Letters to Her Family, 1839–1863.* Edited by Leonard Huxley. New York, 1924. Pp. 335–36.

———. *New Letters and Memorials of Jane Welsh Carlyle.* Annotated by Thomas Carlyle and edited by Alexander Carlyle. 2 vols. London, 1903. Vol. 2, pp. 5–6.

Chitty, Susan. *The Beast and the Monk: A Life of Charles Kingsley.* New York, 1975.

Davies, James Atterbury. "John Forster at the Mannings' Execution." *The Dickensian* 67 (January 1971): 13–15.

Davis, Nuel Pharr. *The Life of Wilkie Collins.* Urbana, 1956. P. 117. Adaptation of the Manning name in *Basil.*

Ellis, S. M. *William Harrison Ainsworth and His Friends.* 2 vols. London, 1911. Vol. 2, p. 170.

Frith, William Powell. *John Leech: His Life and Work.* 2d ed. 2 vols. London, 1891.

Hanworth, Lord [Ernest Murray Pollock Hanworth]. *Lord Chief Baron Pollock: A Memoir.* London, 1929.

Jerrold, Blanchard. The Life and Remains of Douglas Jerrold. Boston, 1859.

Lutyens, Mary, ed. *Young Mrs. Ruskin in Venice.* New York, 1965. Pp. 76, 89. Comments of Effie Ruskin on the Mannings.

Robinson, Mr. Serjeant. *Reminiscences of One of the Last of an Ancient Race.* 2d ed. London, 1889.

Schlesinger, Max. *Saunterings in and about London.* Translated by Otto Wenckstern. London, 1853.

Victoria, Queen. *The Letters of Queen Victoria.* Edited by Arthur Christopher Benson and Viscount Esher. 3 vols. London, 1907. Vol. 2, pp. 319–21.

Wey, Francis. *A Frenchman among the Victorians.* Translated by Valerie Pirie. New Haven, 1936.

Williams, Montagu, Q. C. *Leaves of a Life.* London, 1891.

Literature and Journalism

Barham, Richard Harris. "Hon. Mr. Sucklethumbkin's Story—the Execution." *The Ingoldsby Legends* (First Series). 11th ed. London, 1855. Pp. 299–304.

Carlyle, Thomas. "Model Prisons." *Latter-Day Pamphlets.* 1850.

Jerrold, Douglas. *Douglas Jerrold's Wit.* Arranged by Blanchard Jerrold. Boston, 1859.

Kingsley, Charles. *Alton Locke.* 1849. Novel containing a harrowing description of conditions in the Bermondsey slums.

Ousby, Ian. *Bloodhounds of Heaven: The Detective in English Fiction from Goodwin to Doyle.* Cambridge, Mass., 1976.

Spielmann, M. H. *The History of "Punch."* New York, 1895.

Thackeray, William Makepeace. "On Two Roundabout Papers Which I Intended to Write." *Roundabout Papers. Works.* New York, Kensington Edition, 1904. Vol. 27, pp. 184–91. The Northumberland Street case.

"Street Literature" and Popular Culture

Collison, Robert. *The Story of Street Literature.* London, 1973.

Cottrell, Leonard. *Madame Tussaud.* London, 1951.

Hindley, Charles. *Curiosities of Street Literature*. London, 1871. Collection of broadsides, street ballads, and other street literature, including Manning broadside cited above and a biography of Calcraft and two of his hangmen rivals.

————. *The History of the Catnach Press*. London, 1887.

————. *The Life and Times of James Catnach (Late of Seven Dials) Ballad Monger*. London, 1878.

Tragical Comedy or Comical Tragedy of Punch and Judy, The. Cambridge, 1926.

Tussaud, John T. *The Romance of Madame Tussaud's*. 2d ed. London, 1921.

Sutherland Family

Argyll, Duke of. *Passages from the Past*. 2 vols. New York, 1908. Vol. 1, pp. 27–43.

George Douglas, Eighth Duke of Argyll. *Autobiography and Memoirs*. Edited by Dowager Duchess of Argyll. 2 vols. New York, 1906.

Gower, Lord Ronald Sutherland. *Records and Reminiscences*. New York, 1903. Pp. 1–5.

Topography

Balleine, G. R. *The Bailiwick of Jersey*. London, 1970.

Besant, Sir Walter. *South London*. New York, 1898.

Butler, Ivan. *Murderers' London*. London, 1973.

Darlington, Ida. *Survey of London*. London, 1955. Vol. 25, pp. 20–21. Horsemonger Lane Gaol.

Knight, Charles. *London*. 6 vols. London, 1851.

London as It Is To-Day: Where to Go, and What to See During the Great Exhibition. London, 1851.

Phillips, G. W. *The History and Antiquities of the Parish of Bermondsey*. London, 1841.

Pictorial Handbook of London, The. London, 1854.

Whitbread's New Hand-Map of London for 1851.

Fashion History

Cunnington, C. Willett. *English Women's Clothing in the Nineteenth Century*. London, 1937.

Webb, Wilfred Mark. *The Heritage of Dress*. London, 1912.

General

Annual Register 1849. Pp. 448–457. Description and statistics of the cholera epidemic.

Dodds, John W. *The Age of Paradox: A Biography of England, 1841–1851*. New York, 1952.

Harrison, J. F. C. *The Early Victorians 1832–1851*. New York, 1971.

Kieve, Jeffrey. *The Electric Telegraph in the U. K.* Newton Abbot, 1973.

Page 83, line 4: "guilt" should read "innocence"

Page 321, caption, line 2: "his spot" should read "this spot"